UNDER WESTERN EYES

&

D1446209

UNDER WESTERN EYES

India from Milton to Macaulay

Balachandra Rajan

ଊଊ

Duke University Press   *Durham & London*

East Baton Rouge Parish Library
Baton Rouge, Louisiana

© 1999 Duke University Press
All rights reserved
Printed in the United States of America on
acid-free paper ♾
Typeset in Trump Mediaeval by Tseng Information
Systems, Inc.
Library of Congress Cataloging-in-Publication Data appear
on the last printed page of this book.

This book is dedicated to

The Shining One
Who came out of the first lotus
And who still wears its perfume
In the waterfall of her hair

Contents

Acknowledgments

Chapter 1 of this book was presented at the 1994 ACCUTE conference in Calgary and was published in *English Studies in Canada* 23, no. 1 (March 1997). Chapter 2 was presented at the International Milton Symposium in Vancouver in 1991 and was published in *Of Poetry and Politics: New Essays on Milton and His World*, edited by P. G. Stanwood (Binghamton, N.Y.: Medieval and Renaissance Texts and Studies, 1994). Chapters 4–6 were presented in an earlier form as the Tamblyn Lectures at the University of Western Ontario in 1994. Chapter 6 was published in *Romanticism, Race, and Imperial Culture, 1780–1834*, edited by Alan Richardson and Sonia Hofkosh (Bloomington: Indiana University Press, 1996). Chapter 7 was presented at the 1997 conference of the North American Society for the Study of Romanticism and was published in the *European Romantic Review* (Summer 1998). All published material has been substantially revised for this book. I am grateful for the early exposure given to parts of this book and for the opportunities I have had to benefit from this exposure.

Parts of this book were also read at Queen's University; Brock University; the International Association of University Professors of English; the 1995 International Milton Symposium; the Universities of Delhi, Jadavpur, Goa, and Kurukshetra; Sahitya Akademi; the India International Centre; and the Indira Gandhi National Centre.

Catherine Belsey, Marilyn Butler, David Clark, and Tilottama Rajan read parts of the manuscript and helped me with their comments. Janel Mueller was unfailingly supportive, particularly on those occasions when I felt my reach exceeded my grasp.

I am deeply grateful to all those whose interest and hospitality encouraged me to persevere in the arduous task of completing this book late in my life as a scholar.

UNDER WESTERN EYES

∂∞

Introduction:
Preliminary Navigations

෨෨

This book is in part the narrative of a discourse, tracing its development, its consolidations, and the ways in which it lent itself to its
unraveling. Milton can be seen as a central presence in both the articulation and the dismantling of this discourse. When he published
Paradise Lost, the East India Company had been in existence for
two-thirds of a century. It was a business concern and preferred to remain innocent of the links between profit and empire that Milton's
work disturbingly uncovered. Commerce rather than conquest was
supposed to distinguish English overseas interests from the Spanish
performance. Trade did not follow the flag as in the conventional sequence, but as later events would make evident, the flag inevitably
was to follow trade.

Commerce and conquest could be dissociated in the rhetoric of
nationhood, but mercantilist thought,[1] national security, the competitive advantages of privileged access to raw materials and markets, enlarging the elect nation's territorial holdings and protecting it aggressively from its enemies were powerful stimulants in the
other direction. The Dutch were more matter-of-fact in these matters than the British, their self-interest less camouflaged by literary
confusions. They recognized early and explicitly that commerce and
empire were not merely interdependent but almost interconstitu-
tive of each other. "We cannot carry on trade without war nor war
without trade," wrote Jan P. Coen, the founder of Batavia, in a statement remarkable for its threatening interchanges.[2] A later governor,
Antonio van Diemen, found himself taught not by ripe reflection
but by "daily experience" that "the Company's trade in Asia cannot
subsist without territorial conquest."[3]

The British were slower to reach this conclusion than the Dutch,
but by 1689, we find the East India Company insisting that it

had to become not merely a trading community but a "nation in India." Without the support provided by this expatriate nationhood, the company's employees would remain no more than "interlopers united by his Majesty's royal charter, fit only to trade where nobody of power thinks it their interest to prevent us." The English nation in India is formed here by commercial necessity and perhaps seeks only parity with India's other subnations. No such restrictions mar the robust declaration of Joshua Child, who managed the company's affairs for over two decades. Confident not only of the future but also of its imperial shape, Child wrote in 1687 of "the foundation of a large, well-grounded, secure English dominion in India for all time to come."[4]

At the time of this stentorian prophecy, Britain's dominion in India amounted to little more than a toehold. The narrow strip of land on which Madras was built had been granted to the company by the Vijayanagar Kingdom, then in decline. Its English population was about 300. Before Robert Clive, its most distinguished citizen was Elihu Yale, who arrived from Connecticut in 1672 and rose to become the governor of Fort St. George fifteen years later. His fortune when he left India was estimated at $5 million. To the university that bears his name, he left the sum of £500, two trunks of textiles, and 417 books.

On the other side of the South Indian peninsula was Bombay. It came as part of the dowry of Catherine of Braganza to the English king, Charles II, who, not knowing quite what to do with it, leased it to the company for £10 annually and a loan of £50,000 at 6 percent.[5] The loan was at the prevailing rate, and since Madras was then valued at a mere £6,000 in the company's books, the transaction was less lopsided than it seems. The company dutifully paid the rent until 1730. With an aggressive Mahratta presence in the hinterland and with tropical illnesses rife in Bombay itself, life in that outpost could be brief and unpleasant.[6] Nevertheless, it took three years and the presence of three British men-of-war for the Portuguese to hand over this part of the dowry. Bombay grew in importance, outstripping in the 1680s the trading depot the British had established at Surat in 1612, which was the first footprint of their presence in India.[7]

Although Milton writes of the East India Company's ships as "close sailing from Bengala," Calcutta had not yet been founded. The site was tossed to the British almost negligently by the Mughal regime and survived an inconclusive encounter between Aurangzeb's army and the company's forces.[8] In an unpromising terrain, the specific location of Calcutta was chosen because Job Charnock fancied a banyan tree in the neighborhood.[9] A century later, Calcutta was a prosperous city, culturally vigorous, the home of the Bengali Renaissance, described by some as the Paris of the East.[10] The banyan tree itself flourished in literature from the time that Milton, placing it in "Malabar or Deccan," invoked it as the tree Adam and Eve used to cover up their shame. After the 1857 trauma, Lady Canning painted it symptomatically in the sepia monochrome of India's alienness.

The empire may have been acquired in a fit of absentmindedness, but the discourse that justified it does not give that impression. The discourse was formed by its distancing from Spanish cruelty, by a construction of Ireland ill at ease with that distancing, by the feminization of the Orient that from Virgil onward had been entrenched in Western perceptions,[11] by situating that feminization in Milton's highly hierarchical universe, and by appropriating for imperial purposes the structures and valuations of that universe.

In opening up and filling in this highly compressed summary, we become aware of the deep entanglements of English imperialism in the early stages of its self-articulation. The classical relationship in which a dominant self defines a subjected other and then defines itself by the exclusion of that other is only one of several axes of reference. We have an imperial other in Spain and a theological other in Rome, linked in a formidable and unholy alliance. Perceptions of the New World are poised on an uneasy discrimination between settlement and occupation. Perceptions of the Old World are poised on an equally uneasy discrimination between commerce and empire.

These multiple othernesses and the interplay between them constitute the uncertain and often invaded space in which English imperialism must articulate itself. It is not surprising that the articulation is defensive. It is ironic as we move down the trail of history that an articulation originally defensive should have such expansive and dominating consequences.

The space of self-formation is not simply harassed by multiple othernesses. It is also harassed by an interior imperialism that takes possession of the fallen self and enters into collusive arrangements with the imperial others on the fallen self's horizon. An independence struggle within the self must somehow discover a rhetoric that reconciles its own decolonization with the aims of an empire it seeks beyond itself.

A rhetoric that performs these functions will not be seamless. It will be crevassed with equivocations that, as they are forced into explicitness, will result in the reluctant clarification and the progressive dismantling of the very ideology that proclaims them. The rhetoric will also be characterized by a self-justifying compulsion that is inherent in its uneasiness: its desire to account for and yet to protect itself.

These ambivalences are further complicated because the earliest theater for English imperial constructions was Ireland. England could disavow the black legend, but Ireland, as a Catholic country, had to be seen as participating in that legend. Ireland therefore had to be constructed not simply as backward and consequently pre-Christian but also as backward and anti-Christian.[12] As an outpost of demonic imperialism, a papal Cuba in a Renaissance cold war, it could only be dealt with, made safe as well as made new, by resorting to that root-and-branch propensity endemic to breakaway Protestant thought.[13] In the process, the line was blurred between commerce and plunder, settling and ravaging began to go together, and Spanish cruelty resurfaced in zeal against a people not only barbarous but also given to a religion that was the antithesis of everything for which the Reformation stood. To fulminate against Spain while doing much of what Spain allegedly did when the problem was Ireland was a rhetorical feat calling for some dexterity or for a compartmentalization in which the left hand could remain ignorant of what the right hand was doing; it was more common to stumble into the second course, but neither could give comfort to the literary intelligence.

Discomfort is evident in book 5 of Spenser's *Faerie Queene,* widely treated as the Irish book.[14] It draws back significantly from the policies advocated in *A View of the Present State of Ireland.* Of these withdrawals, the most complex is in the Amazonian cantos. Radigund, the Amazon Irish queen, bears a name whose derivation has yet to be satisfactorily traced, but much can be gained by treating her as representing the militant tradition in the Celtic feminine. Artegall, sometimes identified with Lord Grey, Queen Elizabeth's deputy in Ireland,[15] is unable to overcome Radigund in battle because of his susceptibility to what Milton's Adam describes as "beauty's powerful glance" (*Paradise Lost* 8.533).[16] Stripped of the superiority inherent in his manhood, he is reduced to a compliant femininity that mirrors Ireland's status vis-à-vis England in the hierarchy that Radigund has usurped. It remains for Britomart cum England to kill

Radigund in combat, put her followers to rout, and bring the fallen Artegall back to Englishness.

We can say that the Amazonian episodes dramatize the patriarchal overwriting of a Celtic culture resistant to patriarchy and represented as dangerously subversive both in its militancy and in its beguilements. That culture, however, is overwritten and not eradicated, as *A View*'s cultural politics brutally recommend. It is significant that Talus, Artegall's companion and a figure for violence unrestrictedly used to settle troublesome problems, is made to desist by Britomart from exterminating Radigund's followers (5.7.35–36). Talus is in fact a dubious asset, performing tasks that are unpleasant but necessary as Artegall looks the other way and sometimes acting on his own initiative. Spenser is clearly troubled throughout this book by the difficulties of bringing justice (Artegall's virtue) to bear on intractable situations without resorting to a degree of force that would take charge of these situations. The mob scenes in book 5, which are strikingly frequent, further concede the inevitability and the inevitable excesses of force in attempting to deal with popular discontent.

Despite an anti-Catholic fervor that in the 1640s intensified into hysteria, these misgivings are not abandoned in the book's last episode. Landing in Ireland, Artegall meets the hostile Papist followers of the Roman Catholic monster, Grantorto. Talus immediately embarks on their wholesale slaughter. Artegall restrains him from proceeding further so that the issue can be settled by single combat. Single combat can be seen as symbolically destroying the cause rather than the effects and as freeing Irena-Ireland from a captivity we can treat as foreign to her nature (5.12.4–9).

In charting the uneasy poise between the necessity and the limits of force, the Irish book also suggests that there can be other dragons besides those threatening maidens in distress. Feminine Ireland here anticipates India in its waylaying of mission-driven knights in imperial armor. There are differences, of course, but the differences merely multiply the betrayals possible within the containment of subversive femininity.

English constructions of Ireland and India obviously differ, but they are both "children of the same parent" and the characteristics of the elder child are easily transferable to the younger one.[17] Facilitating this transfer are the claimed Oriental origins of the Irish—an ancestry that Spenser and Sir John Temple, among others, invoke for pejorative purposes.[18] Byron's more tolerant view, which also responds to the habitual feminization of the Orient, sees "wildness, tenderness and originality" as part of "Ireland's national claim of Oriental descent."[19] Shelley, too, recognizes the connection between Ireland and India in the context of a universal humanism, arguing that "the Celt knew the Indian" before Jupiter made such fraterniza-tion difficult.[20] Irish romantic writers play on the connection, using India as a surrogate for Ireland. The praiseworthy aim may be to suggest that the subjection of two peoples distant from each other is spelled out in the same language of dominance. Nevertheless, the consequence is that English constructions of Ireland (influenced, as we have seen, by their Reformation roots) infiltrate the way in which India is perceived and the evangelical devaluations to which it is later subjected.

The reverse strategy of using Ireland as a surrogate for India was not practiced, probably because Indian writing in English did not begin to put itself together until the approach of India's indepen-dence. But India as wayward, treacherous, obstinate, and dangerous, as unfit to be educated and fit only to be governed, is a familiar char-acterization after 1857, reviving memories of Spenser's and Milton's Ireland. The feminization of the Orient softens the accusations into the stuff of which fantasies are bred, which, as might be expected, remains extraordinarily durable. A century after 1857 and ten years after India's independence, M. M. Kaye in *The Shadow of the Moon* continued to speak of India as "a vast glittering, cruel, mysterious land, teeming with violence and beauty" and as hiding "undreamed of depths of cruelty and terror" beneath its "glamour and beauty."[21] Two centuries earlier, the more urbane Oliver Goldsmith, as if in anticipation of later rhetoric, had described the Bengal tiger as the most beautiful but also the most evil of animals. Nature with admi-rable evenhandedness had been obliged to compensate for what it bestowed in excess.[22]

Imperial discourse in the last quarter of the seventeenth century had acquired some of its distinctive characteristics, including a ca-pacity for self-deception that came out of its self-troubling Reforma-tion origins. It could still avoid confronting itself fully by arguing that it had been primarily concerned with fresh religious beginnings in the allegedly empty areas of the New World and that its rela-tionship with the populous Orient would be assertively commercial rather than territorially rapacious. It had yet to come to terms with the acquisition of huge territories, densely inhabited, highly civi-lized, and, until the Mughal decline, effectively governed.

Possession was soon to change perception. One hundred and fifty years after Milton wrote his poem, the British were in undisputed control of half a million square miles of the Indian subcontinent.[23] The French threat had ceased to exist. The Mahratta challenge had been extinguished. The Mughal monarch was now the company's pensioner. Forty years later, the last of a legendary line would proceed into exile, to be erased in the oblivion that was Burma.

Imperial discourse on India responded swiftly and supportively to these changes in the extent and character of imperial power. This book traces the presence and consolidation of that discourse through a series of literary sites that exhibit the collusions of gender, commerce, and empire. Although several of these sites have been previously examined, sometimes extensively, they have been examined little, if at all, in relation to their representation of India. Our perception of them is changed by the collusions we find in them, resulting in readings of canonical and near-canonical works that differ from those to which we are accustomed. These readings are not offered as decisive. They are offered as necessary and as calling for future readings of works of literature to take proper account of the imperial presence in them.

Luís Vaz de Camões, studied in the first chapter, is not an English writer but can be considered crucial in the genealogy of English imperial discourse. *The Lusiads,* his poem celebrating Vasco da Gama's passage to India, becomes, in the words of an eighteenth-century English translator, the epic of those who hold possession of India. It opens the gateway into an imperial terrain by making the gateway itself (a sign of the submissive feminine as opposed to the shield and spear of the conquering masculine) the artwork of a people requesting conquest. The commercial insistences of the last two books also make *The Lusiads* an important event in a continuing commodification of the feminine that is wittily displayed both in Donne's nineteenth elegy and in the metaphors through which Dryden's Indamora is courted by her suitors.

Sir Richard Fanshawe was the first English translator of Camões. His translation, printed in 1655, places the poem in interesting proximity to *Paradise Lost* (which offers among its many realignments a revisionary reading of *The Lusiads*) and to Dryden's *Aureng-Zebe,* the first English literary work on an Indian subject. It is at this point that the discourse of English imperialism begins to gather itself in relation to India. It is also at this point that England begins to secure its footholds on a subcontinent that will later pass into its undisputed possession.

By making his fictional Aurangzeb everything that the real Aurangzeb was not, Dryden elegantly defines India as the site of the utterly other. After the fictional Aurangzeb is transformed by inversion into the ideal English monarch, his marriage to Indamora can then represent England's marriage to India's desirability, with Nourmahal as the emblem of the Indian wildness that the husband-monarch is able to control and to marginalize.

Milton tries to reconcile dissent with obedience (a paradox native to forms of nationhood that were both theologically secessionist and secularly imperial) by postulating a divine imperialism that must prevail unconditionally over the demands of earthly monarchies. His purpose in transcendentalizing imperialism is to sweep the world clean of secular imitations. Instead, the omnipotence of the sacred and its total command over a total containment become the paradigms of imperial power.

By the end of the seventeenth century, it can almost be said that the preliminary draft of a discourse that would govern English constructions of India is lying in wait for India's acquisition. The swift expansion of British control over India from 1760 to 1820 is the stimulus needed to activate and articulate a pre-text that, like the territorial acquisition to which it can be correlated, remained dormant during the first half of the eighteenth century. The conclusive voice in that articulation is James Mill's. Mill and Hegel standardize and harden imperial discourse, putting the other into the lumber room of history as well as at the outskirts of civilization.

The immediate aim of Hegel's German agenda, as distinct from the world agenda that his totalization of the realm of knowledge implies, is to deal with the Indic infatuation of his compatriots, the openness to otherness of thinkers such as Friedrich Schlegel.[24] Sealing off that otherness and reducing it to irrelevance by the march of history are measures that respond decisively to a local malady, but in Hegel's compendious frames of thought, they also provide that philosophical sustenance that the rhetoric of English imperialism has so far lacked. Germany when Hegel wrote was apart from Prussia, little more than a collection of baronies, but England, as a nation-state with a swiftly expanding empire, could be both the current vehicle of the idea and the prophetic statement of what Germany might become. The Hegel-Mill conjunction and the devaluing force of its application to India mark a move in English imperial ideology that is only superficially exotic. Englishing Hegel does not merely acknowledge the international nature of imperialism and Hegel's primacy as an imperialist thinker; it also builds on a root-and-branch disposition toward otherness that is entrenched in English anti-Catholicism and in the construction of Ireland as a subjected people.

The Mill-Hegel consolidation becomes dominant in imperial thought and rhetoric but falls short of hegemonic status. It cannot fully insulate itself from its previous dispersions, dispersions marking a period of contestation that in effect extends over the romantic era. Romantic literature is troubled not simply by the forces of instability, textual and thematic, that reside in any discourse but also by the competitive presence and final overwriting of another discourse (for which William Jones provides a scholarly substantiation) more hospitable to literary undertakings than the view that eventually prevailed. Much of romantic literature acquires its richness by being written on the fault line between these two discourses, by being forced into contention with itself, by being required to comply and called on to protest. Sydney Owenson's effort to question a discourse that she enters by a dramatic act of cooperation with it, Southey's war between his Indian poem and its prefaces, and Shelley's dissociation of India as a country of the mind from an actual India surrendered to Mill-Hegel characterizations are all expressive of an overdetermination that may run persistently through romantic works, even through those to which the empire seems peripheral.

Overdetermination is a concept that tends to substitute the entangled site for the uncertain author. The examples charted above—sharply different in their responses to similar pressures—indicate that the author is not only not in hiding but also obstinately active on the site. More important, they suggest the power of literature to flow around ideologies, to acknowledge and even propitiate their powerful presences but to interrogate them through circumvention rather than through the simpler forms of protest.

When Macaulay's minute eventually puts the seal of approval on Englishing India rather than on reforming India's institutions, it establishes an important prevarication supporting both the permanence and the withering away of empire. India's otherness can be collapsed into likeness, and the effort to do so can sustain the nobility of the imperial project as a self-consuming artifact. But India's otherness can also remain obdurately resistant to transformation. The project will then be frustrated, but the frustration will felicitously prolong an imperial rule to which there is no alternative.

The afterword permits itself some expansion of contexts. It considers contestations between center and margin, unity and diversity, closure and openness, and related polarities and pairings laid down in imperial discourse but also defensively present in nationalist counterdiscourse. It endeavors to clear a space for understanding in which a contemporary India might imagine itself and seeks to reclaim this vocabulary for that space in a manner not controlled by the pressures of either discourse.

This book can be characterized as a historical study with its center of gravity in the romantic era, carried out from a postcolonial vantage point. It might be argued that postcolonialism is at this moment in a state too formative and too involved with its own self-definitions to be able to offer us a vantage point. But postcolonialism's emancipatory difficulties are concerned less with how to read literary history than with how to reduce from presence to irrelevance discourses it has disowned but with which it remains entangled. Eradicating these discourses or seeking recourse to an imagined authenticity behind them are attractive but not effective strategies. Imperial discourse on India in particular makes use of Indian history and thought, appropriating it and resituating it so that a total rejection of it would also reject much that is important in India's understanding of itself. Bypassing these troubles by invoking a prelapsarian, classical India refers us to a location in and out of history. Such a paradigmatic construction has its uses. Distillations of history appeal to the proposition that history should be read as the poem of the possible. But history is also the stubborn story of how the possible has been betrayed. Two kinds of literature must be read in their complex conjunction. Amid the anxieties of liberation, the second story may have more to tell us.

Contemporary difficulties in arriving at a discourse fully emancipated from imperialism's residues are anticipated notably by Shelley. When the Spirit of the Hour in *Prometheus Unbound* describes the "tools and emblems" of humankind's "last captivity" as "not o'er thrown but unregarded,"[25] he is indicating a purgatory we may not yet have entered. The tools and emblems are still anxiously regarded, and their subversive possibilities are by no means a thing of the past.

Reclamation rather than eradication may seem the appropriate route to take. In the final stanzas of Shelley's poem, Demogorgon uses imperial language to articulate not a resurgent imperialism but the way in which that resurgence is to be overcome. His reappropriation can be considered audacious, but the lines remain vulnerable in their self-conscious persuasion by excess, their dependence on a vocabulary that must be both invoked and avoided: "This is alone great, joyous, noble, free / This is alone empire, life, victory."[26]

With India, the problems of disentanglement are compounded because the emancipatory effort may have to be directed not to an imperial discourse but to a nationalist counterstatement that was developed in response to it. The counterstatement was extraordinarily articulate, although it is not, as establishment historians tend to suggest, a paradigm for all resistance movements. Its articulacy makes revisionary treatment of it difficult, and the difficulties are increased since the counterstatement offers itself as an essentialist declaration, so that to accept its validity may be to concede its permanence. We have to treat it historically as a construction appropriate to a time of resistance calling for reconsideration in an India that has assumed control of itself. In reconsidering it, the trope of India's femininity that was retrieved from imperial-hierarchical devaluations of the feminine may have to be relocated so as to emphasize its accommodative strength rather than its essential inviolability. That accommodative strength has deep roots in the Indian past. Unity in diversity, a concept that countered accusations of India's predilection to "wildness" (an observation we find first in Dryden that is raised to metaphysical dignity by Hegel), is also an understanding that may have to be reworked in an India where the fear of fragmentation, reinforced by the partition trauma, has to contend with a respect for diversity that has run creatively through India's history. Hybridity, once a routine charge in imperial invective against India, drawing angry attention to India's wild proliferativeness and wanton confusion of forms, has now become almost a sign of cosmopolitan richness as opposed to the poverty-stricken purity of the provincial. Literature has long recognized the merits of hybridity as one way of escaping the tyranny of genres. But the genres are not lost sight of in the literary blending. There is a distinctiveness in any significant hybridity that can become submerged in the current proposition that all of us are hybrid. With the odium of the word now spent, India needs to rearticulate that distinctiveness in relation to a history that we treat as beginning in an extreme act of hybridity: the union of the Aryan with the Dravidian and with the civilization of the Indus Valley.

Partha Chatterjee has recently argued that an Indian nationalist, postcolonial statement, made predominantly in the cultural realm, was in place well before India's independence.[27] Indeed, the cultural space necessary for this statement had been tacitly conceded by the imperial power. Within it, an imagined community was located, based not on the range of Western options to which Chatterjee finds Benedict Anderson's influential book[28] restricted but on a model differentiated from Western forms of nationhood.

It is not possible in a restricted introduction to do justice to a position as thoughtfully worked out as Chatterjee's, but difficulties attend (and encumber) his claim, some of which he does recognize. First, the nationalist construction has to be freed from the exigencies of having to be put forward as a counterstatement to the dominant imperial statement. Then, as an imagined community comes into engagement with the actualities of power, it must reshape itself within the dynamics of that engagement not by modifying but by reinvigorating its principles, drawing responsively on the depths of what it has imagined. The politics of the fragment, conspicuous in Chatterjee's epigraph, must be placed in a contestational rather than adversarial relationship, necessarily shifting in its settlements, with the politics of a whole that can no longer be imagined as imperial. The aesthetics of the unfinished poem, particularly in the romantic era, are not without bearing on this engagement.

Most important of all, an imagined community conceived almost exclusively within a cultural space is likely to treat economic determinants as indifferent to events within that space. Culture and economics can be thought of as proceeding along independent trajectories, and the extent to which economic universalism is culture generating in a manner that may threaten all forms of distinctiveness is minimized by a dissociation made in the first place because cultural space was treated as not crucial, and therefore as retrievable, within the realities of imperial power.

Economic universalism suggests bleakly that this estimate was correct. It now challenges us to develop a cultural poetics that is not protectively identitarian and defensively essentialist in the face of a powerful movement toward homogenization, all too often portrayed as an irresistible consensus. The challenge is by no means restricted to India, and India is by no means uniquely fitted to respond to it. All it can do is to make a distinctive contribution to the defense of distinctiveness, one that the current discourse of distinctiveness flows into but does not entirely dictate.

To achieve distinctiveness without resorting to fundamentalism is not the easiest of tasks. Multiculturalism by itself is not a sufficiently emphatic marker. Principles of togetherness are necessary to discriminate one multivocality from another. A place in a conversation is not quite enough; there has to be a location, a voice set apart from and yet involved with others that is responsive to what the conversation says because the conversation does not entirely articulate the voice. Distinctiveness has to be a matter of positioning, and the positioning has to be historically acquired rather than adopted as a conversational role. Moreover, the position formed, despite the strength of the convictions that may have formed it, must be open to change in the exchanges of understanding. It must not remain a statement of principles from which there can be no deviance and that the conversation is entered into only to document.

It is not inappropriate here to consider Milton's *Samson Agonistes*, a liberation text that is also disturbingly fundamentalist. As the drama of a people in bondage, it speaks to all peoples who have fallen into bondage because they have not imagined their communities with sufficient conviction and cohesiveness. They have broken their covenants with their identities. Like the animals in Kipling's *Jungle Book*, they have given up their authority by losing possession of their secret names. As a liberation text, *Samson* speaks sternly to subject peoples, pointing out how they have contributed to their own fate. But it also proposes a fundamentalist deliverance, God versus Dagon, integrity versus otherness, and purity versus a hybridity expressed both in Dagon's idolized embodiment and in the mixed marriage with Delilah that was also Samson's betrayal. It is no accident that the first hybrid was Sin.

Samson represents the defensive segregation, the deep fear of being lost in the other, that has been pervasive in imperial discourse. Its threatening irony is that it does so in the name of a subjected people, offering us a deliverance we must learn to avoid. Its challenge is to ask us how we can engineer the avoidance without falling into today's Philistinism, the economic universalism by which we are enveloped.

Evolving a discourse for the future, particularly one that will address an economic imperialism that is evasively transnational, is a responsibility fraught with uncertainty, but viewing the past from the standpoint of a settled agenda (the uncertainty can be said to lie in its implementation) is an undertaking that may seem largely free of problems. It can be argued that all we need to do is detect the imperial presence in a work and then devalue it according to the prominence of that presence. We complicate this straightforwardness by pointing out that works of literature are often ill at ease with the imperial coercions to which they are obliged to be responsive. We complicate it further by adding that the character of that uneasiness varies widely from one work to another. Finding and delineating the individualities of uneasiness are important concerns of the literary historian. Moreover, it is not simply individual works that we should read as troubled by the stresses within themselves. The narrative that flows through these readings and that the readings help sustain and even compose must itself be read as not internally unified; it is hegemonic to the world but not to itself. Its ambivalent origins are never written successfully out of it. The Renaissance preliminaries to the decisive articulation of an imperial discourse on India are not merely preliminaries; they also carry into that discourse the structures, perplexities, and self-examinations of Reformation religious thought.

Apart from our changing views of sites and the delineation of the narrative those changing views establish, we can hope that the reading experience of passing through the sites will change the character of the reading conventions. This book does not make this quite considerable claim. It seeks to refine rather than to redefine or realign the forces that constitute the current reading protocol. But refinements that take proper account of contestations between and within discourses must make our perception of literary sites more complex. They will do so despite the initial simplification of treating those sites as events within imperial history or assessing (as with Milton) their continuing appropriation by that history.

Participation in discourses of dominance is not deficient in nuances, but the dominance should not be submerged in studying the nuances. Nuances presume a standard expectation. They depart from it in order to play against it, to disclose what is not on the expectation's surface, to offer interrogation in acceptance. They can assemble themselves under an overall trope such as the feminization of the Orient, but they also need to be considered in the sheer range of their cultural substantiations if the trope is to be a guide to perception rather than a way of avoiding it.

A tale as neatly told as the one recounted is likely to arouse some skepticism. Narratives are suspect today, and a metanarrative such as the one being offered, emplotted to display the coming to power of a discourse, may be additionally suspect, even though the historian cannot avoid narration and even though any adequately organized argument has to be marshaled as a narrative movement. Narratives are now taken as indicative of the passion for totalization, the lust for closure that bars the door to multivocality and the enrichments of openness. David Quint's carefully worked out identification of epic narrative as the vehicle of the imperial makes the cloud of disapproval looming over the form even larger.[29]

The narrative being put forward is open to yet further erosions since it is not averse to Edward Said's almost notorious proposition that the Occident has been constructed as the other of the Orient.[30] To accommodate these concerns, one can only do what the scholar normally does: the narrative must be exposed to questioning or situated among possibilities for questioning. It must endeavor not to be imperious in its detection and pursuit of the imperial.

It seems undesirable to retreat beyond this point. Thought defines itself by exclusion but must then come to terms with what it has excluded. This is a Hegelian proposition that Hegel fails to observe in *The Philosophy of History*. His failure is evidence of how powerfully imperial pressures bear on the formations of thought and is among the justifications for a scrutiny that seeks to chart the growth and characterize the nature of these pressures.

Said's generalization can be defended as historically necessary, as constituting the kind of beginning that his first book defines,[31] and as opening the door to an extensive critical terrain, the mapping of which is still contoured by what he said in the first place. But Said's statement is important even in the simplifications that we now wish to diversify because imperial energy *is* simplistic, given to obliterating nuances and to making its ideological and rhetorical investments in discourses that are powerfully polarized.

The innovative force of Said's initial generalizations has been apparent in the entire field of postcolonial studies, but resistance to their strongly sculptured character has grown. Said has responded to this resistance in the evolution of his own thought. A crucial essay in 1989 advises us that terms such as "representation," "the colonized," "interlocutors," and even "anthropology" cannot be assigned "any very fixed or essential meaning." The words, Said continues, "seem . . . to vacillate between various possibilities of meaning." In some instances, they even "divide in half."[32]

Said's uneasiness with the "fixed or essential" meanings around which his own discourse seems to be constellating is apparent in his current emphasis on the hybrid and on contrapuntal statements within imperial discourse. These modifications seek to offer a vocabulary for questioning that discourse while continuing to testify to a coercive strength to which the resistance to Said's work is in danger of not doing justice.

Yet the term "contrapuntal" is curiously evasive. A countervoice heard within the imperial music is in the end a contribution to that music, a contained interrogation rather than a dismantling force. The orchestration of protest here makes insufficient provision for an improvisatory space. It is too close to being part of the written score and the compositional requirement.

Exclusionary statements are exercises in purity, and the hybrid that Said now increasingly invokes may seem by definition a contestation of such statements. We can say that hybridity is the intertext brought about by two polarities unable to fully disavow each other because each needs the other to constitute itself. The intertext is not intermediate. It is the alternative established by a mutual rejection, a space that neither antagonist is able to avoid or preempt. As an area of spillages and reabsorptions, it has a life of its own as well as a life uncomfortably shared with its parents. This is one possibility within the term "hybrid," a term that in its nature can be composed in different ways. Said's use of the term is once again evasive or, to put it more understandingly, flexible in a way that responds to the diverse and even divergent strains in the world's principal cultures, including those that make much of their purity.

Said's accommodative response to his critics can be questioned in the realm of theory. The determinist view of discourse that *Orientalism* puts forward allows little space for agency or for voices of protest that are not allotted, even when they seem autonomous to those who take up the voices. Said's musical metaphor shows his interest in enlarging this space but also shows his continuing involvement with the determinist perceptions that made his inaugurating statement so powerful. We can make these observations, but we also need to admit that methodological purity may matter less than making common cause on matters of deeper conviction.

Occident and Orient are simplifications that Said takes over from a self-styled West that has embossed them on history. The self and the other to which these entities are equated are, on the other hand, inventions of critical theory that can now be criticized as questionable in their usefulness. The other, as the site of everything that the self has decided not to be and as the proliferation of all that it must avoid, takes part, we can argue, in a heavily simplified oppositional construction that cannot accurately mirror the complex relationships between subject peoples and imperial nations.

This is an objection that too easily restricts itself to the formal architecture of the imperial statement. The purpose of the self-and-other distinction is to have this architecture put in place not merely so that we can respectfully receive its proclamation but also so that we can examine the ways in which that proclamation has been circumvented, discomfited, or eroded. That power is constitutive of understanding is a fact important enough for us to welcome a distinction that keeps the fact steadily before us, but the contrast is also designed to make us aware of forces which will ensure that the hegemonic claim is not the last word.

Freudian-influenced views of the self-other relationship always stress the complicity (or, even more telling, the fear of complicity) that underlies the oppositional staging and that can be a root cause of imperial anxiety. That anxiety is typically allayed by an intensified energy of repudiation, through which the self is reassured of its stability and of the protection of its identity from the purged elements it has made marginal or monstrous. If power relationships are often marked by a vituperative energy much in excess of operational necessities, the reasons are usually psychological. Because of these undertows that attend the oppositional statement, neither Stephen Greenblatt nor Michel de Certeau confine themselves to a barrenly binary account of the relationship between the self and the other.[33]

Tzvetan Todorov's *Conquest of America*[34] presents a somewhat different picture. The chapter and section headings indicate a wide variety of relationships with the other, including that hybridity once used routinely in invective against India and now seen as a means of deliverance from the monolithic claims of nationalism, fundamentalism, and walled-in ethnic purities. Todorov's discussion of this range of relationships would be more persuasive if it were less dominated by what he sees as Europe's distinctive capacity to understand and assimilate the other[35] — a capacity that throughout his text often seems primarily manipulative and opportunistically dedicated to exploiting vulnerabilities in the other's worldview. At its broadest, that capacity extends to the examination of the other, that self-scrutinizing strength frequently claimed to underlie Europe's uniqueness, a strength that Hegel makes into the driving principle of all thought not condemned to reiterate itself.

In a striking array of contrasts, Todorov argues that the verbal education of Native Americans favors "paradigm over syntagma, code over context, conformity-to-order over efficacy-of-the-moment, the past over the present."[36] The "education" is in fact ahistorical, concerned with time only in its inscription of the timeless. If history, or more precisely the narrative articulation of the meaning and purpose of history, is an invention of the West, it becomes an invention designed to write the Western will triumphantly over the failure of backward civilizations to understand how perceiving the world has changed.

As Todorov himself recognizes, the differences he finds between Europe and its other are remarkably close to the historical differences in Europe itself between pre-Renaissance and early modern modes of understanding.[37] Geopoliticizing the historical, or vice versa, will soon become a familiar strategy in self-and-other relationships. Todorov does not explore this dimension. His book seems humanely concerned with the many ways of understanding the other that offer themselves to the desire to understand. It is necessary to insert the warning that understanding is not the purpose of the self-and-other exercise. The purpose is to settle into discourse power relationships that are formally political but also supportively psychological. Because the other is internal as well as external to the self, the supportive can become the subversive, and that is the dormant irony of the exercise. Todorov recognizes this internality,[38] but the recognition comes late in the book and is not adequately built into its detections.

The sophistications of self-and-other relationships were brought out initially by scholars examining events in the New World. Events on a different continent, within a different time span, form another province of the mind, and commerce between the two provinces has so far been restricted. If this commerce were to be increased, a variety of connections and differentiations might be ventured. Asia's feminization as part of a literary history that goes back at least to Virgil might be set against the lack of such a history in the New World. The feminization of the land in America, allegedly empty and awaiting the masculine imprint, could be contrasted with the feminine civilizations of a populous Orient, on the spaces of which much had already been written. The New World's proximity to innocence (and also to savagery) could be set against a sophistication in Asia perceived as verging on decadence. The relationship with Asia can be psychologically complex not simply because of gender assignations that cultural history has annotated lavishly but also because Islam, the other and the enemy, provided a large part of the bibliographical and cultural resources through which Europe was able to retrieve its own beginnings, thereby fueling a Renaissance by which Islam was eventually overcome.

These are adumbrations indicative of how much more must be studied. Even in their preliminary outlines, they make it evident that imperial rhetoric must be flexible in offering its enlightenments if it is to demonstrate to subjected peoples with markedly different cultures and histories the deficiencies that have earned them their subjection. That rhetoric is also the result of the distinctive stresses and sudden opportunities that have entered each imperialism in its formation. Given the real and not merely the conceptual presence of these variables, the tableau of a monolithic self that is Europe confronting a uniform other that is the Orient is not particularly difficult to discredit. The danger is that the discrediting may overwrite a major revision in understanding that ought not to be banished from our minds.

Few would have wanted to argue, even in the passion for simplicity that inaugurates beginnings, that all imperialisms were identical, that all subject peoples were identically constructed, or even that self and other were inexorably positioned within a discourse that could not be interrogated without disempowering the self and thus dismantling the imperial relationship. Said's accomplishment is not to have invented these simplifications but to have questioned the converse simplifications that before his work were generally taken for granted: to wit, that imperialisms differ importantly and perhaps decisively from one another, that subject peoples are not constructed as others but objectively discerned in accordance with their distinctive characteristics, and that imperial relationships are based not on self-justifying fictions but on perceived actualities that, as they change, will also change the relationships. No one, least of all the resistance to Said, would rush to defend these propositions. The reluctance to do so is Said's real accomplishment.

Imperialisms obviously vary, although in spotlighting their differences, one should remember the quip to which Krishna Menon was addicted: to ask a subject people which imperialism they prefer is like asking a fish whether it would rather be fried in margarine or in butter. Subject nations, like master imperialisms, are undoubtedly constructed in different ways, although here again a book such as David Spurr's, which studies a variety of constructions within a variety of imperialisms under a series of governing tropes, ought to make it evident that dominance everywhere speaks a dominant language.[39]

On the other hand, the reduction of imperial relationships to binary dispositions unilaterally controlled and implacably segregated is convincingly eroded by Gayatri Spivak, Homi Bhabha, Lisa Lowe, and Sara Suleri.[40] Indeed, the resistance to Said—or, more precisely, to those academic constructions of Said that we might call "Saidism"—has grown in strength, reflecting much more than the zeal with which the academy chips away at major generalizations. Its cumulative results can now be called impressive. This book takes in the insights of that resistance and the disarticulating propensities it underlines, but it also testifies to a coercive strength in imperial discourse—a strength repeatedly registered in the literature this book studies—that Said has made strikingly evident and that should not be submerged in the current predilection for rejoicing in the ways in which discourse is undone.

Theorizing the erosion of discourse has now proceeded to the point where Bhabha, in an incisive comment, can discriminate between differential (Jameson), contrapuntal (Said), and interruptive (Spivak) interrogations of discourse.[41] Differential interrogation, particularly in the romantic era, is an important concern of this book. Contrapuntal interrogation, as has been pointed out, offers the ambiguous advantage of placing protest within the imperial music rather than seeing it as an interruptive derailment calling for rearticulation of the discourse thus derailed. Contestational interrogation, which Bhabha does not consider, rests on a parity between the totalizing drive toward the whole and the separatist energy of the fragment. Because it lies in the grain of literature and even of literature pertinent to the imperial statement, it provides a connection between poetry and politics that can be deeply relevant to the manner in which discourses, including those that are imperially safeguarded, generate both their articulation and their undoing. Thought does not beget "its own executioner," as Yeats suggests, in the darkness set aside by its "own increasing clarity and confidence."[42] It does beget the resistance and the alternative understandings that are needed to maintain its own integrity as thought.

Articulation and undoing are two sides of the same cultural coin. The first phase of postcolonial thought tended to concentrate on the coercive strength of imperial discourse. The current phase concentrates on its self-dismantling propensities. It is time to put the two phases together and to study literature as the deeply conflicted locus of the interplay of both sets of forces. Canonical literature, in particular, offers itself both as a stronghold of the imperial presence and as a principal interlocutor of that presence. Both the acceptance of the canon and its current disavowal are oblique acknowledgments of the canon's imperial nature. They need to be supplemented by an understanding of how the canon disarticulates itself and of how strongly that disarticulation works against the imperial perceptions of which the canon can be the vehicle.

No single figure can exhaust or even dominate imperialism's range of relationships with subjected peoples. The self-and-other figure can be criticized as deficient in analytical finesse. Nevertheless, it will remain important because it responds so well to moral, historical, and psychological alienations and because the narrative of its break-down can be regarded as implicit in the figure itself. The percep-tion of India as feminine will continue to instruct our understand-ings because of the elaborate range of devaluations that imperialism has been able to find within the feminine and because the Indian counterpoem is singular in refusing to minimize a femininity that it proceeds to reinstate as the emblem of its resistance. Rape and rehabilitation treatments of the England-India relationship can be perceived as drawing on India's femininity and on a devaluation of the feminine into otherness, made possible by the remoteness and exoticism of India as a site. The figure has its limitations,[43] but its narration in reverse by Forster and Scott is indicative of an anxiety in which retribution mirrors intent. It has by no means outlived its usefulness as a metaphor for imperialism's sexual politics, and its exorcism of guilt by responsibility supports a sequence familiar in evangelical arguments.

Rehabilitation in the evangelical exercise calls for narrowing otherness into difference. The consequence can be the attempted erasure not merely of much that a culture has been educated into finding important in itself but even of the habits of mind that led to those findings. Such procedures draw on the root-and-branch dispo-sition of post-Reformation religious thought and on the paradoxical fusion of tolerance within the boundaries of a culture with extreme intolerance of what lies outside those boundaries. One can argue that the former needs the latter if the self-other relationship is not to be doubly undetermined.

Finally, homosocial treatments of the England-India relationship traverse the figures mentioned, reminding us of the obvious although backgrounded fact that Englishmen ruled India largely through the agency of male Indians. The psychologizing of the power situation (or its reverse) can be brutal in Scott, can be outreaching in Forster, or can express itself in Kipling as hierarchical camaraderie in the togetherness of the great game. The other side of this medal is the memsahib factor, as Raleigh Trevelyan chooses to call it,[44] with its insinuation that the empire might have fared better if it had pre-served its purity as an all-male operation. All these figures can assist us in the patterning of texts, but texts would be less than enlighten-ing if they did not resist as well as respond to these patternings.

The figures that map imperial rhetoric can be varied, but they remain housed within an aggressive, oppositional architecture, an architecture that is not simply part of the history of perception but also part of the way in which perception, driven by power, is able and possibly doomed to fulfill itself. To the scholar safely distant from what must occasionally be retrieved as the injustice of events, the architecture frames a theater rich in ironies. Hegemonic claims within this theater can be treated as made vulnerable by their vehemence, as inviting undoing because they are uneasily recognized as excessive or even constricting by those who nevertheless propound them. Collaboration, which is quite other than collusion, is a reassuring strengthening of these claims. It is the natural outcome of dominance, which prescribes both a collaborative space and a collaborative role. Collusion is antiofficial, the subtext of the explicit text. It is the other of the self-and-other relationship.[45]

As these reflections suggest, the complications of psychic politics are compounded by their enmeshment in a web of textuality. Discourse is constitutive of a dominance that in turn makes operational the articulations from which it issues and the rhetoric it energizes and by which it is also sustained. The interconstitutiveness of the political, the psychological, and the textual makes conversion into a single currency tempting. Textual conversion is the transaction most likely to appeal to those within an interdiscursive formation whose minds have already been shaped to some degree by their practice of literary modes of understanding. The consequent tendency to read textual behavior back into psychological states and political decisions can be strikingly productive but is not without its dangers. Transferring the dynamics of the subtext to self-and-other relationships is one prevalent example of this tendency. Another is to treat the instabilities of discourse as indicative of imperial uneasiness, anxiety, frustration (as in Bhabha's remarks on colonial "nonsense"),[46] or even terror (as in Suleri's intensification of anxiety).[47] Such imperial states of mind undoubtedly have existed. A Passage to India testifies to their reality, and Kipling's Kim can be said to acknowledge them by its highly controlled insulation from their presence.[48] We can wonder, nevertheless, if these states are adequately defined by tying them closely to theories of textual behavior that are themselves open to contestation.

These cautionary remarks are not meant to minimize the enlightenments of exploring the politics and psychics of the textual. Indeed, a book such as this that foregrounds discourse must also foreground the analogies and possibly the connections between political and textual behavior. It must, in addition, raise the question of whether there are imperial genres or at least genres to which imperial statements gravitate.

Quint's work goes far to persuade us that the epic is, of all genres, the one most hospitable to imperial statements. This book acknowledges Quint to the extent of styling as epic even the metagenre of the narrative of imperial discourse. On the other hand, it also considers drama, nonepic poetry, and the novel as vehicles for imperial propositions. It may even point to the discomfiting possibility that no genre is unreceptive to the imperial spirit.

If we associate epic and empire too closely, we face the difficulty that the huge territorial aggrandizements of recent empires took place when the epic was in decline and when the long poem was more inclined to turn in on itself than to assert its mastery over the external world. The novel, as Said points out, proliferated during the age of empire,[49] and that fact may cast suspicion on the novel; but if we are persuaded by Mikhail Bakhtin's distinction between the monologic epic and the potentially dialogic novel, much of that suspicion must be held in suspense. Narrative itself, rather than its manifestations in the epic or the novel, can be singled out as the agent of imperialism, with the natural movement of narrative to closure signifying the advance of imperial power to its ordained objectives. Resistance to closure then becomes the textual sign of political resistance. Penelope in one tradition and Scheherazade in another indicate how that resistance might be feminized.

The refusal to accept closure is an important ingredient in the implicit manifestos of the postcolonial. Parody, irony, and allegory act not merely to postpone but also to undermine the pretensions of dominance to a conclusiveness that would make dominance impossible to undo. Yet from Chaucer onward, the form of the unfinished has complicated the potential politics of narrative, first by contesting the purposiveness of the epic with the errancy of romance and then by making formidably more difficult the long poem's searching of its own assumptions—a search that must be successfully concluded if the poem is to earn its entitlement to move forward.[50] The canon's contribution to its own dismantling makes the politics of genre more intricate and unstable than the simple assimilation of forms to ideologies might suggest. Some forms are more hospitable to imperial uses than others, but the use of a hospitable form (as in Keats's two *Hyperion* poems) can indicate that imperial attitudes are being questioned as much as they are being endorsed or even that endorsement itself, offered as in Keats from the perspective of the rejected, can become a radical form of questioning. *Hyperion* and *The Fall of Hyperion* are poems of the vanquished, but they are poems that accept a victor's poem that is then twice found impossible to write.

Quint's view that the poem of the losers typically restricts itself to disorienting and fragmenting the epic of the triumphant is not quite borne out by Keats's earnest effort to write the poem that the march of mind ordained.[51] His inability to proceed with the epic of the grand advance because of his numbing sense of the tragic human expense of it is a commentary that addresses not only the merits and necessities of change but also that "giant agony of the world" that must be endured if change is to be brought about. The poetry of dispossession is at its most probing in Keats. The two *Hyperion*s speak strongly and disquietingly not only to an England undergoing wrenching modifications in its economic and social structures but also to an India where the Mill-Hegel discourse could be perceived as irresistibly advocating the replacement of a Saturnian by an Apollonian order of things.

Pursuing Quint's view further, we would also need to note that India's countervailing epic—the official narration of the history of its resistance—is not an effort at disorientation but a statement in epic form clearly appropriating the Western model of the recovery of Ithaca.[52] In its dedication to finding form amid the fragments, the Indian narrative can even be called high modernist. It is consciously triumphalist, answering closure with a retaliatory closure, a tryst with destiny, dramatically positioned at the hour of midnight. The question to be asked is whether the dependent styling of the counterstatement allows it to emancipate itself from the imperial narrative it succeeds. The choice is, after all, the *Odyssey* and not the *Mahābhārata* or the *Rāmāyana*, which, harassed at every turn by ethical issues that remain stubbornly problematic, are better models for the complexities of today.

Discourse can be read as ideology entrenched in rhetoric. It is also responsive to being read as literature, particularly when we transfer to discourse the articulating strength and the dismantling energy that have been seen as jointly characterizing literature. The ideal, hegemonic discourse, almost Calvinist in its predeterminations, announces itself as unilaterally decreed, as fully containing and eventually assimilating to its own integrity the energies of protest and resistance within it, as never overcome and only transiently threatened by any excess of the actual over the programmed. These specifications are remarkably close to those used until recently to judge the excellence of a work of literature. The distinction (and it may be crucial) is that the new critical poem generates a difference that it then endeavors to take back into itself. The poem of imperial discourse generates an otherness and proclaims its identity by containing and possibly nullifying that otherness. In this respect, it can be deemed Miltonic. Both poems can be treated as open to erosion by an indeterminacy inherent in the behavior of texts. The world is similarly answerable to power and similarly resistant to omnipotence.

The hegemonic, antithetically organized poem of imperial discourse gives rhetorical substance to and passes into the practice of a hegemonic, antithetical world. The reflections of each in the other offer one more example of the collusions between the world and the text, between aesthetic satisfaction and the satisfactions of power. Such interchanges make problematic the claim that there may be an aesthetic dimension to imperial understanding that can be set apart from the dominance helping to constitute that dimension. Marvelous possessions may adorn the cabinet of one's mind, and the Western sense of wonder as it gazes on these acquisitions may indeed be disinterested (as Greenblatt suggests)[53] and may belong to a realm momentarily indifferent to the imperial. But detaching the aesthetic dimension in this manner simply enables imperial power to function in a context free from cultural embarrassments and to helpfully enlarge the subjected territories that provide the contemplative gaze with its marvelous possessions. Warren Hastings, who combined an educated admiration for things Indian with a remarkable talent for acquiring Indian territory, is an example of this ambivalence bordering on schizophrenia that must sooner or later resoundingly devalue what it initially claims to respect.

If we transfer gender relationships to the imperial theater (as is repeatedly done in this book), it becomes apparent that within the enhancements of possession, some esteem for the inferior gender is not out of place.[54] Civilizations can be imagined as appealingly obsolescent, worthy of art while their conquerors are worthy of history. It is then not inappropriate that the investments of power should offer an aesthetic and psychological dividend, that there should be epicurean opportunities for what Said calls "the pleasures of imperialism." The exotic "replaces the impress of power with the blandishments of curiosity"[55] or, in higher substitutions, with the surprise of difference. But it is a surprise held in the grip of a supremacy that re-assuringly distances what it elevates. The admirable is also the anti-quarian, promoted from the lumber room of history to an honorable place in its museum.

Unfortunately, difference cannot be securely housed in a lumber room or even in a museum. In writing eloquently of the surprise of difference, Barbara Johnson sees that surprise as opening the doors of perception and as vividly revealing how the world of our knowledge has been hemmed in by the very assumptions that formed it.[56] The surprise is the measure of how much needs to be known. It is also, and more threateningly, a discovery of how much must be changed in order to know it. The history of response to difference has seized on the threat and minimized the opportunity. Far from opening the door, it has proceeded to bolt and bar it. Dominance can read differ-ence as a plea for inclusion. It has been figured instead as a demand for exclusion, a demand that unmasks difference as a halfway house to otherness. The surprise of difference can begin in wonder; it ends in anger as surprise by sin. Hegel's self-castigating movement from one to the other in the opening paragraphs of his chapter on India in *The Philosophy of History* traces a psychological route that the West finds it difficult not to follow.

The imperial poem thrives on the other's outrageousness. To pre-sent the other as unfit for dialogue is to subject discourse to a neces-sary dictatorship that claims to be benevolent but that needs to be accountable only to itself. The monstrous in that dictatorship cannot be civilized: it can only be governed and kept in place by the civiliza-tion that has constructed it as monstrous, and its insidious presence in the self that created it makes hegemony all the more imperative. In the aftermath of imperialism, the aggressiveness of this contrast is embarrassing. It then becomes encouraging to concentrate on the instabilities of discourse, on its indeterminate spaces, and on the underground proliferations that subvert its official structure.

In this way, the refusal of the text to totalize can be read as point-ing to other refusals that have taken place in history or at least in literary representations of what may have happened in history. The dispersing text becomes the habitat of the terrified imperialist cry-ing out like Pound that he cannot make it cohere, the difference being that what will not cohere is now the stuff of empires rather than language. Textual politics invites us to consider the inevitable excess of the actual over the programmed, the growth within dis-course of indeterminacies that are indeterminate in extent and that the discourse is unable to cordon off, and the million mutinies that the text mounts against the monologic passion of the oeuvre. The question is whether we can unfalteringly carry the refusal of the text to totalize into a world of events where the will to totalize remains very much in being and where deferral and destabilization have not dispersed the concentrations of power behind that will. Politics may indeed partake of textuality, but that does not mean we can repose our confidence in the textual undermining of political intent.

These caveats are not offered as prohibitions. It is plain that India's reticence, its resistance to being mapped, and its Draupadi-like withholding of itself have been disconcerting to imperial aims. The hegemonic gaze is unsettled when it falls short of omniscience. It is no accident that Mowgli in *The Jungle Book* attains his supremacy over others because he knows the secret name of each inhabitant of the jungle. The secret name is the name of the last withholding, the name surrendered by a nakedness that has learned that it can shield nothing from the imperial gaze.[57] Read thus, Mowgli's knowledge is in direct confrontation with the story of Draupadi's disrobing, the most powerful of all metaphors of India's inviolability and one that the Indian imagination everywhere cherishes. If the Draupadi legend prevails or is successful even in resisting erasure, imperial knowledge can remain anxiously uncertain about what might come together in the unmapped space of its ignorance.

In practice, imperial discourse is satisfied to be slightly less than omniscient and is prepared to accept a space of residual indeterminacy, provided that space can be successfully cordoned off. There may indeed be advantages in conceding that such a space exists. To say that something in India's perception of itself remains obstinately outside intelligent understanding is to make a scathingly adverse comment on the irrationality of Indian civilization, but it is also to argue that imperial power must proceed to contain what imperial knowledge is unable to chart. If 1857 rather than the Bhagavad Gita is India's fundamental scripture (as MacBryde contends in *A Passage to India*),[58] the remedy is to do what Reginald Dyer did at Jallianwalla. Imperial terror, real or tactically exaggerated, may be the origin, but imperial repression is the result.[59]

When political decisions are assimilated to textual behavior, it is usually the indeterminacies of discourse, its figurations of anxiety or aporia, that are read back into historical events. Acceptance of an imperial discourse smacks of collaboration, so little is said about its possibilities. But when the discourse is styled as a self-consuming artifact—as in Macaulay's 1833 speech and the remarks of his colleagues—some discomfiture can be created by assisting the discourse to proceed expeditiously to its extinction and by disposing of the pretexts for deferral contrived by those dedicated to the permanence of empire.[60] The directing images of the Mill-Hegel view are of India's guided advance along the route of civilization and of its growth from immaturity to a fully adult state. Such images foresee their own effacement.

Said in "Orientalism Reconsidered" writes of "the muteness imposed upon the Orient as object" and sees the Orient as "not Europe's interlocutor, but its silent Other."[61] This is a statement that needs some qualification even if we broaden the term "muteness" to cover those stage-managed voices that a sufficiently confident discourse can allot to resistance. From 1890 onward, India was not silent but irritatingly articulate. A range of voices that at the end of the century included Gokhale, Tilak, and Swami Vivekenanda broadened to include Gandhi and Nehru, philosophers such as Radhakrishnan, political novelists such as Mulk Raj Anand, and cultural figures such as Tagore. Scrupulously placed within the flexibilities of the prevailing discourse, these voices put to subversive use the equivocations they found within that discourse. Playing the discourse game with expertise even when translated into political performance was not enough to free India from British rule. But winning the game or making its prolongation more difficult was more than an achievement in a war of words.

The textualizing of events has run through this introduction as a methodology that can offer striking enlightenments but that can also lead to a reductionism we should be careful to avoid. That caution is more strongly called for because the confluence of postmodernism and postcolonialism has greatly increased the persuasiveness of the elision between textual perception and political understanding. Both movements find their identity in resisting containment, in disavowing the center, and in seeking to dislodge the entrenchments of previous discourses by irony, parody, indirection, and the distancing of the real as the conspicuously imagined, its reification in the realm of nightmare.[62] All these literary strategies are translatable into ways of viewing history and ways of interpreting textuality. But they also seem to assemble themselves unhappily around Quint's claim that losers typically restrict themselves to fragmenting and disorienting the poems of victors.

We must remember, though, that as the classic forms of imperialism gave way to the stresses within themselves, grand narratives lost their power to sustain us even before Jean François Lyotard announced their delegitimation. Emancipation itself, cast as a grand narrative, as in India's counterepic of independence regained, has been subject to similar erosions of confidence. Salman Rushdie's *Midnight's Children* is an almost exemplary postmodernist display of those erosions, even if, in Satanizing the independence poem, it comes uneasily close to an inverted grand narrative.

Local coalescences, or Lyotard's *petits récits,* may be all that the form of the unfinishable can offer.[63] The state of understanding, which may be too fluid to be called a state, can no longer respond to the opposition between winners and losers that we detect in Renaissance and Victorian constructions of empire and that prevails not merely in the pages of Quint's book but in the triumphant discriminations of the Mill-Hegel view of the world.

Postcolonialists are clearly not losers, and reflection suggests that they cannot always be characterized as winners, uncertain of their own identity and preoccupied with the stubborn historical and psychological residues of a discourse otherwise defunct. The point being made by writers in the confluence is that imperialism is only a genre of totalization and that totalization, behind its many manifestations, remains the implicit enemy. If that is so, it can be credibly argued that fragmentation is the only possible oppositional strategy.[64]

However, fragmentation may not be enough to combat the newly emerging interlockings of conglomerates of power that owe their loyalty not to national causes but to economic models. Unimpeded commerce, heightened competitiveness, and maximized productivity are among the key concepts in the discourse of this gathering wholeness, a discourse sufficiently powerful to be acknowledged even in defensive propositions such as the level playing field.[65]

It is difficult to fragment an empire that has no center and makes no territorial claim. To engage coalescences and dispersions of power that are transnational, anonymous, and evasive, we need to counter the economic monotheism to which these shifting alliances subscribe with a philosophy of pluralism and of cultural distinctiveness. That philosophy, in resisting homogenization, must contrive to fall short of fundamentalism or of aggressively protected ethnic purities. The problem, although formidable, is not new. The uncertain and wavering course of the endeavor to respond to it is, in large measure, also India's history.

As we consider how imperial discourses are read by events, it becomes evident that two inheritances of textual understanding are involved. Derridean views of language govern propositions about the fissurings, slippages, and fragmentations of imperial discourse, just as Foucauldian views govern propositions about its coercive strength, its constitutive power, its containing capability, and its predestination of all that it contains. We have to seek a via media that is not the implied advocacy of one school or the other. The power of discourse to write events is limited and is further limited by the power of events to rewrite discourse. Equally, the realities of challenging and undoing the structures of imperial power (including the one that is currently emerging) are not always reducible to textual behavior, even though textual behavior can be an indispensable guide to reading those realities. The world is not a text, although it is textured with texts.[66]

The Lusiads and the Asian Reader

&ck

In March 1553, four ships set sail from Lisbon along the route that Vasco da Gama had pioneered for Western commerce. Three were lost on the way. The fourth ship, the *Sao Bento*, dropped anchor in Goa only to be lost on the way back. Among those disembarking from the *Sao Bento* was a common soldier, Luís Vaz de Camões, the author-to-be of *The Lusiads*.

Goa had been seized by Afonso de Albuquerque in 1510, an event foretold by Jupiter in *The Lusiads*, who assures the importunate Venus that Goa will in time be the queen of all the East. Camões had not arrived to savor the truth of this prophecy, regarding a city he described elsewhere as a modern Babylon, to enjoy the fruits of the paradise da Gama had hailed, or even to conduct preliminary research for *The Lusiads*. He came because he may have had no alternative. In a street brawl on Corpus Christi Day in 1552, the quarrelsome Camões had wounded a court official, Garcalo Borges. He was cast into prison for eight months. Borges did not press charges and in fact forgave the poet after receiving an apology. The king's pardon followed on March 7, 1553, presumably with a condition attached to it. A fortnight later, Camões embarked for Goa. "I set out," he wrote dejectedly, "as one leaving this world for the next."

He continued on his colorful course, taking part in an expedition against the king of Chembe on the Malabar coast within six weeks of his arrival in Goa and perhaps in an expedition to Ormuz in 1554. In February 1555, he could "be located with some precision" in Somalia.[1] In the following year, he appeared a third of the way across the world in Macao as trustee for the dead and absent. Opinion differs as to whether this was a promotion or a further degree of exile. In Macao, Camões once again displayed his customary talent for not getting along with authority. Relieved of his post, he was in some

danger of providing his successor with an additional dossier by joining the ranks of the dead and absent. The hospitable Vietnamese rescued him from a shipwreck in the Mekong estuary. Clutched to his
heart was the waterlogged manuscript of The Lusiads. This incident
is a story that seems designed to belong to literature rather than fact.
Camões endows it with a double legitimacy by incorporating it into
his epic poem (10.124). He also anticipates Milton here and elsewhere
in The Lusiads in his infiltration of the epic voice by the personal.[2]

From Macao, Camões returned to Goa and was in and out of
prison, once for not paying his debts and once, it is conjectured, because of the enemies he had made at Macao. He decided to return to
Portugal but languished for two years at Mozambique, unable to pay
for further passage. It was not until 1570 that he reached Lisbon. The
Lusiads was published two years later. The king awarded Camões a
pension of 15,000 reis, which is described as not magnificent but not
a pittance.[3] It compares well with the payment of £10 that Milton
received for writing Paradise Lost.

A life that reads like a tale out of Conrad is reflected in a poem
that is more robust than thoughtful. Innumerable and boastful accounts of Portuguese victories past and future remind one of the
"tedious havoc" that Milton castigates (PL 9.30), although only after
indulging in a fair measure of it himself. Camões assiduously courts
comparison with Virgil by making more than eighty allusions to the
Aeneid and claims superiority over past epics because his hero is
actual rather than legendary. The machinery of the poem, complete
with Greek gods and Olympian squabbling, is also lavishly emula-
tive of the ancients. It becomes something of an embarrassment in a
poem written under Christian auspices, so that at one point (10.82),
Tethys is obliged to warn da Gama that she and the mythological
apparatus she represents are to be regarded as no more than figures
of poetry. It is advice that the reader is expected to apply with discrimination. The future Portuguese empire that Tethys thereupon
proceeds to display to da Gama is clearly not intended to be figural.

The view of The Lusiads that these remarks introduce runs against
the grain of current interpretation. It is put forward to suggest that
current interpretations may rest on reading habits that need to be
scrutinized. Commentary on The Lusiads is almost nostalgically
Eurocentric. Negligible attention is given to the poem's representation of Asia, even though Camões's epic displays the heroic quest as
the discovery of a new route to Asia's riches. This reticence is symp-
tomatic, but it ought to be slightly surprising in an era in which
Western revisionism seems prepared to admit that it needs to listen

to others as well as to learn from itself. Circumstances make it necessary to declare the relevance of an Asian viewpoint in the reading of the poem and to do so perhaps with an assertiveness that would not have been called for in a world of evaluation with more generous boundaries.

Historicizing *The Lusiads* restricts itself at present to considering the poem as an event in the epic genre or as an event in the orchestration of a Portuguese-European identity. The first tactic enables us to separate epic dreams of heroic achievement and glory that are both upper class and in the high style from more prosaic commercial visions that are middle class and in the mean style. The inexorable collusion between commerce and empire is mystified by a disengagement that enables us to read *The Lusiads* as an impure poem or as a poem forced out of the decorum of its genre by the glittering possibilities of a breaking open of commercial horizons to which it was unable to remain oblivious.

The second tactic of considering the poem as an event in a national-cum-European formation of identity can attach considerable weight to the questionings of itself that *The Lusiads* occasionally places at its margin. These questions are treated as part of an internal debate through which Portugal proceeds to write out its meaning and destiny in a manner that can be read as emblematic of Europe, but they also have been treated as troubling the poem or even placing it in jeopardy to a sufficient extent to do away with some of the embarrassments of its imperial stridency in a postcolonial era.

Lacking in this historicizing is any sustained consideration of the poem as an event in imperial history, as an important and strong articulating voice in the coming to power of a discourse of dominance. This protocol of avoidance is not surprising. Placing a poem within a genre or within a history of identity formation is an activity that can seek to remain descriptive; placing it within imperial history makes evaluation difficult to escape. It also means that the evaluation may put in doubt the status of any poem that contributes powerfully and with sufficient single-mindedness to discourses and practices now generally disowned. The protective barriers erected against this way of approaching *The Lusiads* are entirely understandable; they make it helpful (and perhaps essential) to import into the poem's Eurocentric containment a reading from a different space that is formed by a different experience. For the sake of clarity, I propose to pursue and to endeavor to shape this reading before putting it into engagement with other readings that have so far prevailed.

Camões's insistent claim to be measured against Virgil only reminds us that Lisbon was not a second Rome and that *The Lusiads* is not a second *Aeneid*. The difference between the two poems verges on the profound. There is in *The Lusiads* no Dido to abandon, no Turnus to contend against, no devastated Troy to remember, and no lost homeland to reinstate in the pursuit of an imperial destiny. More important, the poem's freight of feeling carries within it none of Virgil's war weariness, his sense of a heroic and world-ordering imperative weighed down by the sacrifices the imperative exacts. Camões's epic seems behind Virgil in imperial time and almost a return to imperial innocence.

Epic poems are exercises in purposefulness and therefore cannot place themselves in jeopardy, but to write poetry at all is to submit to a hazard from which even epics cannot be immune. One possible hazard is Tethys's warning to da Gama that the vision of Portugal's future that she shows him from a hilltop is figural. The imperial dream could be in question here, but Tethys's caution is quite rightly treated as addressed to a suspicious church rather than to a subversive reader.

The most telling and celebrated jeopardizing of the poem is the old man's harangue at the end of canto 4, as da Gama's expedition sets off on its journey. The diatribe expresses the objections of the conservative opposition to the king's overseas policy as well as the potentially Satanic vanity of the quest for glory and fame. For Western critics, the old man's speech is crucial in the recuperative remapping of *The Lusiads*. An Asian reader would be more struck by the manner in which the speech is placed on a horizon that seems to recede into history. The old man is never heard from again, and once aired, his views receive no further attention. We could argue that they needed no further attention, that they were underlined sufficiently by events, that the old man's prophecy rang all too true in the shrinking Portuguese empire of the 1580s. But da Gama's voyage is not presented in that disillusioning aftermath as an enterprise that might need to be rethought. It is presented as a climactic and heroic achievement from which a once noble nation has declined.

The imperial enterprise can be both glorified and doubted. We can be surprised by sin, and Milton surprises us by a resplendent display of classical heroism against which the ninth book makes its tragic turn. But Milton is unique in his capacity to enact pride—and more persuasively poetic pride—not simply as a prelude to but as a basis for poetic repentance. Camões does not seek the poem's self-repentance or even its sustained interrogation. Attempts to find in the old man's speech an enduring site for this interrogation are commendable in their intentions but dubious in their success. It might be more fruitful to see in the futility of the old man's protest some of the poem's authenticity as an imperial document. Da Gama's fleet is sailing away not only from Lisbon but also from a worldview now out of date.

Glory and fame in *The Lusiads* are not, as with Milton, the noble mind's last infirmities. They are epic pursuits, manifest in Portugal's history as it proceeds to the crowning exploit that is both the poem's prize and the history's climax. An Asian reader, understandably resistant to the imperial theme, cannot easily forget that Asia was the soil on which glory and fame displayed their banners.

It is not surprising that heroic statements, however noble as poetry, remain unpersuasive to the victims of those statements. Camões's poem must accept this impoverishment in a postcolonial world. It may not be alone in this deprivation, but it may be alone in its enthusiastic subscription to the commercial rewards that go with honor, dominion, and the discomfiture of the infidel.

To the Asian reader, Camões's world presents itself as a world not of meaning but of riches. The mountaintop from which da Gama is shown the Portuguese future is reached through an impenetrable thicket that reminds one of the approach to Milton's Paradise.[4] Characteristically, it is strewn with emeralds and rubies (10.77). William Mickle responds to such invitations by describing *The Lusiads* in the preface to his 1776 translation as "the epic poem of the birth of commerce, and, in a particular manner, the epic poem of whatever country has the control and possession of the commerce of India."[5] His view has been strongly contested, but the reductionist characterization may reflect some of the poem's difficulties in claiming more for itself. In the exhortation that opens canto 7, for instance, religious divisions are first deplored and unity is called for in contending against the infidel. It is then blatantly argued that those unmoved by religion should at least be moved by the prospect of vast riches (7.11). The exhortation takes place on the threshold of the discovery of India, making it once again clear that the wealth of Ind that Milton infernalizes is, in Camões's poem, the fitting recompense for epic valor.

The purpose of da Gama's voyage was to open a passage to the Orient that would destroy both the Venetian monopoly of the spice trade and the Arab monopoly of the trade routes between the East and Europe. Lisbon would become Europe's richest city, and the blow dealt to the Moslem infidel would felicitously serve both commerce and religion. "I hold it as very certain," Albuquerque opined, "that, if we take this trade of Malacca away out of their hands, Cairo and Mecca will be entirely ruined, and to Venice will no spices be conveyed, except what her merchants go and buy in Portugal."[6] For a brief period, this strategy seemed triumphant. Although one-third to one-half of da Gama's men never saw Portugal again, the cargo he brought home sold in Lisbon for sixty times the price paid for it in India. By the early sixteenth century, Venetian trade with the East was sufficiently disrupted for Portugal to take over 75 percent of Europe's spice imports, reaping profits of 90 percent in the process. "For a time," G. V. Scammell comments, Portugal's "remarkable ambitions came near to success, an astonishing achievement for a tiny country short of ships and men, and with such forces as it possessed thinly scattered through dozens of forts and posts in East and West alike."[7]

Portugal's moment of commercial glory was brief. Despite the capture of Goa (1510), Malacca (1511), and Ormuz (1515), Eastern traffic through the Arab world recovered and, indeed, began to surpass its previous dimensions. The failure to capture Aden resulted in the spice traffic being rerouted rather than cut off, and the porousness of Portugal's blockade was attested to by clandestine Portuguese participation in the very trade it was seeking to intercept. By 1600, only 20 percent of the pepper and less than 50 percent of the other spices reaching Europe were arriving in Portuguese ships. Indeed, as the sixteenth century wore on, the spice trade lost its preeminence for Portugal, and cargoes were increasingly made up of cotton textiles. The Portuguese also developed a carrier trade, conveying the produce of South and Southeast Asia to the markets of China and Japan. Japan had been fortuitously "discovered" by a Portuguese ship blown off course by a typhoon, and for a time, trade between China and Japan was exclusively in Portuguese vessels. These secondary trade gains were scarcely compensation for the shrinking commerce of a waning empire. Seventy years after da Gama's voyage, Camões was writing of a moment already past and prophesying a future that the present seemed insistent on undermining.[8]

Portugal's declining fortunes became catastrophically evident when King Sebastião in June 1578 led an expedition to Alcácer-Kebir to verify Camões's assurance that the Moslem everywhere would quail in terror before the weight of Portugal's armies and the fame of its exploits (1.6–8). The king had reasons for confidence apart from

Camões's poetry. Fifty years earlier, in celebration of a triumph by the Portuguese over the Moors, a subservient Moor had ridden a lavishly caparisoned white elephant, curtseying thrice before the pope and sprinkling the assembled spectators with water. On this occasion, the outcome would be different, even with an invading force of 1,500 horsemen and 15,000 foot soldiers, transported by 500 vessels. Nine thousand camp followers accompanied the expedition, including large numbers of women, to celebrate the victory in the manner of canto 9 of *The Lusiads*. In four hours of battle under a searing African sun, the flower of Portugal's manhood was destroyed. Eight thousand were killed, and 15,000 taken prisoner and sold into slavery. No more than 100 found their way to safety. In the following year, as the plague descended on Lisbon, Camões contracted his final illness, commenting that he was glad to die not merely in but also with his country.

It is not difficult to consider *The Lusiads* as a poem of bombast that history ironically falsifies. The grandiose conception of the state of India (which, in the period's expansively vague geography, included not only India but also Southeast Asia)[9] can be mockingly set against Portugal's limited manpower and its increasingly straitened finances. Yet the defining Portuguese experience may be the extraordinarily swift expansion of nationhood into empire, an empire that, although precariously maintained, was more far-flung than any hitherto in history. The dizzying opening of horizons that sea power suddenly made possible accounts for many of the excesses in the Portuguese imperial vision, and the overreaching becomes more endurable as we remember how events inflated the dream.

The Portuguese effort has its instructive antecedents not in Western but in Indian history. K. M. Panikkar is, of all Indian historians, the most impressive in depicting how South India's expansion into "further India" was achieved by the very sea power that ten centuries later was to open India to colonization by the West:

> At the end of the fifth century the area of the Mekong valley, Malaya and the Indonesian islands were dotted with Hindu principalities some of which, like the kingdom of Funan, had attained considerable importance and prosperity. This was the formative period. Hindu culture and organization had been established on a firm basis, and the local population—at least the higher strata—assimilated with the Indian emigrants and colonists. The next five centuries wit-

ness a great flowering of Indian culture in these areas which properly belong to Indian history, because at least till the twelfth century, these people considered themselves as integrally belonging to the Indian world.[10]

"Further India" was a cultural as well as a territorial concept, the former persisting while the latter dissolved. In the noblest of his many books, Heinrich Zimmer writes of the Indian cultural world:

> Each of the colonial cultures and art styles of Ceylon, Indonesia, and Further India, as well as that of Tibet, China, Korea, and Japan, took over in a worthy way the Indian heritage, giving to it an original and happy local application. Out of various ethnological and biological requirements self-contained styles were formed that were the peers in originality, nobility and delicacy of the Indian.

India remains "the creating hearth": "Indeed, whenever the incredible brightness of the spiritual, the balanced repose of the dynamic, or the brilliant power of the triumphantly omnipotent are made effectively manifest in Oriental art, an Indian model is not far to seek."[11] There is a lesson to be learned here, and some of it is learned in Macaulay's vision of an "imperishable empire" in which the integrating force is to be cultural cohesion rather than imperial dominance.

Sea power established and sustained the Portuguese empire, but long lines of communication and manpower restraints made that empire (unlike the cultural world of further India) an essentially coastal affair. The brief and solitary reference to the Mughals in *The Lusiads* (10.64) is not necessarily a reflection of this skin-deep character. Although the Hispanic Society's editor finds the lack of attention to the Mughals surprising,[12] the fact is that the dynasty had not come into existence when da Gama dropped anchor in Calicut. A reference to the Mughals is only possible in the accounts of the Portuguese imperial future that occupy the last books of the poem. Camões does make such a reference, but the occasion he chooses is the support the Portuguese give to the king of Gujarat in his campaign against Akbar's father, Humayun. The Portuguese reward consisted of permission to build a fortress in Diu. Since Akbar himself was on the throne at the time *The Lusiads* was published, singling out the event was much less than tactful. It also showed the Portuguese wrongheadedness (predictable in a coastal empire) in assessing the balance of forces on the Indian subcontinent. In the year following the publication of *The Lusiads*, Akbar opened his campaign against Gujarat and, realizing like all successful generals that speed was of the essence, surprised his adversary with a forced march that covered the 600 miles to Ahmedabad in eleven days. Surat had been taken six months earlier, and all of Gujarat was now subdued. The Great Mogul, who fortunately had not read *The Lusiads*, exacted no price for Portuguese participation in the alliance against his father. Later in the decade, Akbar was to begin his pursuit of a universal religion and was to summon Portuguese Jesuits to his "House of Worship" in Fatehpur Sikri to articulate the insights of Christianity. Tennyson takes note of the event in his carefully researched poem, "Akbar's Dream."[13] In another five years, Camões's perception of the Great Mogul might have changed, but the period in which he sets his poem remains one in which the Delhi sultanate was collapsing and in which power relationships all over North India were turbulent and unpredictable.

In South India, the situation was quite different. The Hindu kingdom of Vijayanagar had been growing in power and influence for more than a century. Niccolò Conti, the Italian traveler, visited the capital in 1420. His perfunctory reference to it pales in comparison with ʿAbd-er-Razzak's glowing description in 1442: "The pupil of the eye has never seen a place like it, and the ear of intelligence has never been informed that there existed anything to equal it in the world."[14] The Portuguese traveler, Domingo Paes, visited the kingdom's capital soon after da Gama's arrival and described it as "the best provided city in the world."[15] Vijayanagar's suzerainty extended to all of South India, and Portugal respected that suzerainty sufficiently to seek Vijayanagar's permission to build a fortress at Bhatkal. Permission was granted but only after Portugal had demonstrated its prowess by Albuquerque's capture of Goa, although with the assistance of 2,000 Indian troops.[16] Portuguese relations with Vijayanagar were extensive, and indeed, much of our information about the kingdom comes from Portuguese sources such as Domingo Paes; Duarte Barbosa, Magellan's brother-in-law (on whom Camões draws heavily in his account of the matrilineal society of the Nairs); and Fernão Nuniz. Panikkar describes these relationships as "most cordial,"[17] but perhaps they are better characterized as opportunism covered with a diplomatic veneer, as is too often the case in relationships between nations. When Vijayanagar reached its apogee under the rule of Krishnadeva Raya, the veneer of cordiality was sufficient for Portugal to assist Vijayanagar substantially in recapturing Raichur. Nuniz treats that event as decisive in Vijayanagar's attainment of supremacy in South India. As the kingdom became less stable, Portuguese relationships with it became predictably more disruptive. It may not have been altogether helpful to Vijayanagar that "the external trade of the great Hindu kingdom was practically in the hands of the Portuguese."[18] That trade, which, as Barbosa noted, extended from China to Alexandria, included a considerable number of Persian horses. Nuniz, who earned his living as a horse dealer, estimates that as many as 13,000 horses were imported annually into Vijayanagar.[19]

The ruler of Vijayanagar at the time of da Gama's arrival in Calicut was Narsimha Saluva, to whom Camões is almost certainly referring when he speaks of the kingdom of Narsingha.[20] Camões's response to Vijayanagar bypasses the substantial connections between Portugal and the Hindu kingdom. It is restricted to observing that Vijayanagar is more noted for its gold and precious stones than for the valor of its people[21] and that it is the territory in which St. Thomas was treacherously put to death (7.21, 10.108–19). None of Vijayanagar's accomplishments are recognized in a poem that takes it for granted that Oriental nations are incapable of sustaining the forms of civilization and that the best they can do is to provide opportunities for commerce. Others who claim no literary eminence have been able to perceive more in Vijayanagar's history.

The Vijayanagar style, a Hindu anticipation of the baroque, has aroused disparate reactions and can be accused of florid excess. On the other hand, the political statement the style sought to make could be expected to call on the aesthetics of lavishness, using the controlled profusion of Hindu art as a metaphor for the kingdom's ordered plenitude. That statement was soon to come to an end.

A coalition of Moslem-ruled Deccan sultanates disastrously defeated the Hindu kingdom's army in the battle of Talikota on January 23, 1565. They were aided in this crushing victory by two crucial defections from the Vijayanagar forces. The sacking of the capital followed, and in five methodical months of further destruction, Vijayanagar was razed to the ground. "Never perhaps in the history of the world," one scholar writes, "has such havoc been wrought and wrought so suddenly, on so splendid a city."[22] The havoc may have been sudden because the people of Vijayanagar were confident in the victory of their enormous army, but it was also systematic and hideously prolonged. War lust does not explain the 150 days of the capital's ordeal after a conclusive victory had been achieved in the field. It was not sufficient for the city to be plundered; the statement it made had to be erased from cultural memory. Western imperialism possesses no monopoly on the exercise of vindictiveness to otherness.

Camões was in Goa at the time of the battle of Talikota, and when he makes his reference to the kingdom of Narsingha as more notable for its gold and precious stones than for the valor of its people, he may have been commenting on that battle. Despite its more abrasive implications, the comment is indeed necessary to reassure investors in empires such as the Portuguese and the consortiums brought into being by the English, the French, the Dutch, and even the Danes. For venture capital to be called out in sufficient quantities, the territory must be rich in resources and its population easy to intimidate.

A third and more subtle desideratum comes to be added to the imperialist prospectus: the territory must not only accept submission but also acknowledge it as proceeding from its identity. When da Gama is conducted to the Zamorin's palace, he first enters a temple filled with abominable representations of the deity in the manner of the catalog of pagan gods in the first book of *Paradise Lost*. Camões's condemnatory description rectifies an incident in which da Gama is said to have endeared himself (briefly) to the local populace by kneeling in a Hindu temple, thinking it to be an eccentric version of a Christian church. Southey, who considered da Gama to be worse than Francisco Pizarro, seized on the incident as confirming da Gama's stupidity.[23] In fact, da Gama was not alone in his error. It was widely assumed at the time that those in India who were not Moslems must be Christians. The legend of Prester John was potent in preconditioning expectations.[24]

After Hindu idolization of the unnatural has been underlined, da Gama can proceed to the enclosed garden of the Zamorin's palace, a country retreat in the center of the city. A Marvellian disengagement of art from life is suggested, and the barrier, as in Marvell, is porous. Art reaffirms the principles of the real world that are sufficiently powerful to maintain themselves, even in the segregation of the artistic enclosure. The gateway set in the walls surrounding the palace celebrates this infiltration. It is adorned (with a craftsmanship said to be worthy of Daedalus) by scenes depicting previous conquerors of India. These conquerors are specified as Bacchus, Semiramis, and Alexander. The representations are as the shadow to the substance, with the substance attaining its full realization in a final conquest by the Portuguese, of which the previous triumphs are shadowy types.

Of the three conquests, the first is mythical. The fictitious campaign of the second against India was a military disaster, according to Strabo and Arrius. The third conqueror, Alexander, in his brief foray into India, never penetrated to within 1,000 miles of Calicut. Camões is praised for his capacity for direct observation, for writing whereof he knows, unlike Milton, who is compelled to pore over travel books and atlases. The claim is not unjustified but might be more persuasive if *The Lusiads* made less extensive and more critical use of classical historians and geographers. Here, however, Camões is not recording his observations but providing artwork for the imperialist folder. Achilles' shield is the distant ancestor of this artwork, but the depictions on the gateway commemorate submission, not victory, and are carved on a gateway, not a shield. This crucial change, on which Lusiadic commentary is so conspicuously silent, carves out the difference between Occident and Orient, between a masculine, imperial Europe and a feminine, colonial Asia. Were it not for Semiramis, one could argue that domination over the Orient is a Western entitlement so deeply taken for granted that it can even be found incised into the art of subject peoples. Semiramis, an Asian, may seem to represent a problem, but her figure in the gateway may well be an allusion to the matrilineal habits of the Nairs—habits that Camões, drawing on Barbosa's account, has already described in unusual detail. Moreover, since *The Lusiads* draws some attention to Semiramis's lurid sexual practices (which Sir Walter Raleigh regards as invented by "envious and lying *Grecians*"),[25] her imaginary conquest of India can be seen as implanting those practices in the fertile soil of Oriental decadence. India's talent for the unnatural has been emphasized already in the previous stanzas. Conquest by a woman to whom the unnatural comes easily compounds the effeminacy and degeneracy of the conquered. A civilization that celebrates its defeats in this manner has earned the ennoblement of a Portuguese conquest.

Said finds imperialism "supported and perhaps even impelled" by ideological formations that include the notion "that certain territories and people *require* and beseech domination."[26] The gateway to the Zamorin's palace is sculptured as if to demonstrate this proposition, treating it as inlaid into India's understanding of itself. It is a gateway not only to India but also to a way of viewing the colonial world.

The feminization of the Orient is a perception deeply embedded in imperialist discourse, but as the perception accumulates its history, the nuances (or crudities) of that feminization become more instructive. We are not yet at that more sophisticated stage where an Oriental-feminine other comes into being as an object of desire and guilt that a censored self has fashioned from its purged elements. The self's previous collusiveness with what it must hereafter reject and its will to eradicate all traces of that collusiveness can then be reflected in the sternness with which the other is treated. The purged identity is heroically maintained. Exploitativeness can be masked by a defensive anger that then becomes the evidence that the self's illicit relationships with its alternative are being severed and that their tentacular tenacity is being dealt with root and branch. This root-and-branch ferocity is chillingly apparent in Greenblatt's memorable juxtaposition of genocide in Hispaniola with Guyon's destruction of the Bower of Bliss.[27]

Such a specification of the other is best nourished by a religioethical mentality that projects the internal structure of order within the self onto the external relationship between ruler and ruled and that reconceives the nature of subject peoples so as to fit the images of that projection. The Protestant ethic of temperance and thrift is ingenious in meeting these requirements. Although conducive to capital formation, it is also in potential conflict with the consumerism that is the basis of empire. It is therefore driven to set in subliminal motion an argument for empire that would preempt this conflict. An ambivalent construction of the Orient becomes necessary, in which Western morality can denounce what Western cupidity continues to desire. Conquest that allows both condemnation and possession and finally even redemption of the object is the lucrative way out of this self-inflicted paradox. Oriental opulence has been a persisting stereotype, as Third World poverty is today. When the opulence is infernalized, as in Milton, the way is open to self-rebuke conveniently displaced into disciplining of the other and to self-indulgence from the profits of that disciplining. Said's work is indeed supportive of a syndrome in which responsibility follows rape and a hostile relationship with otherness violated graduates into a hierarchical relationship with otherness redeemed.

The Lusiads seems not to be troubled by these entanglements of psychic politics. It invites reading as a work of imperialist innocence. Homeric rather than Virgilian, it is only marginally given to the self-examination that in Virgil undercuts victory with some of the sadness of things. It needs no fictions of self-justification. The economics of plunder and the heroic satisfactions of annihilating the enemy are not emasculated by matters of morality. Wealth and women are the rewards of war. The women are provided in canto 9, and the prospective wealth is displayed in the next canto as if the human and cultural resources of the many-splendored earth were matters of absolutely no consequence. Milton looks down from a mountaintop to ponder the terrible dubiousness of history, hanging suspended in the mixed nature of humanity. Camões looks down as Milton's Comus might have to see the full and unwithdrawing hand of nature pouring forth its bounties, with no other aim than to "sate the curious taste" of an emerging consumerism that has smelled the savor of affluence (*Ludlow Masque* 709-23; *PL* 11.884-86).

One can equate the world that da Gama is invited to view with the banquet Christ refuses in *Paradise Regained* (2.337-91). There is a higher hunger in which Camões shows no interest. When the layers of the Ptolemaic universe are unwrapped to display the Portuguese future as its kernel, the poem also unwraps its identity as scarcely more than a guidebook to the spice trade. India grows rich on gold, precious stones, perfumes, and spices, and Malabar fattens on trade from China to the Nile (7.31, 41). Bengal outranks all other countries in fertility (7.20). The abundance of Chittagong, the looms of Orissa, and "treasure-strewn" Cambay await exploitation by those who control the routes of maritime commerce (10.106, 120, 121). Jedda owes its prosperity to the spice trade (9.3). Banda can offer pepper and mace, the Moluccas provide nutmeg and cloves, and cinnamon presents itself as the fame, wealth, and beauty of Sri Lanka (9.14). Borneo's gift to the Portuguese is camphor. The cloves of Ternate and Tidore are all the more precious because they will be purchased with Portuguese blood. Sumatra offers silk and gold and trees weeping fragrant gums and balms in the manner of the trees in Milton's paradise. The Maldives provide coconut palms, Socotra offers bitter aloes, and the islands of Africa supply ambergris (10.132-37).

The limitations of this inventory are persistent and obvious. One might expect more from a work of literature, and Camões does indeed advise us that gold is the root of all evil and that contempt for riches is a part of human dignity (6.98, 7.98-99). Like the old man's harangue in canto 4, these statements are made in order not to be heard again. All three appear at the end of their respective cantos, marking not the canto's climax but its margin, the sporadic and residual appearance of another poem that no longer matters. We can hear in these distant disturbances the voices of what Quint calls a countervailing epic continuing to be audible at the poem's boundary. Their remote location can be read as acknowledging a text, marginalized as archaic and revitalized as subversive, that has been written over but cannot be erased. On the other hand, the very effort at erasure can be read as pointing to the inexorably diminishing future of these voices in a world now to be constituted by economics, not sententiae.

The reading of *The Lusiads* offered here confirms Mickle's characterization, although the exploitativeness I discern in the poem does not seem to have counted for much with Mickle even in 1776, at a time when the English nabobs were growing rich on the plunder of Bengal and when their misdeeds were a topic of popular literature in their country.[28] My reading differs from those of critics such as Richard Helgerson[29] who would prefer to locate their readings of *The Lusiads* around the poem's heroic-aristocratic core and to regard its commercial content as peripheral. It also differs from the readings of those who see *The Lusiads* as a poem divided against itself and who prefer to centralize rather than to historicize the poem written on the epic poem's margin.

Opportunities for such finessing are not lacking in Lusiadic commentary. C. M. Bowra sees Camões as "a Humanist even with his contradictions" and finds among those contradictions "conflicting feelings about war and empire."[30] Thomas Greene suggests that "*Os Lusiadas* is a poem which turns back on itself."[31] Gerald Moser observes that "every intellectual who has reflected on the episode of the Old Man has seen it in the light of his own times and circumstances." The old man, according to him, speaks today to "worries about man's survival among technological advances."[32] Alexander Parker argues that the voyages of Columbus and da Gama were regarded by enlightened thinkers of the time (such as Camões) as opening the way to an "international community" and to "collaboration between different peoples on a scale never envisaged before."[33] Kenneth Jackson in his study of the dialogics of *The Lusiads* even suggests that "there is some evidence that the re-contact with India is upheld as a Utopian fusion of the Occident-Orient split." The split is apparently to be healed by "love as transformed conquest."[34]

These recuperative efforts bear witness to some uneasiness with the more than occasional stridency of *The Lusiads*, but the poem also needs to be shown as complicating itself by those who find Mickle swaggeringly reductionist. The alternative (as Helgerson clearly sees) is to argue that the true site of the poem is not where Mickle found it. Such restorative readings remain precarious because of their excessive attention to possibilities that the poem sites on its margin or that it raises and then declines to pursue. In fact, the most effective turn against *The Lusiads* takes place not at the poem's margin but in another poem by Camões, the justly admired "By the Rivers of Babylon."[35] Something important is said about Camões's epic when uneasiness with its ideology is placed so explicitly outside its borders. The poem surrenders to the imperial future, and although the surrender may not be without misgivings, the claim of the future is so powerful that the misgivings can only be voices from the past.

A potential counterforce in the poem to which imaginative energy is heavily and by no means marginally committed can be found in the Adamastor episode. Placed with high prominence both at the midpoint of da Gama's journey and at the midpoint of the poem itself, the myth of Adamastor is found by Quint to be "a figure for an Africa that cannot definitively be subdued by European arms."[36] Adamastor's menacing warning to da Gama against proceeding further on his quest picks up elements from the old man's speech and is in the tradition of the epic curse—a promise of resistance to the imperial narrative and of the assiduous undoing of the drive to closure on which the authority of that narrative depends.

In weighing Quint's reading of Adamastor, we must remember that the epic prize sustaining da Gama's quest is Asia and not Africa. The stormy cape (which nearly disposed of the author of *The Lusiads*) is a formidable obstacle, but no more than an obstacle, in a drive to finality that leaves the impediment behind both in geopolitical space and as a continuing threat to epic-imperial closure.[37] Significantly, Asia, the consummation of the quest, is not allowed either a site or an image of resistance. Thus the epic topos is crucially limited, and as Quint's study makes plain, it is deformed even within those limits, with Adamastor reduced from a human counterforce to a "blind fury of nature,"[38] able only to recycle its own wrath. Insofar as resistance is repetitive and even random, it can only struggle ineffectively against the teleological thrust of the imperial narrative, an impetus so powerful that, like that divine providence for which the imperial will habitually makes itself a metaphor, it can even turn resistance to its ends. Thus, the storms that assail da Gama actually blow him closer to the shores of India. This is Bacchus's frustration and not Adamastor's. Adamastor's frustration is to remain perpetually taunted by Thetis, locked forever into the African landscape, while Tethys displays to da Gama the many kingdoms that are to be jewels in the Portuguese crown.[39] Thus even this much-praised episode only suggests "that epic's representation of its losers, its attempt to adopt their perspective, may not be able to escape appropriation by the victor's ideology."[40]

Differences between Western and Eastern readings of *The Lusiads* are ultimately disagreements over how to map its center-margin relationships. One response to these disagreements would be to make the mapping historical. The margin then becomes a previous mode of understanding that the poem places at its boundary but is not prepared to efface. Moving the margin to the center reinstates the previous mode and is too close to nostalgia to be productive. It would be preferable to construct a revisionary critique of *The Lusiads* that makes use of the footholds the poem offers but is written out of the history the poem enters rather than out of the history it leaves behind. Milton, as we shall see, offers such a critique, and contemporary responses may have something to learn from him.

When we historicize the poetics of *The Lusiads*, we can be better aware of our own historical position on what Helgerson calls the hermeneutic spiral.[41] Helgerson uses the figure to account for the difference between Mickle's reading and his, but the figure, once invoked, invites us to carry it further. Readings made in the Elizabethan world of English national consciousness, in an imperial world poised on the threshold of possessing India, and in a postcolonial world that must take into account not only heroic identities but also their exploitative consequences will naturally differ in the way they perceive the poem. The spiral form reminds us not only of these differences but also of the interplay of understandings that ought to take place across them.

Helgerson's reading is located in an Elizabethan world that, in writing itself, is articulating a nationhood that will persist and prevail in future constructions of England. *The Lusiads*, not merely honored but cherished in Portugal as a deep and singular statement of the Portuguese national self, is placed within and read as speaking to this English world. It is the poem of an aristocratic-heroic ethos, set in contrast by Helgerson with Richard Hakluyt's voyages, which speak for a commercial ethos, potentially indifferent to the imperial.

One must question a separation that was influential in the decorum of its day but that subsequent events seem to blur. Mickle resoundingly associates commerce with possession, and that association persisted even though nineteenth-century free traders questioned the empire not on moral grounds but on the grounds of its viability as a business concern. They could have been mistaken, and it was more prudent to be safe. As a place for character building and for exhibiting the British heroic identity, the empire had possibilities that could be said to appeal to an aristocratic code, but it would be rash to conclude that these theatrical opportunities were more important than protecting trade routes.

To these cautions one should add that the separation for which Helgerson argues was not clear-cut, even in Elizabethan England.[42] If "honour, dominion, glory and renown" (PL 6.422) were assigned to a heroic realm and profit was assigned to a practical world free of heroic distractions, that may have been largely to distinguish British matter-of-factness from a confusion of genres that marred the Spanish performance. When Milton displaces the heroic claim with the Satanic manifesto, he does not simply devalue the heroic; he also points, in similes freighted with evocations of the spice trade, to the inexorable link between the heroic and the commercial. Donne's nineteenth elegy, a poem admittedly written in the middle style but one that strains instructively against its boundaries, places material riches and imperial possession (figuratively realized as sexual possession) in an intimate relationship within the much-used trope of the New World perceived as the female body. Bonds, seals, and licenses attest to the mercantile strain that pervades the imagery, and since title to possession is conveniently granted by the person possessed, the images can apply the binding forces of both legal contracts and passionate undertakings to the relationship between imperial power and colonial yielding. We pass through the now familiar gateway of The Lusiads to the surrendered wealth of a territory beseeching dominance.[43]

Today's postcolonial reader is concerned not with how England wrote itself, even in Donne's exuberant complexities, but with how Asia is to write itself in a manner that emancipates it from previous writings by Europe. For such a reader, the heavy commercial freight that the poem carries and the characterizing of every Asian country exclusively in terms of its wealth and vulnerability are too dominantly foregrounded for The Lusiads to be approached as a heroic poem that swerves into the commercial. The reverse reading of Camões's poem as a commercial poem that swerves into the heroic remains possible, but the magnitude of the swerve cannot be made significant to those aware of the exploitative realities, the destructive cooperation of commerce with possession, that history wrote as a postscript to the poem's final cantos.

The relativities of reading must always be borne in mind as we read. The argument being pursued here is that the turn of the spiral into our era has opened the way to a new order of reading that calls for a place among the concerns of this book. It is not suggested that the new reading is the only reading our historical situatedness can authorize. It is suggested that intercultural understanding cannot proceed until the new reading is more than the voice in the margin that the old man's harangue continues to be in *The Lusiads*. The look of a canon, largely imperial, must change as readers from territories, until recently subjected, take their proper place in future reading communities.

If East and West are to approach each other in their readings of *The Lusiads*, they can do so only against the backdrop of that enormous cultural simplification we call imperialism. Some works of literature resist this simplification, others comply with it, and others find resistance in compliance. Two of these categories are honorable today, but the third is not dishonorable and scholarship is not served when it is elided into the other two.

Beginnings simplify in order to generate the impetus that will give them their stamina as beginnings. Beginnings leave something behind. There will always be an old man on the shore whose age is the proof that he no longer matters. If we discern a pathos in *The Lusiads*, it is the pathos of a poem mastered by its burden. It has to define an imperial moment, not of transition but of rupture, that opens a strange road into a different era. To assess the poem's pathos, we must assess what history rejects in order to form itself, what lesser possibilities it places in exile or in otherness, and what stridencies it nurtures in defending the imperial statement against the residue of its own unavoidable guilt. A poem that calls for these assessments may not always be pleasant to read. It is more important that reading it should be enlightening.

2

Banyan Trees and Fig Leaves:
Some Thoughts on Milton's India

ভে

Scholarship on Milton's India is not voluminous, and the student in search of understanding cannot proceed very far beyond the Milton encyclopedia article on the subject. The general disposition is to treat the handful of references to India as unrelated excursions into the exotic, part of an encyclopedic epic's obligation to be encyclopedic even in its naming of places. If the references are taken together, their most conspicuous characteristic is that nearly all of them occur in infernal or postlapsarian contexts. They can then be regarded as collectively proposing the Satanization of the Orient in a way becoming familiar to Milton's time. Milton's contemporaries were not unanimous on this matter.[1] Commercial relations with the East were strengthening, and it was hard to argue that the Devil and his associates were the only possible source of supply for commodities that European nations wanted. The biblical imagination was less entangled in these niceties. Egypt was an abomination, and anything east of it was likely to be worse.

The first book of *Paradise Lost* is indeed heavily laden with pejorative references to the Orient. Both the catalog of false gods and the building of Pandemonium provide rich opportunities for moral invective. The opportunities, although seized with characteristic energy, remain sufficiently routine for J. B. Broadbent to observe straightforwardly that "the oriental similes place the building as a citadel of barbaric despotism."[2] It is to be noted that Babylon forms the eastern limit of these similes, almost as if the true heart of darkness has been set apart for deeper castigation. Nevertheless, Pandemonium is not totally Oriental. Its facade reflects the Mediterranean world, with Doric pillars that may be designed to remind us of the colonnade that Gian Bernini built for St. Peter's. The bee was the emblem of Pope Urban VIII, who consecrated St. Peter's, and Milton duly provides us with a bee simile that deflates the fallen angels and embroils the papacy in Oriental viciousness. We are now in the outer chamber of Pandemonium, and a reference to pygmies beyond "the Indian mount" (1.781) helps us to fix Pandemonium's location in the poem's imaginative space. The reference to "fairy elves" that follows confirms the location.[3] It remembers Shakespeare's *Midsummer Night's Dream* (2.1), where dissension in the fairy realm, sufficient to upset the seasonal order, arises over a young boy given to Titania by an Indian queen who is Titania's votaress (2.121–37). Spenser goes further in *The Faerie Queene*, claiming dominion over India for the world of Faerie (2.10.72). The claim can become more than fanciful in view of Queen Elizabeth's Faerie ancestry.

Pandemonium itself is hierarchically organized, with class distinctions cementing the imperial display. Its great hall is for the democratic multitude, who must contract themselves to cope with the hall's limited seating facilities. "Far within" is the council chamber for the "secret conclave" of the power elite, who are provided with "golden seats" and can maintain without compromise "their own dimensions like themselves" (1.790–97). The first book ends poised on these lines, and as we turn the page, the imagination opens the doors to the interior:

> High on a Throne of Royal State, which far
> Outshone the wealth of Ormus and of Ind,
> Or where the gorgeous East with richest hand
> Showers on her kings barbaric Pearl and Gold,
> Satan exalted sat, by merit raised
> To that bad eminence.
> (2.1–6)

Ormuz was once the emporium of the Orient, and Marvell's deluded voyagers to the Bermudas dream appropriately of "jewels more rich than Ormuz shows." By the time Milton wrote *Paradise Lost*, this legendary splendor was becoming a thing of the past. Ormuz's fortunes declined after its capture from the Portuguese in 1622 by an Iranian expedition with British naval support. Described in *The Lusiads* as a barren mountain of salt (10.41.1–2), important only as a marketplace for Eastern riches, it became in Milton's poem that "island salt and bare" to which Paradise was eventually reduced.[4] On the other hand, the wealth of Ind was very much a matter of the present and was commented on by every traveler to India, including English emissaries such as Sir Thomas Roe and Sir Richard Hawkins.

Their interest in the peoples and cultures of India seems marginal in comparison with their zeal in making inventories, but evangelical fervor can erupt revealingly through the assiduous stocktaking. Thus Thomas Coryat, having first described the Hindus along expected lines as a "gentle people," describes them almost immediately afterward as "brutish ethnicks," as displaying "superstition and impiety most abominable in the highest degree," and as "aliens from Christ and the common-wealth of Israel."[5]

In these circumstances, the "Throne of Royal State" that Satan occupies and that outshines the wealth of Ind could point specifically to the Peacock Throne as the most conspicuous embodiment of that wealth. Since 1634, when Shah Jehan moved the Mughal capital to Delhi, the throne had stood in the Hall of Public Audience, a structure 600 feet long and 370 feet wide, which might have suggested the outer court of Pandemonium. Jean-Baptiste Tavernier, the French jeweler, had examined the throne in 1665, and although his detailed description was translated only after the second edition of *Paradise Lost* was published, reports about the throne would have been widespread in a London where the East India Company had been in existence for two-thirds of a century. With its pearl-fringed canopy supported by golden pillars, the throne was the epitome of the "gorgeous East" in its opulence.[6]

When *Paradise Lost* was published, the monarch on the Peacock Throne was Dryden's hero, Aurangzeb. He could be said to have been raised to his eminence by merit, if by merit we mean the successful killing off of every other claimant. History fits the image, but Milton may not have been aware of the fitness. It is tempting to think that he was aware of the inscription, four times repeated in letters of gold, in Shah Jehan's white marble Hall of Private Audience, which corresponds to the council room of Pandemonium. As a comment on Satan's situation, its layered irony must be deemed Miltonic: "If there be Paradise on earth, it is this, it is this, it is this!"

The direct application is obvious, but the statement becomes more interesting read against the grain, with the triple repetition compounding the force of the "if." Paradise can be not native but alien to the earth, won laboriously against the earth's resistance. Shah Jehan built in this way, and his achievement has become identified with one matchless building demonstrating that death is the mother of beauty. The proud hedonism is really not in conflict with another description to be found over the Victory Gate in Akbar's abandoned palace at Fatehpur Sikri: "The world is a bridge, pass over it but do not build upon it. He who hopes for an hour may hope for eternity. The world is but an hour; spend it in devotion, the rest is unseen."[7] Pandemonium has been built, and the two statements put before us both the elation and the vanity of building. The mind is its own place but can only be its own place by installing itself on the Peacock Throne of the self. The throne is in the inner chamber and is thus a statement of identity as well as a public announcement, a tacit disclosure of the weakness to be found in its strength.

So far, the movement to the center through the precincts of Pandemonium and through a corresponding geography of vainglory and ostentation seems to assign India a decisive place at the heart of the evil empire. The proposition is staged with sufficient persistence to persuade us that no other proposition needs to be made. The moral imagination can be discouragingly simplistic, but Milton is fortunately not a simple writer. In the spice trade simile, which transports Satan on his journey to Asia, he is doing much more than once again presenting India as one of the primary sites of infernality:

> As when far off at Sea a Fleet descri'd
> Hangs in the Clouds, by Equinoctial Winds
> Close sailing from Bengala, or the Isles
> Of Ternate and Tidore, whence merchants bring
> Their spicy Drugs; they on the Trading Flood
> Through the wide Ethiopian to the Cape
> Ply stemming nightly toward the Pole. So seem'd
> Far off the flying fiend.
> (2.636–43)

Ternate and Tidore are Spice Islands in the Moluccas, but the phrase is also an alliterative remembrance of *The Lusiads*, and Satan's voyage, the ancestor of all voyages, is being placed in relationship to da Gama's voyage to India, of which Camões's poem is the epic celebration. *The Lusiads*, as we have already seen, celebrates a voyage not simply from Lisbon to Calicut but also from a medieval to an imperial world order. Not without regret, it leaves the previous view and its voices of protest symbolically at its margins. As the defining of an imperial moment, it made its deflationary appearance in the midst of what should have been another imperial moment. Fanshawe's translation of it was published in 1655, the year in which Jamaica was captured as a consolation prize in Cromwell's failed Western design.

The failure of the design led to the usual reassessment of what

Providence may have had in mind for God's Englishmen. An influential decoding of the divine rebuke was that English expansiveness should hereafter be commercial. England should complete its reformation before dissipating in imperial adventures, an identity that had yet to be bonded into nationhood.

Commerce in such dissociations is always presumed to be innocent of empire. Milton's accomplishment is to have seen with clarity the necessary and potentially Satanic merging of the two realms. In an age uneasily engaged in discriminating the sanctified from the demonic uses of imperialism, Milton moves hesitantly to the proposition that imperialism is itself a form of use and a form of use so profoundly exploitative that its right use is impossible. It is not a proposition Milton can endorse resoundingly. Ireland stands in his way and so does the New World. But to write a poem is to transgress ideologies.

The imperial vision in *The Lusiads* is one in which honor, dominion, glory, and renown go hand in hand with the rich rewards of the spice trade. Milton accepts the integrity of that vision and then uses that integrity to discredit both components. Classical heroism is devalued by Christian heroism, and the main motive of commerce is discerned as consumerist self-indulgence. Milton's treatment of Camões is indeed heavily revisionary.[8] The old man's voice is heard again, but it is a critiquing, not a protesting, voice. It does not helplessly query the new order. It points instead to an immemorial order that cannot be violated without tearing apart those who violate it. The nature of his poem enables Milton to endow his warning with the weight of ancestral authority. But the warning is also culturally focused. It exposes the rottenness at the core of the consumerist apple.

According to one enthusiastic estimate, da Gama's voyage and Columbus's discovery of the New World were the greatest events in history since the Incarnation. More prosaically, the purpose of da Gama's rounding of the cape was to end the Venetian monopoly of the spice trade and to break the Arab stranglehold on the trade routes by which the "spicy Drugs" of Asia came to Europe. Milton's realignment can be approached by noting that Bengal was not on the spice trade route and that European trade with Bengal was not in spices. The detour through Bengal may have been made to include within the scope of the simile the East India Company, for which the Bay of Bengal had been a principal theater of operations ever since the founding of Madras in 1640. But the geographical expansion is also designed to advise us of an expansion in the scope of the term "spicy Drugs." As G. V. Scammell, a leading historian of early European imperialism, observes:

> Spice was a vast and ill-defined generic which also embraced perfumes like incense and musk, medicines and drugs (the galingales of China and the aloes of Socotra), dyes, and the exquisite manufactures of the East, ranging from Chinese silk and porcelain to the carpets and tapestries of Persia. To those were added the products, as we shall see, of the Middle East—the glassware for example of Damascus.[9]

The term is in fact a synecdoche for the entire range of conspicuous consumption, and conspicuous consumption had been an issue with Milton ever since 1634, when Comus produced a bizarre ecological argument in its favor.[10] Thrift needed to be part of the Protestant ethic if the middle class was to be instrumental in capital formation. At this point in the poem, "spicy Drugs" anticipates Adam's and Eve's transgression and the hallucinogenic qualities of the forbidden fruit. The link is invited even though drugs in seventeenth-century usage were not typically hallucinogenic and even though Adam Smith as late as 1776 described tea as a drug.[11] Milton's aim in inviting the link and in departing from his view in *De Doctrina Christiana* that the forbidden fruit was "in its nature neither good nor evil"[12] is to join original sin to all subsequent excesses in consumption ("Greedily she engorged without restraint" [9.791]) and to inscribe the Satanic voyage within subsequent voyages of exploration and commerce as the tainted origin from which they may need to be rescued. In the process, attention shifts from the Orient as a primary site of evil to the Orient as supplier to a clientele who have discovered it and made use of it to pamper the weakness within themselves. It is notable that the fleet described in the simile is en route to Europe, laden with the profits of the spice trade, even though Satan is en route to Asia.[13]

In looking at Milton's similes, we have to pass by their most important characteristic, namely, the extraordinary completeness with which the similes translate what they purport to resemble. We have to restrict ourselves to how India is perceived within the translation. It is already clear that there can be more than one perception, depending on the course of action or the religious or moral imperative to which the construction of India is annexed. The next reference to India occurs when Satan alights on the outer shell of the "pendent world"—an outer shell where limbo is derisively located and that is compared in its desolation to the central Asian plateau:

> As when a Vulture on *Imaus* bred,
> Whose snowy ridge the roving Tartar bounds,
> Dislodging from a Region scarce of prey
> To gorge the flesh of lambs or yeanling kids
> On hills where flocks are fed, flies towards the springs
> Of Ganges or Hydaspes, Indian streams;
> But in his way lights on the barren Plains
> Of Sericana, where Chineses drive
> With sails and wind their cany wagons light:
> So on this windy sea of land, the fiend
> Walked up and down alone bent on his prey.
> (3.431–41)

The crucial element in this compendious simile is the pun that joins Tartar to Tartarus. Milton did not invent the pun; it is attributed to Pope Innocent IV in response to Tartar invasions that, by 1241, had extended into Hungary and Germany. In further response to those invasions, Pope Innocent's successor, Pope Alexander IV, issued the following warning to the princes of Christendom:

> There rings in the ears of all, and arouses to vigilant alertness those who are not befuddled by mental torpor, a terrible trumpet of dire forewarning which, corroborated by the evidence of events, proclaims with so unmistakable a sound the wars of universal destruction wherewith the scourge of Heaven's wrath in the hands of the inhuman Tartars, erupting as it were from the secret confines of Hell, oppresses and crushes the earth [so] that it is no longer the task of Christian people to prick up their ears so as to receive surer tidings of these things, as though they were still in doubt, but their need is rather for admonition to take provident action against a peril impending and palpably approaching.[14]

The similarities between the papal bull and Milton's poem, written over four centuries later, do not need to be labored. Particularly important is the connection between the Tartar invasions and the opening lines of book 4, where the poet wishes that Adam and Eve had been shocked into attention by that "warning voice," that "terrible trumpet," as the papal bull has it, foretelling the "wars of universal destruction" envisioned in Revelation 12:7–12. The conspicuous difference is that the pope's concerns are limited to the penetration of Europe by the Tartars. India is not even on the horizon of calamity. In Milton's simile, on the other hand, India is central. It is the destination to which the vulture flies, leaving an inhospitable and barren habitat in search of a more fertile environment where it can "gorge the flesh of lambs or yeanling kids." It is true that the vulture seeks the sources of the Jhelum (Hydaspes) and the Ganges rather than the plain that those great rivers irrigate and that future invasions of India were to ravage. But its flight, Satan's journey, and the Tartar debouchment into India run related courses, brought together all the more evocatively because the earthly Paradise was reputed to lie where the Ganges had its beginnings. In the opening lines of the seventh canto of *The Lusiads*, for instance, all India is hailed as lying in proximity to this Paradise (see also 4.74). More than one ancient father followed Josephus in making the Ganges one of the rivers of Paradise.[15] Milton, like most of his contemporaries, locates Paradise elsewhere, but his simile remains freighted with these associations.

In linking India to Paradise and the vulture's flight to the Satanic journey, Milton now presents India not as the site of infernality but as its victim. It is a construction reinforced by "lambs or yeanling kids," which, apart from its religious overtones, cannot but suggest the exposure of inexperience and helplessness to the onslaught of power and cruelty. Tamburlaine sacked Delhi in 1398 and is said to have slaughtered 80,000 of its inhabitants, leaving pyramids of skulls to mark the milestones on the city's highways. The Great Mogul, on the Peacock Throne when Milton wrote his poem, proudly affirmed his descent from the house of Timur. Milton's immediate reference is to the Tartars, but the reference can be extended to all the invasions that the snowy ridge of Imaus could not contain and that erupted into India along a much-traveled route of conquest. We can even read the "windy sea of land," which so felicitously materializes the indeterminate nature of limbo, as pointing to a windy sea not of land, which was to become the route of further conquests. Milton obviously did not intend to say this, but poems have a life beyond their boundaries.

In the fifth book, Raphael descends to Paradise not to blow "a terrible trumpet of dire forewarning" but to "bring on discourse" and thereby instruct Adam and Eve on their place in the order of things. He approaches the Edenic pair through a wilderness of "flowering odours," a "spicy forest" that invites us to reflect on the misappropriation of the spice trade (5.291–99). Dinner is served, with an international menu on which India is prominently, although vaguely, featured. The emphasis is not on indiscriminate variety but on "Taste after taste upheld with kindliest change" (5.336). There is no gorging on the flesh of lambs or yeanling kids. The meal is vegetarian, and the three partake of it in order to suffice and not to burden nature (5.451–52).

Commenting on the meal, Alastair Fowler detects a "grim irony." Pontus was notorious as a source of poisons, and Punic figs were best known for the threat to Rome that Plutarch made them symbolize.[16] Good things can be directed to evil uses, as is apparent even from the pre- and postlapsarian connotations of words such as "errant" and "wanton." Milton is at pains to advise us that when the right order of things existed, it was eloquent about itself, even in such matters as serving an appropriate meal to a visiting angel. But the right order of things can no longer be presumed to exist pristinely behind the masks of misappropriation. Shifting depictions of India do not necessarily lay bare an essential India that lies beyond and is uncontaminated by the depictions. Representations may unmask previous representations, but they, in turn, may put in place assumptions that need to be unmasked. Milton's multiple constructions of India place strikingly before us the relativity of constructions and their entanglement with one another in a confused amalgam that both represents the texture of imperial discourse and lays its prevarications open to scrutiny. Milton is complicit in some of the prevarications. He is also committed to the scrutiny.

These entanglements have to be borne in mind as we proceed to the proliferations of the banyan tree passage, which, of all Milton's images of India, is the most compelling and also the most evasive (9.1099–1118). Before doing so, we need to consider Satan's activities in the interval between his expulsion from Paradise by Gabriel and his assistants and his second entry for the successful temptation. Satan has circled the earth three times in an east-west and four times in a north-south direction. The purpose of these peregrinations is not merely to survey his kingdom while he awaits another opportunity but also with "inspection deep" to consider which among the world's creatures might best "serve his wiles." His last stop is the "land where flows / Ganges and Indus," and his final choice, "after long debate," is "The Serpent subtlest Beast of all the field" (9.81–82, 86–87). It is more than arguable that the infernal potentiality of India is once again being underlined and that India as victim or as prime provider of a repast fit for angels has receded into the background.

Satan now enters Paradise but not with his earlier exuberance, when, with "one slight bound," he leapt over the garden's protective barrier (4.181). This time he makes his entry via one of the rivers of Paradise, fortunately not the Pison, which was identified with the Ganges, but the Tigris, which shoots into an underground gulf at the foot of Paradise and surfaces as a fountain next to the tree of life. Satan emerges in the rising mist of the fountain "involved" with the primordial fluidity, as if inextricably part of the elemental nature of things (9.69–76).

The choice of India as the last stop before Paradise and of the serpent, with which India is strongly associated, as the fittest vehicle for the original sin might be regarded as appropriate preliminaries to the choice of the banyan tree for the original cover-up. Milton's emphatic dismissal of alternatives seems designed to pave the way for the cumulative infernalization of India. The subtlety and deviousness of which the serpent is the symbol and the comprehensive concealment afforded by the banyan tree are invested in *Paradise Lost* with the authority of origins. These propositions were soon to be engraved in imperial rhetoric as routinely part of India's representation.

Paradise Lost is a scholarly poem, and when Milton, in choosing his tree, waves aside "that kind for Fruit renowned" (9.1101), he reminds us of an earlier gesture. In the fourth book, the possibility that Paradise may lie at the summit of Mount Amara, "under the Ethiop Line / By Nilus head," is dismissed. It is, Milton tells us, "by some supposed" (4.281–83). In fact, it is hard to find anyone who confidently upholds this possibility, although every discussion of the location of Paradise raises it. The citation count is extensive, but the acceptance count approaches zero. Milton is very much in the majority here, tilting at a windmill in the robust fashion of scholarship. In the ninth book, on the other hand, he may be in a minority, even though Raleigh, in discussing this possibility, is able to cite more than one precedent.[17]

Reasons for going against the majority view can always be found and are most persuasive when they can be shown to be part of the imaginative logic of the poem. If the choice of the banyan tree is striking, so too is the readiness to make Paradise a site for postlapsarian lust. "God attributes to place / No sanctity, if none be thither brought" is Milton's justification for the destruction of Paradise (11.836–37). The desecration of sanctity that Milton's departure from precedent serves to underline deepens the original shame and calls for a more comprehensive cover-up. The connections are plausible, but we still need to argue that an innovation is not justified by referring it to another innovation that need not have been made.

Another view might be that infernalizing India has always been part of the poem's agenda and that the more benign presentations we have explored merely mean that the infernalization is not total. "The proliferating tree is a tree of error," Fowler tells us categorically. "It is an objective correlative of the proliferating sin that will ramify through Adam's and Eve's descendants."[18] If true, this conclusion is a virulent desacralization of a tree that has always been holy to Indians as both the site and the subject of Upanishadic instruction, a tree that Southey, in a poem not particularly sympathetic to India, approaches with respect as a temple of nature.[19] Moore similarly refers to the "sacred shade" of those "holy trees whose smooth columns and spreading roots seem to destine them for natural temples of religion."[20]

Milton's similes invite straightforward readings by their sustained correspondences between tenor and vehicle. But his language can also circumvent and retreat from the dominant momentum it nourishes. The tree "spreads her arms" in an encompassing gesture reminiscent of the crucifixion. The "Daughters grow / About the Mother Tree" (9.1105–6), and the gesture can be read as bringing together and protecting the human family rather than as bringing about the confusion that Gerard describes in his *Herball:* "The first or mother of this wood or desart of trees, is hard to be knowne from the children."[21] The "Pillared shade" that the daughter trees provide suggests a composed architecture rather than a wilderness of reflections. Yet in putting forward his representation, Milton always seems aware of another representation that may be the normal reading and that the turns of his language are not prepared to reject. The pillared shade also recalls the Doric pillars of Pandemonium, and their "High overarched" formations take us back to the Vallombrosa simile, in which the infernal angels were compared to leaves fallen from the tree of life into the valley of the shadow of death (1.302–4). The "Etrurian shade" of the Vallombrosa trees was "imbowered" as it turned in on itself. The bower of concealment is similar and is in designed contrast to the nuptial bower of book 4, lines 690–708. Yet when Kester Svendsen describes the recesses of the tree as a "deep interior sanctuary,"[22] he is not proceeding against Milton's language. The tree serves as shelter, although it can also be used for concealment. It permits withdrawal into meditative depths. It also encourages absorption in a narcissistic coma. Its "echoing walks" can be self-imprisoning, but they can also prolong the cadences of voices that need to be heard (4.680–85).

The contesting interpretations of itself that the spreading tree puts forward do not debar us from seeing it as a temple of nature, but they encourage us to read its proliferations and decentrations as an expanding assault on hierarchical order. Its leaves are not really as "broad as Amazonian targe,"[23] and if bodily concealment were the objective, other trees in India would have served the purpose better. But other trees would not have lent themselves to the emblematization delighted in by Renaissance herbalists and compilers of dictionaries. The Amazons are introduced not so that a passing reference can be made to the size of their shields but as a further source of hierarchical disturbance, with which readers of book 5 of *The Faerie Queene* would have been familiar. They go well with the role reversal that has been prominent in Milton's version of the Fall and with the feminization of the tree, which, blessed exclusively with daughters, compounds by its generative wantonness the destabilization of structure and design.

As we trace the echoing walks of this particular passage, many of the echoes lead us back through the history of the poem into occasions or images of the infernal. The lines are all the more disturbing because the tree's natural attributes lend themselves so easily to demonic appropriation. In addition, Milton compounds the discommoding effect by making gestures toward scientific accuracy, reminding us that the Fall was history to him even though it may be mythology to us. "Columbus found the American so girt," he tells us decisively. Primitive societies are closer to the source, and the characteristics of the source can be discerned more clearly in them.[24] The land that was mistaken for India justifies its erroneous identification by indicating how the resources of the true India were used. The banyan tree is "at this day to Indians known." Any official of the East India Company could inspect it and verify that there was no better way for Adam and Eve to cope with the sudden problem of their nakedness.

It is against the passage's traversals of itself and the received interpretations it accepts and circumvents that we need to consider the figure of the herdsman. Fowler is less than tactful in arguing that "the Indian herdsman is put in because he is primitive and pagan."[25] He is put in to point out to us that, although his responsibilities are far more limited than those of the faithful herdsman in *Lycidas*, he observes these responsibilities, unlike the corrupt clergy whom Milton excoriates and unlike Adam and Eve at this moment. He "tends his pasturing herds," and if he seeks the protection of the tree and cuts loopholes through the "thickest shade" of its foliage, it is not to conceal himself but to perform his task more efficiently and with less likelihood of being incapacitated by sunstroke.

Other revealing images offer themselves as we contemplate the figure of the herdsman. Adam and Eve, like him, are hidden in the tree's recesses, but it is the flock that is now hidden, not the shepherd. The shepherd seeks refuge from the heat of the sun's rays. Adam and Eve seek refuge from the "blaze / Insufferably bright" (9.1083–84) of the Son's presence. The Son is the shepherd, offering a protection symbolized by the tree's outstretched arms, which the guilty pair unknowingly invoke in using that very tree to avoid the Son's gaze. Milton's lines in their dense entanglements work powerfully to persuade us that appropriation is not simply a matter of channeling the properties of the tree to infernal uses. The tree is reinvented by the perspective in which it is installed. And the perspective cannot be said to be optional. It is largely responsible for inventing those who use it.

The final reference to India is in the panorama of the world's empires that Adam sees from the highest hill of Paradise. The *Aeneid* (6.790 ff.) is being remembered, with Milton's typical distancing from that seminal text. The vision is seen from a hill and not foretold in the underworld; it is concerned with all empires, not one; and it turns from those empires to "nobler sights" (11.411), from the sequence of secular pomp to the meaning of sacred history. Camões, diligently Virgilian in his machinery, is intermediate between Virgil and Milton. Like Virgil, he is concerned with a single nation's imperial destiny. Like Milton, his hero is shown the future from a mountaintop. But it is a future in which empire building is glorified, not questioned. Adam looks at the havoc to which his actions will lead. Vasco da Gama looks at the fulfillment of his mission in a future that is only possible because of his heroic accomplishment. The splendors of the Portuguese empire are elegantly displayed to him gift wrapped in the layers of the Ptolemaic universe (*Lusiads* 10.78–91).

Virgil associates the Roman destiny with ancestral statements of the white man's burden, with bringing justice and the rule of law to barbarians.[26] Camões is less concerned with such refinements and shows us the face of imperialism more candidly. Those who chafe under Portugal's light yoke will be made to pay dearly for their insolence. Ironically, the example chosen is Ormuz, which was to pass out of Portuguese hands forever half a century after Camões published his poem and well before Fanshawe's English translation became available.

The mountaintop prophecy, the panorama of empires, and the roll call of place names form multiple lines of connection between *Paradise Lost* and *The Lusiads*. The connections are enforced by the second of Milton's alliterative remembrances—"*Mombaza*, and *Quiloa*, and *Melind*" (11.399).[27] Melind was da Gama's last port of call before setting off on the final stage of his audacious voyage to India under the helpful guidance of an Indian pilot.[28]

The overlap in the view from the two mountaintops is extensive. One might argue that some attention has been paid to making it extensive. To connect the two poems is to become pointedly aware of the sudden blaze and swift extinction of the Portuguese imperial dream. That recognition finds its way back into Milton's poem as a general comment on the transience of empires. What we see from the mountaintop in the first place is the peripheral turbulence and pandemonium of history, not the inner theater of clarified engagement where the forces shaping history are exposed.

Much has changed in the descent from Virgil, and Virgil's Rome is among the empires dismissed. From an Iraqi mountaintop, Rome and "Agra and Lahor of great mogul" (11.391) are approximately equidistant;[29] "great mogul" designates not simply the dynasty but a diamond of unprecedented size (the Kohinoor) presented to Shah Jehan. Stereotypes of Oriental opulence are reinforced, taking us back in one of the poem's many circularities to the wealth of Ind and Satan's throne of royal state. But Rome was also a center of ostentatious excess, as *Paradise Regained* makes clear, and so far there has been nothing in the poem to suggest that Asia surpasses Rome in moral turpitude. We can even conjecture that if Milton had known of it, the Augustinian inscription at Fatehpur Sikri would have appealed to him more than any Roman text.

The inner theater of significance, surrounded by an otherwise meaningless periphery of empires, dramatizes the proposition that the only true kingdom is the kingdom of God. The nature of things in their purity does not permit the rule of one people by another:

> Man over men
> He made not Lord; such title to himself
> Reserving, human left from human free.
> (12.69–71)

Unfortunately, we are dealing not with the nature of things but with their fallen nature. In such circumstances, "Tyranny must be, / Though to the tyrant thereby no excuse" (12.95–96).

The argument does not condone tyranny, but it does suggest that attempts to overthrow tyranny will only reinscribe it unless they are accompanied by a radical change in the structure of the self. One can accept this as an argument, but it needs to be pointed out in reply that Milton unbalances his critique of dominance by too strong an insistence that subjected peoples deserve their own misfortunes. In the England of a failed revolution, this insistence may have been proper to the poetics of the moment. On a less localized scale, we have to observe that phrases such as "Tyranny must be" amount to a de facto acquiescence to tyranny. Tyrants are seldom deterred by the observation that their behavior cannot be excused.

The failed revolution and the need to justify its failure continue to be present in Milton's thought as the temptation of Rome is offered. In *Paradise Regained*, Satan accompanies his offer with the hyperbolic statement that not merely India but also Sumatra and the Malay Peninsula render obedience to "Rome's great emperor" (4.73–76).[30] Christ does not contest this exaggeration. Presumably, he has more important things on his mind. He points out predictably that Romans have earned their fate by their degeneracy. "Peeling their Provinces," already exhausted by lust and rapine, and carried away by the "insulting vanity" of their triumphs, they are luxury loving, cruel, greedy, and "from the daily scene effeminate" (PR 4.136–42). That last and climactic epithet, used extensively by the Romans in the denigration of Egypt, was to be much used again in marginalizing India. Originating in Michael's rebuke to Adam (PL 11.634), it becomes the final touch in the conqueror's inward enslavement to the other he constructs for his contempt.

Milton's description of Rome's degeneracy is not surprising, but his prelapsarian characterization of the Romans as just, frugal, mild, and temperate (PR 4.133–34) seems to invoke Christian rather than classical heroism.[31] The choice of virtues becomes clearer when we turn to the *Second Defence*: "To be free is precisely the same as to be pious, wise, just, and temperate, careful of one's property, aloof from another's, and thus finally to be magnanimous and brave."[32] A parallel between Rome and seventeenth-century England is clearly in the making, and perhaps it is the pursuit of this parallel that leads Milton to observe that the Romans "conquer'd well, / But govern ill" (PR 4.134–35).[33] Government by conquest can never be good government. Human was "left from human free" by the divine edict, and relationships between peoples based on dominance can never be other than deformed. Difference turned into confusion and conversation into the failure to communicate when the original tower of dominance was built. Milton's language at this point moves away from an egalitarian recognition that his previous language has inscribed. In an age when empires were materializing on the horizon and India was beginning to assume its glittering shape as the most coveted of imperial prizes, he cannot quite say that the pursuit of empires can only be destructive and that no people can "conquer well." In addition, his concentration on an inner theater where the principles of a single wisdom are made manifest by their performance in history reduces other wisdoms to peripheral status. At best, the periphery can only reflect the center or be the shadowy type to the center's truth. The design of understanding is potentially imperial. Other designs that are less lofty and humane will sustain themselves on the same geography of privilege.

The appropriation of Milton to this geography of privilege is an important thread in the fabric of this book. His references to India may not be numerous, but his part in India's representation is not merely a matter of six similes that show that he is capable of seeing India in more than one light. *Paradise Lost*, although not imperialist, is imperial as no other poem in the canon is. It is true that the imperial display is consecrated to the pervading and benevolent force of the universal and mild monarchy of heaven, but in the inevitable secularizing of the sacred, other translations of the display must emerge. The center-circumference dispositions, the hierarchical ordering of the poem's principal and almost only human relationship, the omnific word transforming a cosmic chaos that it is not difficult to displace into political anarchy, and the wilderness set against the ordered garden that must be tended and watched over if it is not to relapse into its origins are all perceptions that play a crucial part in the imperialist statement as an apparently timeless work of the literary canon, symbolically blind to the contingent, finds its way back into the arena of power.

Paradise Lost is the work of a totalizing energy by which dreams of empire cannot but be nourished. That nourishment sustains not merely the rhetoric of imperialism but, more fundamentally, the fictions of self-justification that stabilize that rhetoric and endow it with its necessary dignity. The chapters that follow will consider some of the ways in which representations of India within imperialist discourse rest on foundations that can be called Miltonic. Ironically, the poem's foundations (as distinct from those of the imperialism that appropriated it) include a concept of Christian heroism that can be perceived as leading through *Prometheus Unbound* to the nonviolent strategies that gained India its independence. That fact is not simply to be savored with relish; it educates us in the extent to which the canon itself, in its sometimes troubled self-awareness, can be instrumental in its own dismantling.[34]

3
Appropriating India:
Dryden's Great Mogul
ಖಃ

Dryden's *Aureng-Zebe* is a drama without precedents or successors. It is the only play directed to a contemporary monarch that sets before him for guidance the exemplary behavior of another contemporary monarch. The monarch to whom the play was addressed was King Charles II, who apparently read the manuscript and even suggested the modeling of "the most considerable event of it"[1]—a suggestion that has since been the subject of vain speculation among scholars. The monarch placed before Charles as an example was neither from the courts of Europe nor from the world of the noble savage. He was the Great Mogul whom Milton had infernalized in a poem, the second edition of which had been published the year before Dryden's play was performed.

The moral imagination had its view of the Orient, but self-interest called for prudence in the Orient's infernalization. Commerce in its nature might be traffic with sin, but one did not enter into compacts with a party resoundingly named as the Devil merely for the sake of more liberal trade in spices. Mughal India, moreover, was still being treated as a sovereign state and not as a potentially subject territory. A regime from which trade concessions were sought could scarcely be exposed to continuing vilification from the party seeking the concessions. The East India Company made one attempt to speed negotiations by force but withdrew discomfited, respecting for the time being the strength of Aurangzeb's army. It would take a century for the Great Mogul to become the company's pensioner.

In Samuel Johnson's *Rasselas*, published in 1759, two years after the battle of Plassey, Imlac is presented to the Great Mogul and finds himself "astonished at his wisdom, and enamoured of his goodness."[2] The Mughal regime at that time was in a state of almost total disarray. Six years later, it was to cede to the East India Company the rights of revenue collection that made the company the effective master of Bengal.[3] Imlac's encomium possibly looks back to the golden age of Akbar, which Western historians were increasingly disposed to perceive in contrast to the deterioration ushered in by Aurangzeb,[4] but the commendation also appeals to the Enlightenment postulate of a universal human nature that is common to all of us and contains all that is essential in us. Citizenship of the world and not the domination of one people by another is the natural consequence of such a postulate, and exemplary behavior in exotic places is one sign that the postulate is being recognized.

It is therefore not surprising that Dryden should have put it to us that examples for Europe are to be found outside Europe. It is surprising that he should have invited us to consider as exemplary a fictional Aurangzeb unrecognizably transformed from the original monarch then on the throne at Agra. The transformation is not for the worse and could hardly have been for the worse, but it raises problems that scholarship ought not to bypass. L. A. Beaurline and Fredson Bowers observe hesitantly that Dryden "makes the protagonist much less aggressive" than he actually was.[5] J. A. Winn is more decisive and goes as far as any other scholar in pointing to the extent of Dryden's misrepresentation: "The historical Aureng-Zebe was a Machiavellian manipulator, but Dryden's character is a perfect example of filial piety, fighting to preserve his father's throne."[6] Unfortunately, this is all Winn has to say on the subject. Dryden commentators, even when they draw passing attention to the difference between the literary and the actual, seem silently unanimous in assuming an unrestricted right to appropriate India in the interests of making a political statement about contemporary England. Freed of the encumbrance of a double answerability, they can then proceed to concentrate on the fictional constructions necessary to provide dramatic voicing for the English statement.

Dryden's appropriation of Mughal India is perhaps too methodically perverse for abysmal ignorance to be pleaded. Ignorance, moreover, would have been difficult after the publication of François Bernier's book. Dryden could have read Bernier in the original French, but the popularity of the work was sufficient for an English translation to be published in 1671. Its title, *The History of the Late Revolutions of the Empire of the Great Mogol*, indicates its pertinence to the moment in a way that *Travels in the Mogul Empire*, its modern title, does not.[7] Waldemar Hansen, in his richly evocative study, *The Peacock Throne*, aptly describes Bernier as "a wandering Montaigne:

analytical, sceptical, yet humane." He goes on to caution us that Bernier's narrative is full of flaws, bias, and misrepresentation, even if it is often "astonishingly precise."[8]

Bernier's was not the only voice on the subject, but the readability and vividness of his book, with its fluent combination of history, politics, economics, and reportage, made his the voice everyone heard. Percival Spear concludes that "to a large extent Europe's idea of India in the late seventeenth and eighteenth centuries was Bernier's."[9] It is standard practice to regard his book as the "source" for Dryden's play. Beaurline and Bowers, Winn, and George McFadden are representative.[10] We might expect Hansen, as a historian of the Mughal era, to be more skeptical, but he too is a member of the consensus: "No less a master than John Dryden based his historical tragedy, Aureng-Zebe, on Bernier's account of Mogul Hindustan."[11]

It is tempting but not correct to conclude from the evidence that Dryden scholars have not read Bernier and that Mughal historians have not succeeded in reading Dryden. McFadden has clearly read both texts, and his account of discrepancies between them,[12] while far from exhaustive, should be sufficient to pose a problem, but it does not pose one, even for McFadden. A source transformed into unrecognizability should cause us to wonder if it is a source at all. The wonder dissipates because the play is universally thought of as aligned exclusively along the coordinates of English history. Mughal history, even as reshaped by Bernier, is evidently a matter of no importance.

Samuel Johnson is the first critic, and seemingly the only one, to raise the question of what Aurangzeb might have thought of Dryden's play. He finds it fortunate that distance in space is as effective a safeguard as remoteness in time: "Aureng-Zebe (1676) is a tragedy founded on the actions of a great prince then reigning, but over nations not likely to employ their critics upon the transactions of the English stage. . . . His country is at such a distance that the manners might safely be falsified and the incidents feigned."[13]

Aurangzeb may not have been displeased but he may have been puzzled by Dryden's portrait of him as the new model of the Restoration hero, triumphant through moderation rather than destroyed by excess, combining patience with the capacity to act decisively, able to stand and wait but also able to seize the day, but only in the interests of the nation. Bernier admired Aurangzeb for his skills in realpolitik, but the emperor may have preferred an appreciation that was based on the necessities of survival in Mughal India. Without reading *The Prince,* he acted on its principles, as well as on the principles of the Indian improvement on Machiavelli, Kautilya's *Artha-Śāstra,* which was actually written several centuries earlier. Aurangzeb could have contemplated with amusement his reflection in the mirror of Dryden's representation. In the real world of the Mughal struggle for power, Dryden's prince would have lasted for no more than five minutes.

English history in the 1670s was dominated by the succession problem, as Mughal history had been two decades earlier. Dryden may have been attracted by the apparent parallel, but the Mughal route to power, repeatedly trodden and ancestrally bloodstained, was scarcely one he could recommend for English adoption. *Taktya Takhta,* a Mughal proverb on the perils of power, can be translated as "throne or coffin," but no translation can reproduce the pun's grim proximities. Jacobean tragedy is the proper genre of Mughal history, but its sense of inexorability, of destructive energy seeping through vain containments, was no longer fitting for an England that had placed the order of things within appropriate boundaries. If Dryden began by being attracted to a parallel, his next discovery may have been that he could pursue the parallel only by dismantling one of its constituents.

It is time to rearticulate the proposition regarding Bernier. Bernier is not the source of Dryden's play, but his book may be its indispensable background. Dryden is not ignoring Bernier's text; he is writing a critique of it. Mughal history is exemplary, but the example is negative.

If we do not see a negative example in Dryden's treatment of Mughal history, it is because we are looking too fixedly at the relationship of his text to English circumstances and ignoring the events in India that the text overwrites and comprehensively reverses. There is a point in Dryden's use of Bernier apart from making use of the interest in India that his book had aroused, satisfying the current vogue for drama set in exotic places, practicing one-upmanship on Elkanah Settle, and providing guidance on the Stuart succession. If Dryden revised his conception of the hero, abandoning his commitment to rhymed drama in the process,[14] the historical Aurangzeb may well have been the other that his heroic ideal needed to articulate itself. Some confusion, of course, is unavoidable when the new model hero is also called Aurangzeb.

It is not difficult to find examples that will make evident a consistency which cannot be accidental in Dryden's reversals of the historical text. The fictional Aurangzeb is the legitimate successor to the throne; the historical one is a usurper who gained the throne by defeating in battle and later putting to death the legitimate successor, Dara Shikoh. The fictional Aurangzeb is unfalteringly loyal to a father "beleaguered by his sons and despised by his second wife."[15] The historical Aurangzeb wrested the kingdom from his father, putting him under a form of house arrest that as time went on turned into close confinement. He was not freed from captivity even on his deathbed. The fictional Aurangzeb magnanimously forgives the three brothers who contest his legitimate right to the throne. The historical Aurangzeb forgave nobody. Forgiveness was a weakness he did not cultivate. He paraded Dara Shikoh humiliatingly through the streets of Delhi facing backward on a mud-plastered elephant, had him found guilty in a trial for heresy, and put him to death while in prison to avoid the popular anger a public execution might have aroused. He drove Shuja out of India to a presumed death by exhaustion in Arakan. He incarcerated Morat in the grim recesses of Gwalior Fort, rendered him comatose with repeated infusions of opium (a process that took several months), and had him done away with when he could no longer be said to be living. In Dryden's play, this situation too is reversed, with Morat deciding to do away with Aurangzeb and Nourmahal reserving for herself the pleasures of actually administering the "deadly draught" to her stepson (3.313–16). Both the fictional and the real Aurangzeb showed patience, but the patience of the latter was that of a tiger stalking his prey. The fictional Aurangzeb served the kingdom. The real Aurangzeb seized it. Descending from the broad strokes of characterization to the niceties of language, we can note that the fictional Aurangzeb is described contemptuously as a "preaching *Brachman*" (3.216). The historical Aurangzeb spent a good part of his life persecuting Brahmans who were foolish enough to preach. In short, to avoid being hissed off the Restoration stage, the fictional figure would have to totally disavow the real one. This is precisely how he proceeds to fashion himself.

Once the main line of transformation of Dryden's play has been established, it is possible to look at movements across and against that line. Indamora (the name is not casually chosen) is described as "a Captive Queen" in anticipation of the captive queen India was later to become. She serves her true master (not his competitors) with loyalty, showing us how fully imperialism looks forward in its metaphors. Dryden professed to admire the constancy of Indian ladies, which may have appealed to him in itself or because it fitted better into male fantasies: "Those *Indian* Wives are loving Fools, and may do well to keep themselves in their own Countrey, or, at least, to keep company with the *Arria's* and *Portia's* of old *Rome:* some of our Ladies know better things."[16] The Indian lady to whom Dryden is referring at this point is the passively adoring wife of Morat, impossibly named Melisanda. Her self-effacement reaches its climax in an act of suttee, which "cruel Laws to Indian Wives allow" (5.385). Indamora is made of more spirited stuff. All four men in the play are in love with her, and if Dara and Shuja are not, it is probably because they are not among the play's participants. Nourmahal jealously describes her as "this Fatal Helen" (5.257), voicing once more the unexpected knowledge of Greek mythology that Dryden's Indian characters habitually display. Indamora is not above manipulativeness, but it is all for a good cause, even though Aurangzeb has a chained hero's suspicions about which side she may be on, politically or sexually. Relieved of his suspicions, he gives vent to his feelings:

> Love mounts, and rowls about my stormy mind,
> Like Fire, that's born by a tempestuous Wind.
> Oh, I could stifle you, with eager haste!
> Devour your kisses with my hungry taste!
> Rush on you! eat you! wander o'r each part,
> Raving with pleasure, snatch you to my heart!
> Then hold you off, and gaze! then, with new rage,
> Invade you, till my conscious Limbs presage
> Torrents of joy, which all their banks oe'rflow.
> (4.533–41)

Michael Alssid is much too charitable in claiming that this outburst of sexual greed "marks, so to speak, the saint's return to the human condition."[17] It is a further and a vigorous step in the continuing feminization of the Orient. The use of the word "invade" must be found notable, even in this orgiastic outpouring of the will to plunder, of which India cum Indamora is the object. Commerce, in the economic sense, is not absent from the horizon of Dryden's play, and its conflation with sexual images is underlined rather than discouraged. Indamora can talk (in strange language for a captive from Kashmir) of making port with full sails (4.525) and of finding security in convoys (5.360–61). But it is Morat who, having relinquished the crown for the sake of the brightest jewel in it, reduces the high romance of the world well lost for love to the profit taking of the East India Company:

'Twas not for nothing I the Crown resign'd;
I still must own a Mercenary mind:
I, in this venture, double gains pursue,
And laid out all my Stock to purchase you.
(5.126–29)[18]

If Indamora represents India's desirability, Nourmahal represents its disruptiveness. "A spirit so untam'd the world ne'r bore" is Shah Jehan's weary conclusion regarding her (2.376), but his inability to cope with her can be read as a lesson on how not to govern India. It is widely assumed that Nourmahal was Dryden's invention, but the name was also bestowed on Nur Jehan who, far from being Shah Jehan's second wife, was the wife of his father, Jehangir. This identification has not been made by Dryden scholars because of the transference from one generation to another, but Dryden, as we know by now, thinks nothing of such displacements.

Mehrunissa, as she was called before Jehangir bestowed her titular name on her, has fascinated biographers with her extraordinary beauty, her ambiguous origins, and a deviousness that she sometimes seemed to pursue only to create opportunities for further deviousness. Harold Lamb, in a sympathetic fictionalization, maintains that she only did what she had to do to keep the kingdom together during Jehangir's frequent bouts with alcohol and opium.[19] In T. J. Murari's novel, *Taj*, she is, more typically, a woman richly fascinating but always to be feared for her insatiable ambitiousness.[20] Hansen at one point describes her as a "scheming bitch," although his overall characterization of her is fortunately more complex, and Dutch merchants in Agra labeled her as "that vicious woman who is filled with cunning up to her throat."[21] She was also symbolically an expert rider and hunter and, on the other hand, a person of taste and cultural accomplishment. Her ability to compose verse spontaneously in Persian enchanted Jehangir during his fits of sobriety.

Dryden is not wholly insensitive to these complexities. Nourmahal can more than hold her own in her exchanges with Shah Jehan, and despite the latter's prating on the identity between monarchs and husbands (2.330), he can eventually only exert his "Despotic pow'r" over her by calling on a palace guard to seize her (2.346; compare *Samson Agonistes* 1054–55). Winning arguments is not Shah Jehan's strong point, but in Dryden's depiction of him, it is difficult to see where his strong point can be hidden. In her dealings with Aurangzeb, Nourmahal is a different person, thus showing that

India can be effectively governed. At first (vile woman that she is), she looks forward to witnessing his "hourly ebbs of life" as she administers the "pois'nous draught" to him in carefully measured installments. But Aurangzeb's fortitude in the face of adversity brings about a change of heart, and in one of those sudden volte-faces beloved by Restoration dramatists, she confesses herself in love with the Mughal Englishman. Warned by a scandalized courtier that she treads on the verge of incest, she replies in a manner that could be called charmingly artless: "Count this among the Wonders Love has done: / I had forgot he was my Husband's Sone!" (3.354–55). It does not take long for her to collect herself sufficiently to justify continuing in her course:

> I stand with guilt confounded, lost with shame,
> And yet made wretched onely by a name.
> If names have such command on humane Life
> Love's sure a name that's more Divine than Wife.
> That Sovereign power all guilt from action takes,
> At least the stains are beautiful it makes.
> (3.364–69)

By the time she bares her heart to Aurangzeb, she has become considerably more ingenious:

> Promiscuous Love is Nature's general Law:
> For whosoever the first Lovers were
> Brother and sister made the second Pair,
> And doubled by their love, their piety.
> (4.132–35)

This unusual reading of Genesis is angrily received by Aurangzeb, who seems to have read the same book in an orthodox masculine manner (4.489–92). His indignation poses no obstacle to the tidal wave of Nourmahal's infatuation: "In vain this haughty fury you have shown / How I adore a Soul so like my own!" (4.143–44). Repulsed again, she offers Aurangzeb a dagger. If he cannot grant her love, he can grant her death. He refuses to do her this favor. She decides he can live no longer. As he is about to drink of the poisoned cup (comparing himself inappropriately to Socrates and revealing once more the odd reading habits of Mughals), Morat enters. He has promised Indamora a day's stay of Aurangzeb's execution. Nourmahal's response is characteristic, making it clear that monarchs value their "perks": "What am I, that you dare to bind my hand? / So low, I've not a Murder at command!" (4.187–88). Nourmahal's spiritedness and her energetic defense of her behavior have a place in the scheme of things, but only if those inhabiting the place learn to respect its boundaries. A Mughal court is a convenient place to lay down principles not altogether unquestionable in Restoration England, and in the reassuring dispositions of that court, Nourmahal needs a monarch and a husband. Lacking both, she is understandably frustrated. Her wildness calls out for government, but another queen has to go with the kingdom, and if she did not, a pun would have to be sacrificed. Indamora's advantage is that she does not exist except as a different name for India. Nourmahal's disadvantage is that she did exist historically, as the wife of Aurangzeb's grandfather, so that marriage to her would be a comic absurdity not to be contemplated. Nourmahal has no alternative but to run amok. It is difficult to go mad in heroic couplets, but Dryden shows extraordinary skill in maneuvering the disintegrating metrics of madness within the tight confinement of the verse form. Indeed, the passage might be described as metaphorical metrics in its continuing transgression and unavoidable reinscription of its boundaries. Fittingly, the climax is a parody of suttee, immediately following Melisanda's death by fire. Nourmahal dies in a blaze of poetic justice, consumed by the fires of passion within herself.

Despite Dryden's apparently casual treatment of Mughal history, it will be apparent by now that we need to read that history with some attention if we are to hear its echoes satisfactorily in his play. In the set piece review of the qualities of the claimants for the throne that opens the first act, we are told that Dara is inclined to "implacable revenge" (a prominent characteristic of the real Aurangzeb) and that Morat's courage is a slave to his envy (Aurangzeb's behavior was marked by envious hatred of Dara). Bestowing the hero's defects on the competition is one way of keeping those defects sufficiently alive in the play to remind us of the quite different historical reality. But the judgment of Shuja that follows is more than a sloughing off of defects. It is resonant with political implications:

> From *Sujah*'s valour I should much expect
> But he's a *Bigot* of the *Persian* Sect:
> And, by a Foreign Int'rest seeks to Reign,
> Hopeless by Love the Sceptre to obtain.
> (1.94–97)

The reference to James is evident and startling and can be read as a warning to the duke to rely on the affections of the people and the legitimacy of his succession rather than on foreign aid.[22] The Mughal allusion, however, is not to Aurangzeb via one of his contenders but via one contender to the leading contender, Dara. Shuja was pleasure loving rather than valorous, and his interest in religion was minimal. Dara's very name was Persian, a variant of Darius. He was deeply interested in Sufism, which Islamic orthodoxy might regard as a Persian sect. But he was an eclectic, not a bigot, and his trial for heresy was based on treating as deviance not merely his eclecticism but even the readiness to give dissent a hearing. He was in fact found guilty and condemned by bigots, with whom Aurangzeb, a fundamentalist, was fully in sympathy. Finally, he did not rely on foreign assistance. He was the legitimate successor and the popular choice.

Dara embarrasses Dryden to such an extent that these few lines are almost all that is left of him. The difficulty is that many of the qualities Dryden wished for in an English successor—legitimacy by merit as well as birthright, popular support, and tolerance of religious variety—were to be found in the unfortunate Indian prince. The systematic misrepresentation of Dara so that these qualities could be bestowed on Aurangzeb was always a possibility, but rather than paint him methodically in false colors, it was better not to paint him at all. Dara's disappearance is the main cost of Englishing Aurangzeb. The other principal expense is Shah Jehan's reduction to a travesty of himself, whose incompetence and helplessness justify a struggle for the succession and make all the more noble Aurangzeb's filial loyalty. Morat remains as an example of that overstated hero whom the Restoration stage had offered for admiration and whom Dryden's new model was fashioned to replace.

Even the title pages of *Aureng-Zebe* play their part in the appropriation of India. The scene is described as "Agra in the year 1660." By 1660, the struggle for the succession was over. Dara had been found guilty of heresy and beheaded. Shuja had been driven out of India. Morat was a prisoner in Gwalior Fort, and Shah Jehan was under house arrest. But 1660 was the year of the Restoration. The coming to power of the legitimate claimant to the kingdom was the crowning event of 1660 in England and is the climactic event in Dryden's play about India. A history fictionally contrived to echo itself in space is called on to repeat itself in time.

It can and should be argued that Mughal history is treated by Dryden with a disrespect that no writer would have thought of bringing to bear on the Greek and Roman past. Such a disrespect points to a stubbornly resident devaluation of the Orient. It is, to put it plainly, not to be taken seriously. On the other hand, it can be said that if Dryden pillages Indian history, he does so only to construct examples for England and that the examples include not only Aurangzeb but also Indamora and Melisande. The counterargument recoils on itself and may have been intended to do so from the beginning. The distance between the fictional and the historical, between the golden world and the bronze one, is also the distance between England and India, and it is a distance increased rather than decreased by the drastic rearrangements shown to be necessary if Aurangzeb is to be satisfactorily Englished. The play offers itself as an endeavor to display India as exemplary, but the very comprehensiveness of its effort to do so draws attention to a historical reality that is quite the reverse of the play's apparent intentions. A promise of likeness becomes a statement of otherness and so takes its place in a familiar tradition of perceiving India. It is strategy rather than content, the way of arrival rather than the state reached, that makes this particular articulation distinctive.

If the historical Aurangzeb's unveiling as a negative example represents the otherness of India, Indamora and Nourmahal are sharply different yet intertwined manifestations of the feminization of India by a soon-to-be-dominant West. India as desirable yet dangerous, as welcoming but also unpredictable, and as finding its identity under the guidance of the husband-monarch are possibilities that discourse makes explicit and that history is soon to make substantial. It might be noted that the spousal metaphor points not only to an India that wishes to be governed (as in *The Lusiads*) but also to an India that wishes to be English. It would be obviously untrue to argue that Dryden recognizes this wish in his play's determined abstention from even scenic Indianness. Nevertheless, appropriation is a form of marriage and a form that will become variously embedded in future constructions of India by the English.

4
James Mill and the
Case of the Hottentot Venus

ᘒᘓ

The battle of Buxar is more important than the battle of Plassey, which has been reduced to the status of a skirmish, but battles are no longer acceptable as signaling changes in the direction of history. In seeking an alternative, we might wish to consider representations of history as not merely cast in the narrative form but as formed largely by the argument between narratives. It then becomes instructive to consider the spate of British histories of India after Plassey and Buxar and the changing characterizations into which those events were fitted. An outline history of histories can be enlightening in indicating why the specific version that proved decisive prevailed.

Robert Orme wrote the first of these studies in 1763, a military history of the British in India, chronicling the repeated triumphs of the British fighting spirit against Indians doubly weakened by an enervating climate and a protein-deficient diet.[1] As military history, the account is not notable, but it was sufficiently invigorating for the East India Company to appoint Orme as its official historiographer. In undertaking to purchase at least fifty copies of any book written on India, the company provided further evidence of its earnest concern in having its rapidly growing assets valued.

Orme's book was followed by Alexander Dow's three-volume study (1768–72); by Francis Gladwin's examination of Mughal India during the reigns of Jehangir, Shah Jehan, and Aurangzeb (1788); and by Thomas Maurice's seven-volume history of Sanskrit and classical Hindustan (1800) and his further history of modern Hindustan (1802–10). To these should be added Mark Wilks's history of South India (1810–17),[2] which Thomas Moore drew on for his notes to *Lalla Rookh*.[3] The climax came in James Mill's three-volume history of British India (1817), a work that became prescribed reading for officials of the East India Company and that was predictably described by Macaulay as the greatest achievement in historiography since that of Edward Gibbon. We must also take into account the survey of India, begun in 1801 and not completed until nearly half a century later. An effort of determined and mind-boggling diligence, the survey mapped India with exemplary thoroughness through the laborious process of triangulation.[4] It was an imperial statement geographically complementing the act of possession implicit in the histories.

Nearly all of these copious histories were written by soldiers and servants of the East India Company. That fact exposes their ideological investment, although it does not follow that the work of scholars would have been more disinterested. Hegel, an academic, writes Mill very much larger. He does so by integrating Mill's views on India into a systematic philosophy that claims all human understanding as its province.

The different views of the past that eighteenth-century histories of India provide do not, as Milton leads us to hope, show "truth closing up to truth" out of the confusion and the ferment of error. The convention may be that one seeks to know the past in order to install it as the future's instructor. The reality can be that one constructs the past in order to enlist it as the future's accomplice. We can look at these successive histories of India as providing those about to attain possession of the subcontinent with a range of managerial options called for by readings of India's past that were constructed to support these options.

The option adopted will not be chosen because its projection into the past is more faithful to the "facts" or because it is narratively more persuasive. It may be chosen because it is congenial to prevailing ideologies, and since ideologies and historical narrations are both responsive to power dispositions, the choice may exhibit the maximum collusiveness between the intellectual and the historical fictions. These are considerations urged on us with some force, but there is a further consideration arising from the link between commerce and empire that has been repeatedly pointed to in these pages. That consideration, put with an unavoidable drabness that may fail to draw attention to its importance, is cost-effectiveness. The East India Company was a business concern. It is not out of order to ask to what extent the political and cultural world that its relationship to India brought into being was the result of decisions congenial to its balance sheet.

Dow's *History of Hindostan,* principally a compilation drawn from Persian sources, shrinks away enlighteningly from the promised scope of its title. It reduces itself to a history not of India but of its rulers and, more restrictively, of those Moslem dynasties that ruled India by right of conquest—a right that, as we shall see, can be claimed or conceded by figures as diverse as Hastings, Jones, and Macaulay. As in *The Lusiads,* which Mickle revealingly calls the epic of whoever held possession of India, India's submission is incised into its psyche. The Hindus, according to Dow, are "of all nations the most easily conquered and ruled." They "permit themselves to be transferred from one tyrant to another without murmuring."[5] Such language might be read as paving the way for the arrival of a new tyrant, but the British intention is more charitable. It is to provide the dominance India seems to seek but to add to it the benevolence that only England can offer.

The most abusive characterization of India's propensity for submission comes not from an East India Company historian but from the more lettered pen of Oliver Goldsmith:

> The Indians have long been remarkable for their cowardice and effeminacy; every conqueror that has attempted the invasion of their country having succeeded. . . . They are slothful, submissive and luxurious; satisfied with sensual happiness alone they find no pleasure in thinking; and contented with slavery they are ready to obey any master. . . . Fed upon rice and clothed in effeminate silk vestments they are unable to oppose the onset of a European army. . . . Upon the whole therefore, they may be considered a feeble race of sensualists, too dull to find rapture in any pleasures and too indolent to turn their gravity into wisdom.[6]

Dow and Goldsmith define India as a chronically subject nation, and such a nation naturally exposes itself to the utmost liberty of representation. It can be coerced into becoming whatever the conqueror beholds. The conqueror's gaze is that of the inheritor in the first place and will only become that of the reformer as moral self-esteem intrudes into the elation of power. Thus the first proposals are those of continuity, that dominance be exercised along lines already in being. The British are to take over and operate more efficiently (and somewhat less onerously than Aurangzeb) the administrative and fiscal apparatus of the Mughal state. Akbar's tolerance is to be prudently substituted for Aurangzeb's fanaticism, which stiffened internal resistance, reduced extractive efficiency, and made the payment of imperial dividends vastly more difficult.

Imperial dividends had been adequate before Plassey. Trade with India had prospered sufficiently for the Harlowe family in Samuel Richardson's *Clarissa* (1747–48) to have built its fortunes largely on that trade. The East India Company had outdistanced its Dutch counterpart, with textiles overtaking spices as the main component of commerce with Asia. The Bengal silk trade had surpassed that of China. Tea, in turn, was overtaking textiles, and the East India Company's predominance in the tea trade was strengthening. But the balance of trade was disturbingly adverse. Two-thirds of British imports from India in the decade before Richardson's book had to be paid for not in goods but in bullion. Gold and silver obtained from the New World could be disposed of at a considerable profit in India, but the trade pattern depended precariously on a single source of supply.[7] Safeguarding steps were needed that did not involve curbing the consumer demand on which the company's fortunes were based. The conquest of Bengal rearranged the trade balance so that India thereafter became a debtor nation. It also eradicated the sometimes thin line that separates commerce from plunder.

Tragic events in a world six months away from England by a still-hazardous sea voyage would not normally have been a matter for even abstract concern, but the influx of nabobs with fortunes built on the ruin of India created stresses in the English social fabric. The aristocratic and the mercantile had coexisted in England in an uneasiness raised to a principle by Milton's statement that one was "By merit more than birthright Son of God" (*PL* 3.309). As mercantile wealth reinforced the claims of its owners for a more decisive place in the national order, it became desirable to insist that not all mercantile fortunes were made by merit. Class conflicts and Enlightenment ideology combined at this point to create a brief interval in which the equity of empire could be questioned.

Thus, while East India Company historians were taking the imminence of possessing India for granted, English opinion was not without its misgivings. The nabobs became the focus of a resentment considerably beyond the customary irritation provoked by the nouveau riche. Macaulay is not exceptional, and may even be representative, in seeing these years as "the most frightful of all spectacles, the strength of civilization without its mercy." He finds "the misgovernment of the English . . . carried to a point such as seems hardly compatible with the very existence of society." The *Life of*

Clive, from which these remarks are taken, devotes an informative paragraph to the unpopularity of the nabobs and their satirizing in contemporary literature. Samuel Foote's play *The Nabob,* first performed on June 26, 1772, is among the most striking of these depictions. A dialogue between Touchit and the mayor of the small English town where the play is set is a virtual translation of contemporary events in India:

> *Touchit:* Here are a body of merchants that beg to be admitted as friends and take possession of a small spot in a country and carry on a beneficial commerce with the inoffensive and innocent people, to which they kindly give their consent.
> *Mayor:* Don't you think now that is very civil of them?
> *Touchit:* Doubtless. Upon which, Mr. Mayor, we cunningly encroach, and fortify little and by little, till at length, we growing too strong for the natives, we turn them out of their lands, and take possession of their money and jewels.
> *Mayor:* And don't you think, Master Touchit, that is a little uncivil of us?
> *Touchit:* Oh nothing at all. These people are but a little better than Tartars or Turks.
> *Mayor:* No, No, Master Touchit; just the reverse; it is they have caught the Tartars in us.[8]

The persistence of the medieval papal pun on Tartarus is striking (Byron uses it in his poem on the death of Keats), but its transference to the predatory West from the savagely gorgeous East is a refreshing comment on the imperialist adventure. Later, when Matthew Mite (the nabob) offers Lady Oldham the fiendish alternatives of marriage to her daughter or foreclosure on the mortgage, she spurns the proposal with opulent indignation: "I would much rather see my child with a competence, nay, even reduced to an indigent state, than voluptuously rioting in pleasures that derive their source from the ruines of others."[9] Lady Oldham's stern judgment is not peculiar to her plight. It is, she insists, "the voice of the public," and Mite, shrugging it aside as "the common cry of the times," has to reply by demanding that gratitude should be shown to those who have given England "dominion and wealth." The argument is decisively rejected: "Your riches . . . by introducing a general spirit of dissipation, have extinguished labour and industry the slow but sure source of national wealth."

Mite exaggerates to dismiss when he refers to Lady Oldham's protest as "the common cry," but the cry was considerably more than audible. "Man over men / He made not lord" is not a statement reassuring to imperialists. Not everyone was as forthright as Roger Williams in asking what difference there was "between Asia and Africa, between Europe and America" in "respect of the Lord's special propriety to one country more than another."[10] But the hero in Henry Mackenzie's widely read *Man of Feeling* (1771) speaks in the same tradition when he asks, "What title have the subjects of another kingdom to establish an empire in India?"[11] Cowper, a schoolfellow of Hastings, asks:

> Is India free, and does she wear her plumed
> And jewelled turban with a smile of peace,
> Or do we grind her still?[12]

Most important of all is Samuel Johnson, who, in a formidable parenthesis, describes 1498, the year of Vasco da Gama's voyage to India and of Columbus's arrival on the American mainland (in what is now Venezuela),[13] as "a year hitherto disastrous to mankind."[14] "The Europeans," Johnson says resoundingly, "have scarcely visited any coast but to gratify avarice and extend corruption: to arrogate dominion without right and practice cruelty without incentive."[15] Johnson's comment comes toward the end of a period of cultural self-criticism in which Dryden's Montezuma, Montesquieu's Persian, Swift's King of Brobdingnag, Voltaire's Micromegas, and Goldsmith's Chinaman attempt to look back at Europe, although within the perspective of the Western gaze.[16]

The change taking place becomes evident when we contrast Johnson's statement with Adam Smith's conclusion that the "discovery of America and that of a passage to the East Indies by the Cape of Good Hope, are the two greatest and most important events recorded in the history of mankind."[17] Hegel's view (as will be seen) is similar, and the felicities of chronology do indeed call for the coupling of these voyages that brought the whole world into the imperialist embrace. But the two encounters, although intimately related, also differ significantly in their representation before the imperialist will. One calls for civilizing the wilderness; the other calls for taking over and amending the institutions of an existing nation-state. In the end, the rhetoric of civilizing the wilderness infiltrates the encounter with India as supplanting institutions rather than reforming them becomes the shaping force behind the imperial agenda. It is less complicated to deal with savages and animals than with peoples pretending to civility. Spenser's Artegall makes this discovery in *The Faerie Queene*. Nevertheless, India cannot be governed without the large-scale collaboration of Indians. There is therefore a boundary to the slighting of Indian culture, even if that boundary is sometimes not easy to detect.

As has been indicated, the first proposal to come before the British was that of continuity with its Mughal predecessor. The regime, especially under Akbar, had shown itself capable of extractive efficiency without arousing a dangerous intensity of resentment. Its administrative and particularly its fiscal apparatus could be taken over without major alterations. As the British positioned themselves along the line of continuity with the Mughals, it was natural that they should see Islam as the state's official religion and Hinduism as circumferential, a folk culture rather than a religious alternative. Moreover, Hinduism was known almost exclusively through its mythology, and the proliferative exuberance of that mythology tended to confirm its decentered character. Sanskrit was, for practical purposes, a language unknown to the West,[18] and Hindu philosophical, religious, and literary texts remained locked up in the inaccessibility of Sanskrit, except for scanty and fragmentary renderings into Persian.

In a characterization that grows in strength as we ponder it, Wendy Doniger treats the relationship between Hindu mythology and philosophy as the relationship between the Dionysian and the Apollonian.[19] Other pairings can be proposed, but this contestation negotiates yet once more the creative entanglement between unity and diversity that is so pervasive in the texture of Indian thought. The moral is that the philosophy and the mythology should not be considered apart from each other. The architecture of the Hindu temple —the totality that holds in a massively announced and yet precarious relationship, the multitudinousness of the facade, and the inner sanctum, with its "condition of complete simplicity"—is a reminder of this necessary copresence.[20] When attention settles exclusively on the mythology, the Western intelligence is likely to find it monstrous, and this is indeed the standard adjective. Yet it is the proliferative mythology and not the Apollonian philosophy that has been India's principal cultural export to the further India that Zimmer's work surveys.

The marginal status of Hinduism and the dangers of the margin as a subversive site are evident in William Beckford's *Vathek* (1784).

This novel is a retelling of the Faustian legend as an Arabian Nights fantasy with a liberal admixture of the Gothic. The familiar fable appeals to the proposition of a universal human nature that is subject everywhere to the same temptations. It normalizes Islam, and the normalization is further secured by the first in a series of lavishly scholarly notes that testify to the awakening interest in Orientalism and seek to claim documentary accuracy for the exuberant inventiveness of the story. The note defines the solemn status of a caliph as vicegerent of God and as prophet, priest, and king to his people (the traditional functions of Christ).[21] This particular caliph is involved in the capricious pursuit of forbidden knowledge, which seems to fascinate him largely because of the price that has to be paid for it. The giaour who tempts him (the word is a corruption of "kafir," meaning infidel) is an extremely unattractive inhabitant of India. Hinduism is thus made the infernal circumference of an Islam that was itself the infernal circumference of Christianity. The double devaluation indicates the lack of esteem in which Hindu religion and practices were coming to be held. A quite unnecessary note in the scholarly apparatus draws due attention to the absurdity of these practices.[22] This is not to denigrate the elegance and zest of Beckford's novel, which comes to a fine climax in the halls of Eblis, modeled on the metamorphosis of the fallen angels in the tenth book of *Paradise Lost*. Southey may have drawn on it for *The Curse of Kehama*.

The notes for *Vathek* are sufficiently up to date to include references to William Jones, who had founded the Asiatic Society of Bengal seven years before Beckford's novel was published. In glancing at Jones, they show no awareness of the alternative that his construction of the Indian past was building. If a proposal for continuity such as Dow's is to be debated, it must be challenged by a proposal that is reformist. Jones in effect offered such a proposal by putting forward a different version of the Indian past that called for a different style of future management. Hinduism is now seen as central rather than marginal and even as a cornerstone of the edifice of civilization or a lost chapter of the Western identity. Sanskrit was a parent language of humankind, and Sanskrit philosophy and literature were distinguished statements in the history of civilization. Far from being the emissary of Eblis, Vathek's giaour might well be the bearer of an ancient enlightenment.

Jones translated Kalidasa's *Śakuntalā* in 1789, four years after Charles Wilkins published his translation of the Bhagavad Gita. In 1786, Duperron published his *Recherches historiques et chronolo-*

giques sur l'Inde. The second volume contained translations of four Upanishads not from the Sanskrit but from a Persian rendering made, we are told, at the behest of Dara Shikoh. Jones's translation of Kalidasa swept Europe. Hastings read Wilkins's version of the Gita and prophesied that its wisdom would endure long after the British presence had departed from India.[23] Having said that, he proceeded to strengthen and greatly enlarge that presence.

Raymond Schwab writes with deep scholarship and persuasiveness of the importance of the discovery of India as a shaping force in the romantic project.[24] The sustaining vision of that project, as Schwab perceives it, was to bring about a world humanism, enlarged to be free of Greco-Roman constraints, that would fully open up the future of human creativeness to the sum of the best that had been known and thought. But the dominance of the West in any scheme of world understanding is not to be easily relinquished. "Thought's empire over thought," Shelley's memorable and latently self-annulling metaphor,[25] proclaims the transience of intellectual empires, which in their nature cannot join self-knowledge to world knowledge and must repress the "mutiny within" that challenges thought in its imperial pretensions. It is a caution counting for little when empires not of thought were being put together by means that would soon call for the manufacture of ideological empires.

Jones and his colleagues provided a different and inconvenient history of India, but it was not a history offered to suggest that the march of conquest be suspended so that a subject people could be given back its rights. Jones himself, in putting forward a tract containing some mildly progressive proposals, went out of his way to reassure Lord Ashburton that he would "certainly not preach them to the Indians," who, he believed, "must and will be governed by absolute power."[26] With an appointment as Supreme Court judge at Calcutta in the offing, this may have been the only thing to say. But Jones's uneasiness with the reassurance he offers is made apparent by his immediate retreat from it: "Yet I shall go through life with a persuasion that they [the Indians] are just and rational."

It is hard to see why a just and rational people should be subjected to the exercise of absolute power, unless the purpose of power is to free that people from institutional confinements that previous exercises of power have imposed. The view that India should be governed by its own laws and customs, that it should be brought back to itself by an enlightened despotism, is thus for Jones not simply a way of enlisting Indian support for British authority but an important part of his troubled justification of the right of the British to govern India.[27] A more pragmatic and more typical view, concerned with the efficiency rather than with the responsibilities of imperial government, is put forward by Hastings:

> Every accumulation of knowledge and especially such as is obtained by social communication with people over whom we exercise a dominion founded on the right of conquest is useful to the state. . . . It lessens the weight of the chain by which the natives are held in subjection; and it imprints on the hearts of our own countrymen the sense and obligation of benevolence.[28]

"The weight of the chain" is a phrase that must be called brutally frank, and the entire passage makes it apparent that Hastings is considering not the rights of the Indian people—the Magna Carta that Burke optimistically found embodied in Fox's East India Bill, which he himself may have drafted[29]—but simply the optimal strategy of management. To maximize collaboration and minimize resistance, it might be desirable for a people to be governed by their own laws. The Orientalist contribution was to argue that the laws should be those appropriate to the heritage of Hindu civilization rather than those promulgated by the Mughal regime. In this sense, the Orientalist proposal was revisionist. It sought to move to the center what had hitherto been at the circumference. The "obligation of benevolence" was to further lessen "the weight of the chain" and also purge away the guilt of conquest by reinstating what had so far been overlaid.

Jones planned a heroic poem to be entitled *Britain Discovered* that he did not live to write and of which only the "design" exists. It was to be modeled on Spenser, not Milton, whom Jones worshiped.[30] Jones may have turned to Spenser because he saw in *The Faerie Queene* an ancestral poem of the intertwined relationship between the patriotic and imperial selves. A text more enlightened than *The Lusiads* and revelatory of a nation more distinguished and self-searching than Portugal was needed to replace Camões's poem as the epic of those who held possession of India. As the argument to book 2 makes apparent, much of Britain lies waiting to be discovered in India. Kipling's refrain, "What can they know of England who only England know?," is anticipated in a design in which the core of a nation is disclosed to itself on its periphery:

> The gods of India convened on Mount Cailas, by Rudra or *Mahadeva,* the power of destruction; their names, numbers,

characters, attributes, and attendants. The goddess Ganga announces the views and voyage of the *Tyrian* hero: expresses her apprehensions of his ultimate success, but advises the most vehement opposition to him; declaring that his victory will prove the origin of a wonderful nation, who will possess themselves of her books, profane her waters, mock the temples of the Indian divinities, appropriate the wealth of their adorers, introduce new laws, a new religion, a new government, insult the Brahmins and disregard the sacred ordinances of Brahma.[31]

A similar but less detailed prophecy is made in *The Lusiads* (7.46) by a soothsayer inspired by a demon who is surprisingly said to have spoken truly. Ganga's much fuller account of the havoc anticipated from the British takes us aback by its admission that the British victories in India will nevertheless exhibit "the origin of a wonderful nation." Her prophecy verges on the oxymoronic. Its decoding must depend on the undoing of the typical agenda of conquest that she foresees, by the quite different behavior of the British as conquerors. The inventory of destruction spells out the weight of a chain that must not materialize. In doing so, it indicates the formidable extent of a task that calls out for a nation that must be no less than "wonderful" if it is to falsify Ganga's natural expectations.

The implicit claim for England's imperial uniqueness expresses Jones's hopes. The agenda the claim must set at naught itemizes his anxieties. The distance between the two and the extreme imbalance between the comprehensive prophecy of havoc and the brief and solitary countervailing reference to a "wonderful nation" open a fissure that even imperial power may be unable to accommodate. Significantly, Ganga's forebodings are not addressed in the design of *Britain Discovered* until the final book, where a safeguard is offered that seems scarcely in proportion to the fears that have been voiced: "The nuptials of *Britain* and *Albion,* or allegorically, of *Royalty* and *Liberty* united in the constitution of England. The attending Druid ... recommends the government of the Indians by their own laws."[32]

The Ganges is a river that seems to draw Jones into the current of politics. In his "Hymn to Ganga," Aurangzeb is seen as "a ruffian king / The demon of his empire, not the grace," whose misdeeds lead to the throne being rent by discord and to its capture by "nations yet unknown."[33] The argument to the hymn advises us that the poem is "feigned to have been the work of a BRAHMAN, who, by a prophetical spirit, discerns the toleration and equity of the British government and concludes with a prayer *for its peaceful duration under good laws well administered.*"[34]

The Brahman's views seem notably different from those voiced in *Britain Discovered* by the goddess Ganga, whom one might take to be a higher authority. It is an inconsistency more striking than real. The Brahman is in effect giving his prophetical assent to the subtext that will hopefully nullify Ganga's prophecy and that Ganga herself oxymoronically acknowledges. "Toleration and equity" do indeed call for a spirit of prophetic discernment, given the plight of Bengal when Jones wrote his poem. But perhaps because of Bengal's abjection, toleration and equity no longer extend to the "government of the Indians by their own laws." The Brahman's prayer seeks no more than "good laws well administered." The final couplet leaves the Indian content of those laws uncertain: "As they preserve our laws, and bid our terror cease / So be their darling laws preserv'd in wealth, in joy, in peace."[35]

The passage teeters on a difficult balance, suggesting that terror (a word compounded in effectiveness by its almost casual use) can be bidden to cease if the laws of the victor are respected and adding that the laws and customs precious to the hearts of Indians (hence the word "darling") can also be protected at the same time. The word "preserv'd" on both sides of the balance announces a symmetry as if it were a harmony. It is a literary sleight of hand that circumvents a harassing anxiety over a gap in political reality that may not be bridgeable.

Jones's uneasy positioning of these poems between the "absolute power" that accrues from conquest and the counterclaim of a culture he had learned to respect encourages us to read him between the lines. Aware of imperialism as potentially culture exterminating, he seeks to restrict its destructiveness by advocating safeguards that cannot be effective because their comprehensive implementation would be uncongenial to the imperial purpose. To carry on the government of India as far as possible through Indian laws and customs is no more than pragmatic. But the implications of Jones's scholarship and of the romantic enthusiasm over India that Schwab has so impressively documented went considerably further and sought recognition of India as a parent culture rather than benign tolerance of its oddities. To concede this would have been to grant India parity in a dialogue with the West, and both parity and the very notion of dialogue are opposed profoundly to the logic of dominance. Dialogue would not simply lessen the weight of but eliminate the chain "by which the natives are held in subjection."

It was time for a new construction of India's history. Continuity and revisionism both entrenched the past, although in different ways and with sharply different primacies. It was time to argue that the past had had its day, which could not be reinstated, and that all that could be learned from studying the past was the basis of its inability to advance beyond itself. The British mission was not to improve on Akbar or to resurrect the Mauryas. It was to write a new text and not to amend an old one. The moment called for a construction of Indian history that would provide the future with a different empowerment. James Mill was the spokesperson of that moment.[36]

The deifying of history and the entrenching of progress defined by the standards of those whom history has chosen are important features of nineteenth-century thought. Mill's work is in the tradition represented by such clichés as the "ascent of man," the "onward march of events," or even the "grand march of intellect," to use Keats's phrase, which he spent his poetic life questioning. Even the title of Mill's book—A History of British India—is important for the way in which it appropriates that march, enlarging a special interest so that it can become the voice of an imperial constituency. There was no "British India" at the time Mill's book was written. There was only a land grab of unprecedented dimensions by a showpiece of private enterprise known as the East India Company. To call the results of this operation British India is not to write history, but it is to provide the judgmental framework within which history is hereafter to be viewed.

When Spear compares the quality of life in Mughal India with that in seventeenth-century Europe, he concludes that there may be good ground for thinking that "the average peasant had more to eat than his European counterpart and suffered no more oppression from the lords. Mughal India, with an estimated one hundred million inhabitants, had for about a century and a half a standard of life roughly comparable with that of contemporary Europe, though arranged on a different social and economic pattern."[37] Angus Calder agrees with Spear that the Indian peasant may have been better nourished than the European and was no more subject to the pressures of tyranny. He goes on to add that "Mughal India was overall as cultured, well governed and comfortable as any part of the world."[38] These findings are typical and contrast with Mill's conclusion, noted by Patrick Brantlinger, that India nearly two centuries later had not even attained the stage of civilization that Europe had attained in the Middle Ages.[39] Even more arbitrary than the verdict is the way in which India is situated on a European-invented trajectory of development that all civilizations are obliged to follow, with England pressing on from the furthest point yet reached. The undeviating "march of passion and endeavour" that Keats was pondering even as Mill wrote was to result inexorably in the triumph of the Apollonian.

When Mill published the book that, according to William Bentinck, made him rather than Bentinck the real governor-general of India,[40] there were 850,000 slaves under British proprietorship, most of them in the West Indies. A man could be executed for stealing a shilling in Barbados. The Hindu penal code, severe though it was, is judged by Calder to have been much less savage than the English.[41] Mill makes much of the allegation that punishment in India was proportioned to caste, but no honest person can say that punishment under British rule was not proportioned to color. Child marriage (or, more accurately, betrothal) was indeed deplorable, but it was not more deplorable than forcing children to work for sixteen hours a day under conditions likely to lead to their early death. The act charitably reducing that period to twelve hours came into force only a few years before Mill's book. Suttee was a monstrous social practice, not called for in Hindu religion, as even Southey notes,[42] and resisted by Hindu reformers. The burning of witches all over Europe and North America in the previous two centuries can scarcely be called less monstrous. Aurangzeb has been justly described in these pages as a bigot, but compared to the Spanish Inquisition (not abolished until 1820), his regime must be hailed as a model of tolerance. In Australia, where a count seems to have been kept of the number of lashes legally administered to miscreants, the number had risen in 1835 to the staggering total of 332,810.[43]

Compilations like these on both sides of the ledger indicate that people who throw stones are likely to live in glass houses. But they may also point to an unexpected subtlety in Mill's agenda. It is not just India that must be reformed or regulated. England must eliminate or restrain within itself the negative collocation that is India. India is merely the geopsychic site for a cluster of undesirabilities that continue to be illicitly desired. Enlightened civilizations must make these undesirabilities alien to themselves.

Naming at this level is an extreme intensification of the self-other relationship. It is not altogether without precedent. Dryden wittily pursues India as a negative example, but Mill, who is no Dryden, is writing in a genre that is not Dryden's. A book that is to become standard reading for officials of the East India Company cannot be treated in the same manner as a play whose insinuations can be elegantly oblique. Mill's project answers to his temperament. There is a straightforwardness about him that should discourage deft deflections, even among those anxious to complicate the dour movement of his thought. Self-and-other diagrams invite the suspicion that the other is being officially dismissed in order that it may be clandestinely entertained. Mill's work does not exclude a space for the self-scrutiny that should follow upon such healthy skepticism, but moving into that space is a responsibility left to the reader.

One measure of an enlightened civilization is the manner in which it treats its women. Thomas De Quincey apparently found this idea in Kant.[44] Feminine India gives women a high metaphysical status. Its social praxis has been less commendable, but it may be England that here provides the most lurid manifestation of that area of darkness bearing the name of India. In 1810, a woman described as the Hottentot Venus was exhibited in a cage in London and prodded with canes by curious spectators.[45] Tamburlaine's similar treatment of Bajazet had been held up before Elizabethan audiences more than two centuries earlier as an example of Oriental barbarity. The justification for this obscene episode was that the woman did not object to and may indeed have appreciated the anatomical curiosity exhibited by her viewers. After she died, her body was surrendered for further investigation. Speculations that Africans represented a lower form of human life, simian rather than Edenic in its ancestry, were current and are reflected in the imperialist games that the young De Quincey plays with his elder brother.[46]

Scholarly authority is important in imperial games, and the authority behind De Quincey's version is Lord Monboddo's six-volume work, *Of the Origin and Progress of Language* (1774–92). Monboddo considers orangutans and human beings as similar animals. He does not restrict this observation to Africans. The elder brother, who dominates the games, does not deny that the inhabitants of Tigrosylvania (the imperial power in these exercises) once had tails. His point is that they no longer have them, unlike the inhabitants of colonial Gombroon.[47] But this is only because the sedentary postures more common in higher civilizations have, over long years of adaptation, worn off the tails of the inhabitants of Tigrosylvania. In the psychopathology of imperialism, laughter can be important in retrieving excess.

"I had a perfect craze for being despised," De Quincey writes. "I doted on it and considered contempt a luxury that I was in continual fear of losing. Why not? Wherefore should any rational person shrink from contempt, if it happen to form the tenure by which he holds his repose in life?" (1:59). Such masochism fits well into an imperialist framework, providing sites of colonial victimization that can be psychologically coveted even while the consequences of inhabiting them are bewailed. The game obliquely authorizes imperialism since it is seen as the result of the collaboration of both participants. But the game's rules are also exposures of imperialist premises, such as the premise that distance is no barrier to dominion or the proposition that in "a contest between two parties, of which one possessed an article whilst the other was better able to use it, the rightful property is vested in the latter" (1:90).

Most important, the game concedes the hegemonic nature of imperial discourse: "It was the understood necessity of the case that I must passively accept my brother's statements so far as regarded their verbal expression." The claims of the discourse cannot be rejected. They can only be deflected "by some distinction or evasion lying within this [verbal] expression, or not blankly contradicting it" (1:90). Fortunately, there is "in almost everybody's words, an unintentional opening left for double interpretations" so that "undesigned equivocation prevails everywhere" (1:77).

Undesigned equivocation became important in the later stages of the game in India, as the independence movement began to gather strength. In the early nineteenth century, the task was to lay down the game's rules and, even more crucially, its ruling rhetoric. In performing this task, Mill was a principal agent.

It has been suggested that people who throw stones usually live in glass houses. Mill is not content with throwing stones. He proceeds to lay down a barrage. "Rude," "ignorant," "superstitious," and "credulous" are epithets he uses of Hindu civilization so frequently that it is difficult to find occasions on which they are not employed. In two particularly abusive consecutive sentences, Hindu religion is described as gross, disgusting, incoherent, disordered, capricious, rife with passion, laden with portents and prodigies, violent, and deformed.[48] Śakuntalā, which caught the admiration of the West, contains a few beautiful passages of poetry but nothing else "which either accords with the understanding, or can gratify the fancy, of an instructed people."[49]

In the face of this invective, it is difficult to comprehend William

Thomas's characterization of Mill's work as a philosophical history,[50] but if we listen with determination, the sound of thought can be heard behind the thumping. Mill's purpose is to devalue Hindu culture beyond the possibility of reinstatement. The number and severity of his references to Jones indicate that Jones had become an embarrassment, opening doors that ought to have remained closed by naively suggesting that there might be something to be learned from subject peoples. Mill writes a "philosophical" history in which history is defined so as to rule out this unpleasant possibility. Those who are furthest along civilization's learning curve have already assimilated everything that previous locations have to offer. Thus the revisionist proposal can be dismissed, and Hindu civilization can be found inferior at every point to Islamic civilization without the continuity proposal being revived.[51]

Mill's devaluation beyond the possibility of reinstatement can be linked to Elizabethan perceptions of Ireland, and indeed, the rhetoric of abuse is strikingly similar in both instances, going beyond the sameness that attaches to all abuse. Romantic perceptions of Ireland were made less harsh by the political marriage accomplished by the Union Act, by the entry of Anglo-Irish writing into the mainstream of English letters, and by the sympathy for Ireland voiced by leading romantic writers. Indeed, it can be argued that the two histories of representation—those of Ireland and India—begin to diverge at this point and that Ireland becomes the alternative to India rather than its parallel. Arnold's potentially dialogic view of the relationship between the Saxon and the Celtic is significantly never applied to India. It is interregnum Ireland that, extracted from its time frame, is brought to bear on the construction of nineteenth-century India. As an offshore bastion of Antichrist inhabited by an obstinate, treacherous, and deceitful people, whose much magnified uprising in 1641 was soon to be uncannily reenacted in the events of 1857, interregnum Ireland had much to offer the scenario now in the making for India.

One consequence of the scenario can be the demand for a tabula rasa as opposed to a palimpsest—the slate must be wiped clean if what is written on it is not to be nullified by previous writings. The other extreme would be that imperial management should cease endeavoring to reform what is beyond amendment and restrict its intervention to the minimum necessary to prevent an "incorrigible" country from ruining itself. Mill himself may be more inclined to the latter course than the former, but both in Elizabethan Ireland and in nineteenth-century India, British policy shifts considerably between the extremes that radical devaluation offers as its boundaries. The immediate historical consequences are, at least conceptually, heavily interventionist and perhaps build ironically on the beneficent intervention that is taken for granted in the Jones agenda. The direction of intervention (and of beneficence) now changes, moving away from a reinstatement of Hindu culture that is hereafter to be seen as regressively nostalgic and moving toward India's alignment with the march of civilization led by the West.

The new option is also cost-effective since it does not require the creation of an Orientalist cadre at the top level of management. Instead, the interfacing of the European and the Indian can be accomplished at a lower level by an Anglicized Indian elite whose investment in the system will ensure its continuing loyalty.

A further advantage of Mill's reading of India is that it provides a "philosophical" basis for the distaste for India that is the common bond of utilitarians and evangelists. Spears's anthology of European opinions on India documents this growing distaste by showing the mixed comments of an earlier period steadily giving way to comments that are almost uniformly adverse.[52] Although Southey writes a preface to *The Curse of Kehama* dutifully denouncing the monstrosities of Hindu religion, his poem's castigation of that monstrosity is too hesitant for the mounting zeal of his reviewers. When Jones rashly compares Kalidasa to Shakespeare, the retort in *Blackwoods* devalues considerably more than Kalidasa: "Neither the human mind nor human life did ever so exist in India, as to create such kind of faculties as those of Shakespeare or to furnish fields for their inspiration."[53] The discovery of the Elephanta caves produced speculations that Egyptians, Greeks, or Jews were responsible for their origin. When J. Goldingham, an astronomer of the East India Company with extensive antiquarian interests, turned to the obvious conjecture that the caves might be the work of Indian hands, his article was forwarded with the following comments by his superior, General John Carnac: "The immense excavations cut out of the solid rocks at the Elephanta, and other caves of like nature on the island of Salsette, appear to me the operations of too great labour to have been executed by the hands of so feeble and effeminate a race as the aborigines of India have generally been held to be."[54]

Utilitarians and evangelists both preached conversion of this feeble effeminacy, secular for one school and sacred for the other. Conversion rests on the emphatic perception of unlikeness, and propositions such as those of Jones and his colleagues about India's ancient culture, about classical languages that lay in proximity to a unified lost language, and about the common features of the Greek and Hindu pantheons were claims concerning likenesses that needed to be erased. In positing a single learning curve along which all civilizations are obliged to travel, Mill does not wish to suggest that Indian civilization is to be given even the minimal dignity of being viewed as a stage in the attainment of a triumphant European truth by which it can be recuperated rather than dismissed. At the end of a long period of tutelage and "management," otherness can conceivably begin to give way to likeness. India can approach the West along a line of advance that now consigns it to a period more remote than the Middle Ages. Meanwhile, it is the space of difference that matters, and Mill's real concern is to enlarge that space by making it historical as well as cultural and psychic.

We thus arrive at a situation in which likeness can be preached as an objective and otherness recognized as a reality, in which management is based on estrangement, and in which the alienness of India is constructed as everything that the European self has shed and that India must be taught to shed in its turn. A previous generation had mingled with India. Mingling now carries with it the danger of infection by a previous self, of regression into an unacceptable past.

Aloofness from India as a sanitary precaution, prudent for the historically advanced, is apparent in Mill's own resolute avoidance of the possibility of experiencing India. He never visited India and made no attempt to interest himself in any of its languages. He merely wrote the book that became a grammar of Indian civilization for officials of the East India Company. In prefacing his history, he invites attention to these potential drawbacks and, in five tautly reasoned but wholly fallacious pages, converts the drawbacks into a major asset: "Whatever is worth seeing or hearing in India can be expressed in writing. As soon as everything of importance is expressed in writing, a man who is duly qualified may obtain more knowledge of India in one year, in his closet in England, than he could obtain during the course of the longest life by the use of his eyes and ears in India."[55]

Those in the field report; those at the center analyze. This is a commonplace of bureaucratic arrogance, but it goes well with the hauteur of the British administration, with the deepening conviction of India's intractable otherness (side by side with an official policy of making it more English), and with endeavors such as Philip

Mason's in *The Guardians* to give philosophical dignity to the shunning of social contacts. Mason's book makes considerable claims for Plato's ultimate influence (mediated by the master of Balliol, Benjamin Jowett) on the manner in which British civil servants perceived their Olympian role in India. Plato, Mason notes, "wished to prevent his guardians from owning land or houses, gold or silver, or mingling with their fellow men."[56] The British followed the more convenient part of this advice. Even this limited adhesion ensured that "the aloofness often charged against the English as a fault, was in fact in the special circumstances of their empire in India, doubly a virtue. It provided not only impartiality but the ability to disengage; the English could complete their job and go home."[57]

Memories of home were reassuringly preserved in the English cantonment, segregated from the town (as it was typically called) and ironically reproducing in its status delineations the caste distinctions that utilitarians and evangelists denounced. The cantonment is an enclosed garden, an "Eden rais'd in the waste wilderness" (*PR* 1.7), a fragile enclosure watched over by Providence, against which the chaos of India beats "outrageous as a sea" (*PL* 7.212). Its reversal and complement is the cage in which the Hottentot Venus was confined, where chaos is contained by the garden of civilization surrounding it, where outside and inside exchange their allotted locations, with hell at the center and the heart of darkness within. Both arrangements are modelings of the Ptolemaic universe, the first being Milton's immensely influential version. Their common ancestry points to their natural collusiveness, notwithstanding their structural inversions of each other. If the first version fits imperial power at its origination, the second fits it at its zenith, when it is able to cage a conquered people, to examine and pronounce on its anatomy (as was literally true of the Hottentot Venus and figuratively true of the survey of India), and to subject it to controlled experiments in government, the consequences of which are inevitably verified by the coerced behavior of the experimental object. The empowerment the figure confers is heady indeed, but its consequence is that what is in the cage remains irretrievably in the hearts of those who cage it. It can and must be contained, but it cannot be exorcised. The captor's identity and the lucidity of the captor's self-image depend on its subversive and persistent life.

Olympian aloofness and the way in which that aloofness sustains constructions by the imperial gaze are matters negotiated with extraordinary finesse in E. M. Forster's *Passage to India*. The opening pages of the novel almost succeed in making the movement from the cantonment to the town a microenactment of the difficulty and illusions of a passage that Whitman had made into the mind's ultimate adventure. The two worlds share nothing "except the overarching sky."[58] The town is reduced to a pervasive featurelessness by a rhetoric that consistently strips it of any features. There are no steps leading to the riverfront. In fact, there is no riverfront. The streets are mean, and the temples ineffective. The bazaars have no paintings and hardly any carvings. The few fine houses that exist "are hidden away in gardens or down alleys whose filth deters all but the invited guest." The very wood of the carvings that are to be found "seems made of mud, the inhabitants of mud moving." The overall impression is of abasement and monotony, of "some low but indestructible form of life."

In these opening pages, India is more backward than Mill ever found it, but Europe, represented by the Civil Station, improves on it only by providing a different and less disturbing lack of distinction. "It charms not, neither does it repel," Forster says, with the affectation of the phrase advising us that the cultivated nondescriptness of the cantonment may also be an affectation, not a "form of life." The Civil Station is "sensibly planned," and its bungalows "are disposed along roads that intersect at right angles." Order prevails, but order is throughout only the avoidance of disorder. "It has nothing hideous in it and only the view is beautiful."

The view is of Chandrapore, which, seen from the Civil Station, "appears to be a totally different place." Distance provides imagination with the clues not for one text but for several. "It is a city of gardens. It is no city, but a forest sparsely scattered with huts. It is a tropical pleasance washed by a noble river." In each case, the imagination models the exotic so as to amend the tidy and sterile triteness of the vantage point from which Chandrapore is perceived. The trees play an important part in this modeling, like the trees Emma Roberts saw in 1837 framing and concealing the city of Lucknow. As the river on which Lucknow is situated wound its course through lofty, arched gateways, she saw "a bright confusion of palace and temple shadowed and interspersed with trees of gigantic growth and redundant luxuriance."[59] Forster's trees "screen what passes below," but even when scorched or leafless, "they glorify the city to the English people who inhabit the rise." Newcomers "have to be driven down to acquire disillusionment," to see things as the evangelists saw them.

Forster's paragraphs agitate important questions about the contingency of constructions, the proper distance, and the appropriate vantage point, but amid all these relativities, one important gathering of perspectives is ignored. Everything is seen from the hill and nothing from Chandrapore. The multiple readings that constitute and undermine the project of a text that might be India are conveyed with extraordinary sensitivity, but the possibilities all fall within the gaze of dominance.

Ironically, this gaze is held within and given back by the philosophy of the very culture on which it looks down. Both the imperial perspective and the elemental resonances of the caves at Marabar testify to the unavoidability of a world of representations, representations that contain and characterize the effort to know reality and its inextricable entanglement with the passion to command it. The featureless mud of Chandrapore offers itself as clay to the imperial artist. Marabar's deeper denudation tells the creator that he can know only himself, that the match he has lit will show not the undiscovered country of reality but only the transient flame of its own life, fancifully latent in the cave's stone. The self-reflexive nature of understanding, its coiling back into its own limitations, may indeed be the substratum of Forster's novel, its hidden connection between the metaphysical and the political. It is also a cornerstone of Indian thought. That the nearest Western equivalent to Maya is not illusion but representation[60] is a fact that Schopenhauer, among Western thinkers, was singular in seizing on and in incorporating into a philosophy of his own. Since he wrote, the relativity of constructions and the impossibility of avoiding them have become standard propositions in our classrooms. The West has indeed gazed on India's caged body. But it is Indian thought that may have successfully philosophized the caging of the mind that views that body within the gaze it has created and willed.

5
Hegel's India and the
Surprise of Sin

ଚ୍ଚ

There is a point in Hegel's *Philosophy of History* at which the grand march of the idea is suspended. The drumbeat of the argument is no longer heard. The writing takes on a gentler, more reflective cadence, faintly disturbing because it is so uncharacteristic. We move away from the irresistible progress of the chariot of history's life, driven forward by the totalizing imperative. The trumpets cease to sound as we step like Calidore into the pastoral beguilement.[1]

The moment when Hegel's book forgets itself occurs at the opening of his chapter on India. "There is," he tells us, "a beauty of a peculiar kind in women, in which the countenance presents a transparency of skin, a light and lovely roseate hue, which is unlike the complexion of mere health and vital vigour."[2] He proceeds to three feminine mirrorings of this "almost unearthly beauty," a beauty "breathed, as it were, by the soul within." It is "perceived in women in those days which immediately succeed childbirth." It is also seen in them during that "magical somnambulic sleep which connects them to a superterrestrial world." Finally, the artist Schoreel has "given this tone to the dying Mary, whose spirit is already rising to the regions of the blessed, but once more, as it were, lights up her dying countenance for a farewell kiss." Such a beauty, Hegel announces beckoningly, is found "in its loveliest form in the Indian world."

At this point, the nightingale's singing grows fainter, the loveliness that distracted us is exposed, and the bell summons us back to the stern reality of self-making. Destiny calls on us to seize the era. It is trivial to seize the moment, even when the moment seems in and out of time. The beauty by which we have been beguiled is now described as "a beauty of enervation in which all that is rough, rigid, and contradictory is dissolved." We might think it desirable to rid ourselves of roughness and rigidity, but "enervation" reminds us to be vigilant and an earlier phrase has already characterized India's unearthly beauty as "soft, yielding and relaxed." History is written by men, and the wrong gender must be kept in the margin, its allurements held in check. The charm of the "Flower-life," which India typifies, may be "rich in imagination and genius," but dreams have no place in the world. For a philosopher of mind such as Hegel, they have no place even in the mind's world, and the poem he had all but written must be defaced: "Should we look at it more closely, and examine it in the light of Human Dignity and Freedom—the more attractive the first sight of it had been, so much the more unworthy shall we ultimately find it in every respect."

We are surprised by sin here, and Hegel's use of this tactic is at least comparable in effectiveness to anything Stanley Fish found in Milton.[3] Milton uses the tactic with sufficient persistence to justify its treatment as a method. With Hegel, on the other hand, this may be the only occasion on which the book forgets its duty. It is not accidental and it may be crucially important that India is the place of this forgetfulness. Bengal's notoriously enervating climate had softened and relaxed the minds of too many scholars, and Hegel is enacting the Orientalist infatuation with India so that it can be both mirrored and dismissed.[4] His text, in its cumulative yielding to the momentum of that enactment, seems to lay bare the unsuspected strength of his vestigial sympathies, but it is also rebuking a specific and influential readership that has yet to free itself from a digression dangerous to the true tasks of history.

The site that is India in Hegel's ultimate geography has been visited many times by the Western mind. It is the land of the lotus-eaters, Dido's Carthage, Cleopatra's Egypt, and Spenser's Bower of Bliss,[5] with its reminder that Asia is part of the spelling of incontinence. When Nirad Chaudhari entitles one of his books on India *The Continent of Circe*,[6] he is drawing on a tradition of imperialist denigration that, one hopes, is temporarily absent from his mind. Hegel forgets his book in writing of India because India is another traditional name for forgetfulness. It is the place where the will to move on is challenged because moving on is irrelevant to the dream state. This dream state, moreover, is not simply a pastoral hibernation. In its progress from absolute East to absolute West, history has passed through it and willed itself out of its snare. It remains vulnerable to its residual blandishments.

To leave intact a text that acknowledges more than it should is a claim to honesty and a title to anger. Hegel's anger with India runs strong and deep. China, which is at the same stage or prior to India in the East-West movement of the sun of consciousness (p. 103), is spared this vituperation, but China is not the site of the sudden unveiling of the self's need in the other that demands retaliation as the price of its exposure. Only Africa is treated more abusively than India, and that may be because by 1820 Africa was the only continent still available to the newly arrived imperialist. Philosophically, Hegel sees Africa as ineligible to enter history, as the site of a consciousness that is totally unreflective, anterior to any organization of itself (pp. 93–99). Like other Hegelian characterizations, this is a construction made to fit the Procrustean bed of his system, but even within these distortions, the statement that one must abandon all normal criteria of humanity in seeking to understand Africans cannot be considered less than appalling.[7] Equally reprehensible are Hegel's comments on the gentle Taino people who greeted Columbus with innocent hospitality:

> A mild and passionless disposition, want of spirit, and a crouching submissiveness towards a Creole, and still more towards a European, are the chief characteristics of the native Americans. . . . The inferiority of these individuals in all respects, even in regard to size, is very manifest. . . . The weakness of the American physique was a chief reason for bringing the negroes to America, to employ their labor in the work that had to be done in the New World. (pp. 81–82)

Hegel does not add that the slave trade became necessary because of the decimation of Native Americans in an act of depopulation for which it is difficult to find a parallel.[8] In the face of these comments, some effort is required to remember that the dialectical progress of the idea is from freedom for one (China, India), through freedom for some (Greece, Rome), to freedom for all (Germany). "All," moreover, is specifically not restricted to those whom history has chosen as its vehicle. "*We* know that all men absolutely (man *as man*) are free" (p. 19; Hegel's italics; see also p. 104). Unfortunately, the consistent actuality of Hegel's rhetoric (as distinct from the not infrequent nobility of his thought) makes his commitment to the human community run a poor second to his racism.[9]

Racism is not inherent in *The Philosophy of History*. The idea, in its Olympian loftiness, ought to be color-blind in the choice of its agents. In the climate of the day, this impartiality may not be possible, but it can scarcely be said that the tree of Hegel's thought bends reluctantly to the imperial wind: "It is the condition of the inferior, the animal and spiritual inferior making itself more visible which is the objective superiority of the white skin colour."[10] When we move to a higher plane, "it is in the Caucasian race that spirit first reaches absolute unity with itself. It is here that it first enters into complete opposition to naturality, apprehends itself in its absolute independence, disengages from the dispersive vacillation between one extreme and the other, achieves self-determination, self-development, and so brings forth world history."[11]

Lesser people may seek to emulate the Caucasian example, but Macaulay's brown Englishman will have England in his behavior, not in his blood. The "declining nation has lost the interest of the absolute; it may indeed absorb the higher principle and begin building its life on it, but the principle is only like an adopted child, not like a relative to whom its ties are immanently vital and vigorous."[12] The black condition ranks still lower, being "capable of no development or culture" (*Philosophy of History*, p. 98).

As we might expect from these declarations, Hegel's remarks on India are appropriately rough and rigid, showing scant respect for the "charm rich in imagination and genius . . . permeated by the rose-breath of the Soul" that his text subversively courted for twenty lines. Such a slippage must never again occur, and Hegel is only superficially contradictory in his eagerness to take back whatever has been conceded. The imagination that once populated a "garden of love" becomes Bacon's imagination, joining what nature has severed, severing what nature has joined, and making unlawful matches and divorces of things. India is the home of mixed genres, hybridization, and, of course, monstrosity. It is a "wild tumult of excess" (p. 157), a "wild extravagance of fancy" (p. 155), the world of a "monstrous, irrational imagination" (p. 166), a dream state "revelling in the most extravagant maze, through all natural and spiritual forms" (p. 167).[13] Unable to integrate the material with the spiritual, India vacillates between flagellant asceticism and "a voluptuous intoxication in the merely natural" (p. 167).[14] As for the wisdom of India, its "widely bruited fame" has been greatly diminished by "a more accurate acquaintance with its real value" (p. 159).[15] If Hindu culture was once highly rated, it was in "the enthusiasm of discovery" (p. 159). The extensive diffusion of Indian culture is no more than a "dumb, deedless expansion" (p. 142). "The people of India have achieved no foreign conquests," Hegel adds, making clear how expansion should proceed if it is to be considered articulate. On the contrary, the Indian people "have been on every occasion vanquished themselves."[16] Hegel's thinking is proceeding through that much-used gateway opened by *The Lusiads.* India, he continues, has an essential place in "General History" but only as a "*Land of Desire*" (p. 142; Hegel's italics). This is not the desire of the self seeking its margin and speaking from the margin in the name of all it has excluded. It is not the mind's enlargement of its ancestral boundaries, its overflowing of those defensive constraints within which it may have lived in order to know itself. Hegel does indeed mention India's "treasures of wisdom" but only after he has given priority to "pearls, diamonds, perfumes, rose-essences, elephants, lions, etc." The "etc." devalues what follows in relation to an inventory that has trivialized itself. Hegel can now tell us momentously and mockingly that "the way by which these treasures have passed to the West, has at all times been a matter of World-historical importance, bound up with the fate of nations" (p. 142). Commodifying feminine India's relationship to the West and waving aside its possible contribution to world wisdom come together at this point in a derisive climax. No more need be said regarding the romantic delusion that saw India as a primary site of the mind.

Hegel, in writing of the Indian people, does not find the individual nobler than the institution, as Southey finds himself doing in *The Curse of Kehama:* "Deceit and cunning are the fundamental characteristics of the Hindoo. Cheating, stealing, robbing, murdering are with him habitual. Humbly crouching before a victor and lord, he is recklessly barbarous to the vanquished and subject" (p. 158).

In his 1883 lectures delivered at Cambridge, Max Müller found it necessary to devote an entire class to the honesty of Hindus and their abhorrence of deceit.[17] Some of the sources he quotes were available to Hegel and are indeed used in *The Philosophy of Religion.* They count for nothing in this tirade. "The Brahmins," Hegel goes on remorselessly, "are especially immoral. According to English reports they do nothing but eat and sleep. . . . When they take any part in public life they show themselves avaricious, deceitful, voluptuous." He continues to rely on the English (some of whom thought differently) as uniquely qualified to report on a strange phenomenon inaccessible to the rest of the civilized world: "'I do not know an honest man among them' says an English authority." Little can be expected of the younger generation with such models of behavior before them: "Children have no respect for their parents: sons maltreat their mothers" (pp. 158–59).[18]

Hegel finds nothing in India that has not been found by Mill and the missionaries, but he would be less important if he were more original. He dignifies existing stereotypes by blessing them with a philosophical ennoblement. Mill initiates that ennoblement by placing the stereotypes within a view of history. Hegel carries the process further by placing history, in turn, within a completely inclusive frame of understanding.[19] It becomes a province of the mind supported by the same underlying principles that regulate all of the mind's other provinces. The nature of those principles and of the deeply embedded empowerments that world history obtains from them are tersely presented in Hegel's introduction to his lectures:

> Universal history—as already demonstrated—shows the development of the consciousness of Freedom on the part of the Spirit, and of the consequent realization of that Freedom. This development implies a gradation—a series of increasingly adequate expressions or manifestations of Freedom, which result from its Idea. The logical, and—as still more prominent—the *dialectical* nature of the Idea in general, viz that it is self-determined—that it assumes successive forms which it successively transcends; and by this very process of transcending its earlier stages, gains an affirmative, and, in fact, a richer and more concrete shape;— this necessity of its nature, and the necessary series of pure abstract forms which the Idea successively assumes—is exhibited in the department of *Logic*. Here we need adopt only *one* of its results, viz. that every step in the process, as differing from any other, has its determinate peculiar principle.[20] (p. 63, Hegel's italics)

Milton talks of the contracted palm of logic opening into an ornate and graceful rhetoric.[21] The figure is conventional among classical rhetoricians. With Hegel, the hand is not designed to be graceful. It is designed to encompass the world, to grasp it firmly in the text of the hand. Logic is not a mere "department" but the directing force at the center of an empire. Robert Young is right in describing Hegel's philosophical system as "a form of knowledge which uncannily simulates the project of nineteenth-century imperialism."[22] But it is also menacingly more than that. Mill can be called an imperialist thinker. In *The Philosophy of History*, Hegel appears as the proponent of an imperialism of thought who invites us to consider whether thought, as we have come to know it, is worth pursuing on any other basis.

Despite its resolute and characteristic self-confidence, the paragraph we are examining wavers between an evolutionary view of history expressed in the term "gradation" and a transformational view expressed in the reference to "successive forms" that the idea "successively transcends." The major metaphor Hegel employs is consistent with "gradation." The sun of consciousness rises in the Orient and waxes until it achieves its Germanic apogee (at which point Hegel felicitously drops the metaphor). Similarly, a world history that proceeds from infancy to maturity passes through a series of gradations, and old age can even be regarded as a sign of the West's wisdom rather than its decline. Hegel merges both metaphors in his characterization of Africa, along with a judicious injection of the primeval: "It is the Gold-land compressed within itself—the land of childhood which lying beyond the day of self-conscious history, is enveloped in the dark mantle of Night" (p. 91).

Dialectical progress is presented as self-diagnostic. Civilization moves forward by educating itself, by identifying its distinctive limitations, and by finding a way to overcome those limitations within a larger inclusiveness that enriches rather than imperils its identity. This is the path of gradation. To replace it by the forward leap of transcendence, we have to postulate civilizations that, without outside assistance, cannot proceed further along the learning curve of world history. This is the imperialist postulate, and Hegel is powerfully attracted to it because of his commitment to the principle of a chosen people, singularly fitted to the advance of the idea at each specific stage of its realization and therefore taken up and empowered by the idea in the course of its irresistible drive to self-fulfillment.

To make transcendence not only possible but also essential, Hegel treats world history in its passage through the Orient not as a series of gradations but as a sequence of blind alleys, impasses from which there can be no deliverance because the structure of the problem has been articulated so as to make deliverance impossible. Thus India is described as a people without a state, and China as a state without a people (p. 161). These characterizations have little to do with either India or China, but if we look at them diagrammatically and not on the basis of their factual justice, it is obvious that with exclusions so fundamental, neither civilization can find or even invent the other. If we pass to the relationship between existence and transcendence that is the propelling force behind Hegel's view of history, neither India, China, nor Islam can make any progress in inscribing this relationship because none of these civilizations is capable of inventing immanence.

Inventing immanence is a privilege of the West, possible only when there is audacity enough to secularize the sacred and when the subtle knot of the human and the divine still stands at the center of the Western view of history. China, India, and Islam have between them the pen, the ink, and the paper. The presuppositions exist for a crucial movement forward (p. 116), but without a transcendental disclosure, these presuppositions remain only fragments shored against the half knowledge of successive civilizations.

Appropriations of Christianity form a considerable presence in Hegel's thinking about history. That presence becomes stronger when we realize that it is in the nature of a type to be incapable of arriving at the truth. Typology inscribes a decisive difference between world history as it passes through the Orient and world history under an illuminating dispensation that rescues it from the impasses to which it has hitherto been subject. To the imperialist mind, typology also makes available the deep distinctions it embeds in historical time for translation into geopolitical space. In addition, the concept of the elect nation, so potent in Reformation thought, can be transposed into the concept of a people chosen by history whose right to make the future in the image of the idea can be militantly safeguarded against any dissenting will. The strength of the Hegelian ideology is not the strength of argument alone. There are powerful convergences in the history of thought and in the accumulation of the rhetoric of empire by which Hegel's argument is profoundly sustained.

Correcting Hegel's misrepresentations of India would involve us in many pages of pained and pointless protest. It is more important to identify and trace the forces that control the misrepresentations. Only an extraordinary dedication to the imperialist agenda could enable Hegel to write as he does of India with the "that art thou" of Hindu philosophy staring him in the face.

"That art thou" is a recognition of deliverance from individual limitations not into unity but into identity with the ultimate. It is not normally translated into a social text, but if we consent to the move, "that" can reasonably be read as the telos that the collective self seeks and "thou" as representing the growing immediacy and comprehensiveness with which the telos is inscribed and discovered in social performance. We are not far from Hegel at this point, but Hegel cannot afford to treat Hindu understanding as a state on which future understandings can be built. Repudiation and not recuperation is the demand of the imperial agenda and of the dismissive force generated by self-and-other relationships. Hindu understanding must therefore be constructed as a state of incarceration from which no forward movement is possible.

Deliverance from the prison house is comprehensively frustrated because of that dispersive vacillation from which only Caucasian thought is free. The vacillation fragments any potential relationship between the extremes that thought inhabits and between which the dialectic flows. Hindu thought is particularly given to this dispersive vacillation and uniquely unable to break away from its disintegrating force because its extremes have been constructed as mind and antimind and not as two positions that consciousness can occupy without ceasing to be consciousness.

Sublation can take place between a proposition and its negation, but it obviously cannot take place between a proposition and its erasure. If the Hindu ultimate is constructed as the erasure of all propositions, then one can only recoil from it into a delirium of possibilities deprived of any anchor in significance. There is no point in insisting that the world is the text of the idea if every conceivable text is aimless doodling.

Hegel's insistence on the "stupefaction" of the Hindu union with the ultimate is thus a misrepresentation that he had to invent. It gave him a metaphysics dedicated to severance rather than to immanence and a textuality so prolix that it was incapable of writing the world. It offered to the European gaze the sterile yet edifying spectacle of a civilization profoundly unable to analyze itself. All that the West could learn from such a civilization was the necessity of utterly disowning it.

A further consequence of the ultimate distancing between stupefaction and the wild whirl of possibilities is that the ethical vacuum between them can be filled by power according to its caprices. Marlowe's Tamburlaine anticipates Hegel in his pursuit of freedom for one, of unlimited power as the basis of unfettered self-expression. Tyranny must be, although, as Panikkar notes, India was the site of the longest-lived republic in world history.[23]

A corrective essay should be written, but this chapter restricts itself to offering a postscript. In his preface to *The Principal Upaniṣads*, Radhakrishnan reminds us that "Brahman" "is derived from the root *bṛh* 'to grow, to burst forth.' The derivation suggests gushing forth, bubbling over, ceaseless growth." The real, Radhakrishnan adds, "is not a pale abstraction but is quickeningly alive." Since "Atman" is derived from "an," "to breathe," the Atman-Brahman identity is doubly directed to the plenitude of life rather than to the emptiness of the void.[24]

We could conclude that Hegel's disinterment of stupefaction at the core of Hindu thought (being buried alive is used by him as an implicit metaphor) is metaphysically uncalled for and etymologically outrageous. It is more important to recognize that "the whole is the true" is a proposition native to Upanishadic as well as to Hegelian thought. It is on this basis that Sri Aurobindo, the foremost of India's modern philosophers, sees human consciousness evolving out of its limitations into progressively higher and more inclusive states. The aim is world enlightenment and not the providentially encouraged march of the Western will.[25]

Immanence can have more than one meaning, even within Hegel's parameters, but not when the text it inscribes is filled with contempt for those who do not win battles and when the contribution of the Orient to the substance and spirit of world history is reduced to variations on the theme of failure. That India should be devalued by taking a central principle of Indian religious philosophy and installing it as the uniquely Western foundation of an understanding from which India is thereupon excluded is an injustice notable for more than its astonishing magnitude. India, according to the West, conspicuously lacks a view of history that can make history itself a vehicle of human significance. Its failure to keep accurate chronological records is only a symptom of a much deeper malaise. This is Mill's finding (*History of British India*, p. 329) and Hegel's (pp. 161–62) and is echoed thereafter by innumerable voices. It is poetic justice that a crucial principle of Indian thought should be installed as the basis of an understanding India is now said to lack. It is also appropriate that those designated as indifferent to history should have pride of place among history's recurring victims.

Hegel's setting apart of a West capable of progress by gradation and an Orient for which transcendence is necessary but impossible entrenches Western superiority in a manner difficult to overturn. It might be argued that once the way forward has been shown, the East can emulate the West within its own distinctiveness. But the West progresses by debate within itself, by identifying and working through its exclusions, and these are characteristics that Eastern absolutism lacks. Civilizations come to a standstill because they are imprisoned in their own mystiques. This is true of the West too, but Hegel was not considering the problems of a world that stands on the threshold of the twenty-first century. For his time, the weaning of the East from its distinctiveness, its exposure to the gaze of rational understanding, called for tutelage, guardianship, wardship, trusteeship, paternal care, and related recuperations in imperialism's moral armory. These benevolent metaphors do not appear in Hegel, who may be more prepared than others to insist that the inevitable must also be the morally just. They do appear with the numbing monotony of an unscrutinized consensus in the self-justifying fictions of British rule in India.

The feminization of the Orient is as ancient as Western perceptions of the Orient, but Hegel bestows a new dimension on the devaluation of the feminine by making it not only inferior but also obsolete. Rough and rigid honesty, for all its awkwardness, takes precedence over the highly wrought culture of Oriental societies as substance takes precedence over etiquette. If "the Character of Spirit in a state of Dream" is "the generic principle of the Hindoo nature" (p. 140), the dream world can be a garden of love, but it can also be a place of wild extravagance and tumultuous excess, with the outcome indeterminate as long as the dream is its own arbiter. If feminine fancy is not checked by masculine judgment, it will produce results consistent only in their capriciousness. Some of the results may be charming and a few may yield moments of unearthly beauty, but history has to be philosophized as a grammar of change and cannot be written as an anthology of accidents. India is the world of the feminine, "the region of phantasy and sensibility" (p. 139). Jones had imprudently pointed to India as the site of poetry, but there is a time as well as a place for literature, and that time comes to an end when the sun of reason rises, bringing to a close the extravagance of the age of fancy.[26]

The aggressive linear movement from East to West, from feminine to masculine, and from irresponsible fancy to answerable reason can be contested by the spiral, a form of thought often associated with the Hegelian dialectic. The spiral is notable for its recuperation of itself, its extraordinary openness to its history. Every point on it is a point of both arrival and departure. The form unites gradation and transcendence but only if it circles back on its past, lifting it into a different discourse so that the constituents of its life are renewed in another pattern. In Eliot's *Four Quartets*, the most sustained enactment of the spiral form in literature, the point of the poem and the purpose of thought is to persistently unsettle and revalidate itself.

Herbert Marcuse is prominent among those philosophers who argue for the dialectic's openness, who find it proceeding by unsettling and revalidation rather than by progressive consolidation, the cumulative assimilating of the world to the idea. "Dialectical logic," Marcuse tells us, "reveals modes and contents of thought which transcend the codified pattern of use and validation." It "recovers tabooed meanings," he continues strikingly, "and thus appears almost as a return or rather a conscious liberation of the repressed."[27] In a similar vein, Hans-Georg Gadamer stresses the self-undermining nature of the master-slave relationship. The dominant term is defined not by an imperious act of exclusion but by its eventual dependence on the forces it has marginalized: "The truth of self-consciousness will have to be sought not in the consciousness of the master but in the servile consciousness."[28]

As these remarks make evident, there can be more than one way of writing Hegel. Theodor Adorno adds significantly to these ways by offering us a negative dialectic conducted from the site of the other not as an overthrowing but as an extension of Hegelian thought.[29]

In opening up the Hegelian dialectic, Marcuse, Gadamer, and Adorno point to potentialities that Hegel has both offered and suppressed. Dialectical thought, when it is not imperially directed, is unsettled by the exclusions that define it, and it can be argued that this self-disturbance must eventually leak back, even into imperialism's certainties. "Every one is also the other of another," Hegel says, probing a segregation that forms the axis of postcolonial theory. "If this mutual alienation is comprehended," he continues, "being negates its negation and thereby affirms itself as the one *in the other*" (italics added).[30] More sinuously, Hegel argues that negation "posits what it excludes" and that the "Absolute differentiates itself and mediates itself to itself through its own *negativity*" (Hegel's italics).[31] The status of the other in these mediations and discoveries is far from conforming to an imperialist model.

Hegel can even substantiate uncannily Gadamer's reading of the master-slave relationship: "The independent master becomes dependent on the skills and virtues of the servant. . . . The servant now ranks higher in value than the master who merely beholds the shallow sign of his freedom in the servant."[32]

Hegel's rhetoric, like his thought, can display another side when the text is less engaged with events than *The Philosophy of History*. *The Phenomenology of Spirit* has more than one passage that indicates the mind's unhappiness with the boundaries which have formed its present but which in doing so, have inhibited its future. The act of exclusion that constitutes thought generates a desire to overcome the exclusion, to take into thought whatever thought has made marginal. The following is perhaps the most eloquent expression of the discontent with itself which can be for Hegel almost a condition of consciousness: "Lacking strength, Beauty hates the understanding for asking of her what it cannot do. But the life of spirit is not the life that shrinks from death and keeps itself untouched by devastation, but rather the life that endures and maintains itself in it. It wins its truth only when, in utter dismemberment, it finds itself."[33]

Self-discovery in "utter dismemberment" is scarcely an imperialist recommendation. In this statement, Hegel approaches a condition of humility before otherness. The beyond must not merely be recognized. It must also be sacrificially entered, as the crisis zone for the unavoidable life-in-death of consciousness. For the imperial mind, the beyond is beyond the pale. The mind constitutes itself and maintains itself by refusing to recognize what lies outside its just limits.

There is indeed another side to Hegel. The somber instructiveness of *The Philosophy of History* lies in watching him proceed against the best part of himself. Imperialism's constricting strength becomes apparent when a thinker of his stature resolutely shuts down the potential openness of the modus operandi of his own thought. In mapping his system onto history, he finds himself obliged to concentrate compulsively not on the spiral's capacity to recuperate its past but on the forward and eradicating thrust of the line running through the spiral's center. If the present is to be adequately privileged, the past must be relentlessly devalued.

We "leave" Africa, "not to mention it again" (p. 99). We "quit" the "Dream-State characterizing the Hindoo Spirit" (p. 167). The present is implacably Eurocentric. The "magnificent territory on which Carthage once lay . . . *must* be attached to Europe." The French, Hegel adds encouragingly, "have lately made a successful effort in this direction" (p. 93). The possibilities of attachment do not end with Mediterranean Africa. Alexander "opened the Oriental world to the Europeans," bequeathing to the world "one of the noblest and most brilliant of visions which our poor reflections serve only to obscure." The quality of those reflections can be improved by following more diligently the trail blazed by this "great World-Historical form" (p. 273).

With Africa kept off the premises, the Orient brought in only to set the stage, and the Slavs allowed on the stage as a respectable civilization but not the voice that the time needs (p. 350), the curtain can lift on Western Europe's assumption of its destiny. The chosen people have been chosen by the disqualification of all other candidates, as well as by their distinctive relationship to the idea, their unique ability to articulate it as history. In fact, the chosen people have accumulated overwhelming privileges that override any protest others may wish to make about their concept and execution of the world will. God does not merely speak first to the English, as Milton suggests in *Areopagitica*.[34] God sees no point in speaking to anyone else.

That the idea should be carried forward by a succession of peoples whom it has anointed is not a necessary consequence of Hegel's thought. We could argue at least as plausibly that world history should be given its shape by all the world's peoples. Indeed, it is difficult to see how "freedom for all" can be established when the greater part of that "all" is permitted no voice in defining the institutions that might secure that freedom. Much must turn on the definition of freedom. *The Philosophy of History* conspicuously refuses to minister to this need for definition, treating freedom throughout as if its nature were self-evident. Implicitly, it can be said to argue that the real extent of freedom is in proportion to the accuracy of society's alignment with the idea. Popular opinion and a fortiori world opinion can be judged as irrelevant to this geometry. The argument can then call for a leadership fully responsive to the current status of the idea in history and for social engineering as a monopoly of that leadership. Against the elect of the idea, the rights of all others are decisively extinguished. The following passage is quoted in Walter Kaufmann's translation since Kaufmann has rightly objected to those who mistranslate Hegel and then use the mistranslation to sustain an interpretation that would not otherwise stand. It is among the most brutal statements made by Hegel:

> This people *is* the *dominant* one in world history for this epoch—*and it can be epoch making in this sense only once.* Against this absolute right which it has to be the embodiment of the current stage of development of the world spirit, the spirits of the other people have no rights, and they, even as they whose epoch has passed, do not any longer count in world history.[35]

Kaufmann's specific objection is to Karl Popper, whose critique of Hegel in *The Open Society and Its Enemies* is not an exercise in moderation. Yet much that Popper says is justified by this single paragraph, in which the arrogance of election attains dimensions that can only be described as overbearing.

In characterizing the thinking in Hegel's statement as "ruthless imperialistic nationalism" and as "a new event in the history of political thought, an event pregnant with far-reaching and fearful consequences," Ernst Cassirer is representative in his distress. He seeks to mitigate the adverse impact of this passage by arguing that the idea "develops itself in three moments"—namely, "Art, Religion and Philosophy"—that these moments constitute "ends in themselves that have to be respected and furthered," and that Hegel did not argue for the subjection of these realms to the overriding authority of the state.[36]

These autonomies may hold *within* a given civilization that has appointed itself as the standard-bearer of the spirit, but it does not follow that outdated civilizations contain cultural possibilities that need to be "respected and furthered." Civilized nations, Hegel says bluntly, are justified "in regarding and treating as barbarians those who lag behind them in institutions which are the essential moments of the state." This relegation to barbarian status is not simply a cultural demotion: "The civilized nation is conscious that the rights of barbarians are unequal to its own and treats their autonomy as only a formality" (*Philosophy of Right*, p. 219).[37]

We can sense insecurity behind this imperial arrogance. The "absolute right" of the chosen people is militantly claimed not simply because of their uniqueness but because of the necessary transience of that uniqueness. The title to dominance will pass to others, and those empowered to sweep aside all dissent today will become part of the silences of tomorrow. One must seize the moment with energy, even ferocity. The page must be written decisively before the page turns, relegating its omniscient narrators to the ranks of those whose epoch has passed and who "do not any longer count in world history."

The overwhelming privileges of the elect make it important that they should be convincingly identified, but Hegel has nothing to say on a matter that should be bristlingly problematic. We can speculate that the chosen announce themselves by being uniquely fitted to the next stage in the realization of the idea, but this authentication is less than overwhelming when it is the chosen who decide the nature of the next stage. Yet it is hard to see how the situation could be otherwise. In the absence of a democratic forum to recognize and sustain the dictatorship of the chosen (a paradox that history has occasionally entertained), military dominance becomes not merely the most reliable but, for practical purposes, the only sign of election. The respect for military dominance and the contempt for those unable to exercise it that Hegel displays throughout *The Philosophy of History* become understandable in this light but are not for that reason less disturbing.

As the sealed train of the idea's journey leaves the country of the chosen in search of its future, we are tempted to ask what its destination might be. Hegel warns us that predicting what is to come is not the proper business of the historian. Nevertheless, he provides us with a fascinating conjecture:

> America is therefore the land of the future, where, in the ages that lie before us, the burden of the World's History shall reveal itself—perhaps in a contest between North and South America. It is a land of desire for all those who are weary of the historical lumber-room of old Europe. Napoleon is reported to have said: "*Cette vieille Europe m'ennuie.*" It is for America to abandon the ground on which hitherto the History of the World has developed itself. (pp. 86–87)

Abandoning the ground suggests that the New World can give us an altogether new text, but the reference to Napoleon puts us on notice that it may not be wholly a territory of the mind that Hegel seeks. A further set of reflections on America as the land of the future develops the unsettling implications of the remarks in *The Philosophy of History*. It is quoted prudently in Kaufmann's translation:

> Suppose that, after having considered the greater epics of the past [*The Iliad, El Cid,* and Tasso's, Ariosto's, and Camões's poems] which describe the triumph of the Occident over the Orient, of European measure, of individual beauty, and of self-critical reason over Asiatic splendour . . . one now wished to think of great epics which might be written in the future: they would only have to represent the victory of the living rationality which may develop in America, over the incarceration into an infinitely progressing measuring and particularizing. For in Europe every people is now limited by another and may not on its part begin a war against another European people. If one now wants to go beyond Europe it can only be to America.[38]

There is much to note in this paragraph. First we have the proposition that the "greater epics of the past" are greater because they describe the triumph of the Occident over the Orient. *Paradise Lost* is significantly not mentioned, even though Hegel elsewhere contrasts the pursuit of empires on which the sun never sets with a simple German monk (Luther) seeking the new world within (pp.

414–15). The superiority of the Occident over the Orient is implicitly drawn as the triumph of measure over excess, of individual beauty over proliferation, and, explicitly, of self-critical reason over Asiatic splendor. Similar formulas in a similarly martial context are recited in Yeats's poem *The Statues*.[39] All of this is standard bludgeoning of the Orient, with great literature taking part in the castigation. There is, then, an unexpected turn in the argument as the measuring and particularizing that were the basis of the European triumph became the dimensions of its incarceration. The idea is continental, impeded and deflected by regional conventions and boundaries. At this stage, the submerged territorial metaphor takes over the thought, and Lebensraum becomes a demand of the mind that requires that other minds be evicted from the premises. A collective identity must turn in destructively on itself if it cannot wage war against those who constrain that identity. America's moving frontier gives the living rationality of the idea the space it needs in order to become itself.

Militaristic images stride through Hegel's writing, proclaiming themselves in his dismissal of India's dumb, deedless cultural expansion, his withering remarks on the physique of the Tainos, and his contemptuous portrayal of Tainos and Hindus crouching abjectly before their European overlords. Great epics enlist literature in ideological warfare, recording and celebrating the necessary conquest of the Orient by the Occident. The world-historical form of Alexander was the initiation and prophecy of that conquest. The voyages of Columbus and Vasco da Gama that completed the encirclement of the world by the West "may be compared with that *blush of dawn*, which after long storms first betokens the return of a bright and glorious day" (p. 411). Napoleon, the contemporary version of the great form of Alexander, is idolized by Hegel: "I saw the Emperor—this world-soul—riding out of the city on reconnaissance. It is indeed a wonderful sensation to see such an individual, concentrated here at a single point, astride a horse, reach out over the world and master it."[40] The tramp of Napoleon's armies over Europe resounded thrillingly in Hegel's study: "The world-spirit has given the age marching orders. These orders are being obeyed. The world-spirit, this essential power, proceeds irresistibly like a closely drawn armoured phalanx." Those foolish enough to oppose the advancing giant are characterized by Hegel as "powerless vermin."[41] These statements make more comprehensible the otherwise bizarre depiction of a Europe weakened by peace, tied hand and foot by settlements and boundaries, and incapable of carrying history forward in the grand march of the heroic ideal.

"The History of the World," Hegel writes, "is not the theatre of happiness. Periods of happiness are blank pages in it, for they are periods of harmony—periods when the antithesis is in abeyance" (pp. 26–27). It is an ancient thought and a modern one. Aeneas can abandon Dido. Auden, writing in the 1930s, can tell us that building the just city matters and that we must not settle in the village of the heart.[42] But the great poets (Virgil is not in the Hegelian canon) write not simply of the mind's purgations but of its entanglements and of the necessity of those entanglements if mind is to be mind. Hegel writes monolithically of the mind's betrayal in the Indian garden of love. His chapter on India is a response to that betrayal. Elevated by Hegel's own prose into a delusive timelessness, India stands revealed as a present and lasting danger, not part of the mind's mixed loyalties but that interior enemy from which the mind must be cleansed. Its siren call, all the more dangerous because of its masquerade as the call of the spirit, must be identified and debased so that it is never again taken seriously in history.

In moving through the contest between discourse as hegemonic and discourse as self-interrogating, this book endeavors to steer a course that keeps the contest alive instead of collapsing it into either of its terms. The second term is adding to its following, and one might prefer it if only because it is able to take back some of the treason of philosophy and scholarship. To bring about this recovery from a disillusion that may have set in with Said, philosophical and scholarly texts that are ideologically tyrannized in their formal conclusions will need to be laid open to literary retrievals.

In Hegel's case, the acknowledgment and emphatic disavowal of the other in himself on the site that is India is deeply revelatory and, once recognized, can be seen as the driving force behind the otherwise inexplicable vehemence of his rhetoric. The scene and its consequences become an almost exemplary display of self-and-other dependencies. Clandestinely incorporating Indian insights into a Western world system built on the rejection of India is a tactic psychologically consistent with this display. So also is the insistence on withholding the openness of dialectical thought from relationships between cultures and confining those opennesses to the chosen culture of the historical moment. But in the end, it is the denigration of India that counts, as the anxieties of empire become converted into the fuel for the imperial engine's assertiveness. To read scholarship as literature can be instructive, but it is not inappropriate to persist in asking ourselves whether those who ruled India read it in this way.

6

Feminizing the Feminine:
Early Women Writers on India

಄

This chapter deals largely with two novels: Elizabeth Hamilton's *Translation of the Letters of a Hindu Rajah* and Lady Morgan's (Sydney Owenson's) *Missionary*. Both novels were widely read in their time but are scarcely known in ours. Hamilton's novel is hard to find, and commentary on it is strikingly scanty. *The Missionary*, kept alive until now by Shelley's commendation of it, was once far more celebrated than anything Shelley produced. Despite some revival of interest in Owenson, it remains the least commented on of her novels.

To write on these novels is not simply to search the margin in yet another of the incremental operations of scholarship. Recontextualization of these works restores their topicality and helps to explain why they mattered in their time. But recontextualization also retrieves a literary sophistication that would otherwise not be present in our reading of these novels. Their relationship to the discourse of imperialism is befittingly complex, but to savor that complexity, we have to situate them with some care in relation to a quite brief time span in the development of that discourse. Significantly, much of the writing of the romantic era is in alignment with this time frame and can be read as responding to its possibilities and coercions.

By 1830, the Mill-Hegel construction had taken over English perceptions of India. Macaulay's minute of 1835 established English as India's language of higher education and the English achievement in civilization as the standard of excellence India must seek to approach. Utilitarians and evangelists came together in a common zeal for reform by making use of the space of difference between "superior" and "inferior" cultures to argue that reform in the English direction was essential if India was not to be trapped in itself. The reform experiment, moreover, would be less contaminated than it might be even in England since custom and error, those twin sisters, could be disallowed any voice in the proceedings. A subjected country is not without its advantages as a laboratory for the social scientist.[1]

The "obligation of benevolence" for Hastings[2] consisted of the responsibilities (unilaterally determined) that made power seem respectable to itself. More self-righteously, it was presented by evangelicals as an atonement for past injustices, including those for which Hastings was responsible.[3] "We cannot now renounce them without guilt," Charles Grant said of the Indians in 1792, halfway through the Hastings impeachment. He went on to add prophetically that "we may contract great guilt in the government of them."[4] His agenda for atonement consisted of the "moral improvement" of those subject to British rule in India and the rooting out of the "internal principles of depravity" in their cultures.[5]

It cannot be said that India was particularly eager to accept Grant's atonement; it was inflicted, moreover, on hundreds of thousands of square miles of territory that had been spared the original sins of Clive and Hastings. The point to be made is about effectiveness, not justice; two converging movements of reform produced a momentum difficult to resist, particularly in the exclusive boardrooms of a private company that could still make decisions affecting the future of a subcontinent. Yet the reforming impetus, although vigorous, was short-lived, impeded from the beginning by institutional resistances both Indian and English. Two decades later, the events of 1857 shifted the emphasis from social engineering to preserving law and order.

Mill's own agenda, before reformist zeal enlarged it, had sought no more than peace preserved and justice impartially dispensed. The Olympian aloofness offered by this formula fitted the British mood after 1857. The introduction of English as India's higher language and the beckoning possibilities of conversion to Christianity had been presented as the means for collapsing the otherness of India into a space of difference that could be progressively reduced. The original otherness that had been conceived so as to justify these measures was now reinstated in all its intractability. Bengali babus could never be honorary Englishmen. Imitation had been amusing once, but it could be parodic as well as flattering. More threateningly, it could be a form of usurpation.[6]

On the whole, it was better for East and West not to meet. It was preferable for India to be a place of exile where the Great Game was played on a frontier resembling the American West, with the English identity realized at a periphery and not at a center lost to the cosmopolitan. To manage India, the site of passion, deceit, and irrationality, with firmness and with wisdom was to enact in the theater of empire the conquest of the self.

There could be alternatives, even for the same author. In Kipling's world, India is not the madwoman in the attic but a prized possession to be cared for and guarded, externally from rapacious Russians and internally from the wildness in itself. Dryden's Nourmahal, it will be remembered, anticipates that wildness side by side with Indamora's embodying of India's desirability. We can see the wildness as amiable rather than hysterical. We can see the desirability as dangerous rather than rewarding. Perceptions can shift widely between these elasticities, leaving their containment discursively in place. India can also be a jungle where we discover reassuringly that the fundamental law, as in civilized societies and empires, is the obedience of the lower to the higher. On the other hand, Kim can live in an enclosed garden where the events of 1857 have left no scar on the smiling earth. As with the view of Chandrapore from the cantonment in Forster's novel, more than one construction can be shaped and sustained by the gaze of the beholder. But India endearing or dangerous, reticent or treacherously secretive, as not a promise but an appeal or as a promise that becomes an appeal remains consistently feminine India.[7]

Perceiving India as feminine is a familiar practice of the literary imagination. Scholarship should be a different matter. It is factual and not fictive, neutral and not partisan, entrenched protectively in the disinterestedness that Matthew Arnold once called the Indian virtue. Claims to this effect have not ceased to be heard, but they are considerably less persuasive than they once were. It is not easy after Said to believe fervently in the disinterestedness of scholarship, although a mild persuasion along these lines may be desirable in order to continue with these pages. Ronald Inden's important study, *Imagining India*, provides little ground for reaffirming scholarly impartiality.[8] The various scholarly disciplines, as they apply themselves to India, consistently devalue it, and they all eventually do so by subscribing to the fictive dispositions they might be expected to resist. They provide different scholarly names for India's femininity.

India is the anima and the id. It is a proliferating jungle where the garden of civilization must be maintained with great difficulty against the invading undergrowth. It is prolixity instead of order, wayward passion and wild extravagance instead of purposive reason, and serpentine Oriental deceitfulness instead of straightforward Western candor. It is tribal and inherently fragmented. It is the primitive feminine, masculinized too late. It is the Aryan ship foundering in the Dravidian ocean. It is tropical rather than temperate; the very wordplay in this contrast underlines the nature of Indian irresponsibility.[9]

A common rhetoric sustained by metaphors both explicit and buried percolates through the discourse formation of religious, philosophical, socioeconomic, anthropological, and psychoanalytical scholarship. There is an impressive homogeneity in the findings, which may mean that the truth identifies itself by remaining the same irrespective of the approach to it or simply that one usually finds what one is looking for and that the Western gaze looks only in one direction. But, of course, in a hegemonic era, it is the cumulative concurrence that counts and not the cautionary skepticism that is becoming audible only with the passing of territorial empires.

The solidarity of the discourse formation facilitates migration from one discipline to another and increases the coercive force of each discipline. Investigations can lead to vigorously disputed conclusions that seem to bear witness to the integrity of scholarship, but there is no real disagreement on how the investigations are to be channeled. India is a stage on which the feminine can be enacted and given its full range of representations with a luxuriance of rendering that is itself feminine in its elaborations. The elaborations feed back into the originating principle, so that the relationship between gender, culture, and race becomes symbiotic rather than overlapping. When Inden tells us that Mill and Hegel are hegemonic in Indology,[10] we have to recognize that Indology is not just the study of the history and culture of a specific geographical area. If India is thought of as the theater of the other, Indology can appropriately become the didactic productions mounted in that theater.

The completeness of envisaging that characterizes feminine India, the comprehensiveness and the interlocking nature of its rhetoric, makes escape from its constraints remarkably difficult. The directing strength of discourse, its writing of the self that writes the novel, and the heavy investment of identity in the assumptions of empire are particularly to be borne in mind when we consider women writers on India. A subjected femininity might be expected to reach out to a subjected India, defined as meriting subjection because it is feminine. But Benita Parry finds very little of this empathizing in her chapter on women novelists of the Kipling era.[11] Brantlinger's fine chapter on 1857 suggests that the rhetoric enveloping those tragic events remained much the same irrespective of the sex of the author.[12] In the most recent and probably the most thoughtful consideration of this problem, Jenny Sharpe recognizes that "a rejection of the gender hierarchy the domestic ideal enforces does not similarly negate the racial superiority it implies. It may, in fact, reinforce it."[13]

These findings should not surprise us. The sacrifice of family life and the self-effacing exile in an ungrateful land that were needed to maintain British supervision of a wayward and potentially vicious India enshrined Victorian domesticity by immolating it on the altar of empire. The Englishwoman in India was thus captured and sometimes captivated by a discourse that offered her both heroic dignity and limited empowerment. A double seduction was held out in return for the compliance with the script that the discourse expected from participants in its theater. The reward was more than sufficient to contain and render insubstantial any potential generosities of gender.[14]

To study the feminine view of India's femininity under conditions less warped by the pressures of discourse, we must return to an earlier phase of Britain's relationship with the subcontinent. The sudden elevation of India's past in the first wave of Oriental scholarship opened a moment of opportunity for understanding between peoples. The moment passed almost before it had articulated itself. The years 1785 and 1810 might be said to mark its limits, and even during that brief period, the view from the window was clouded. The literary attractiveness of the Jones perception of India merely meant that for the time being, literature would be one step behind in the imperial march. It was the swiftly changing power relationship between England and India that mattered, and that relationship was obliged to place out of bounds the mutual respect that is a condition of dialogue. Subject peoples are to be educated, not listened to. Indeed, the very decisiveness with which the moment was sealed off makes apparent the priorities it threatened.

The first novels in English about India began to be written during this moment. The earliest may have been *Hartley House, Calcutta* (1789). It was published anonymously, but because of the epistolary form and because the letters are from Sophia Gildborne to a close friend in England, we can conclude that the author was a woman. Anne Mellor identifies her as Phoebe Gibbs.[15] A. L. Basham, who draws attention to the novel, finds it of "small literary merit."[16] Nevertheless, it was of sufficient interest for a pirated edition to appear in Dublin during the year of its publication and for a German translation to appear two years later. The novel seems to have attracted a reading public that expanded notably for Hamilton's *Translation of the Letters of a Hindu Rajah*, five editions of which were published between 1796 and 1811. Owenson's *Missionary*, also published in 1811 (the year after Southey's *Curse of Kehama*), was reprinted no less than four times in the same year in three elegant volumes with a portrait of the author, as the publisher, Stockwell, enticingly chooses to put it. The title page also assures us that a portrait of the author will be among the reader's rewards for paying a guinea. The novel's literary, as distinct from its commercial, success was not restricted to the Shelley circle. Schwab notes that in France the "stir regarding Sanskrit" began with Bernardin de Saint-Pierre's *Chaumière indienne* in 1790 and also included *The Missionary*.[17] Indeed, the currency of the novel was such that Owenson, at the time of her death nearly half a century later, was working on a revised version of it (*Luxima the Prophetess*) responding to the events of 1857.

The novel about India was originated by women. It found a significant reading public before the genre (unfortunately including the work of those women writers who practiced it) was made to collaborate in the masculine domination of a feminine Orient, now stereotyped so as to make that domination desirable. Part of the attraction these early novels held for their public was the displacement of gender relationships onto an intercultural plane where issues not otherwise easily negotiable could be discussed through surrogate representations. Sophia Gildborne's admiration (letter 12) for the mildness, gentleness, and inoffensiveness of the Hindus (Mill, thirty years later, is an instructive contrast)[18] recognizes not only a feminine nature that has yet to be given its due but also the capacity of that nature to engender a civilization worthy of respect. Suttee can be taken as implying that a woman exists only as the wife of her husband and that her life ends when that meaning is extinguished. Gildborne treats it as evidence that heroism of the highest order is not excluded by gentleness. Her platonic attachment to a teacher at the University of Benares foregrounds the *idea* of India rather than its bizarre customs or exotic fascinations. In her conversion to Hinduism (letter 26), she rejects not only the West but also the masculine principle the West embodies in favor of a feminine alternative. When her friend and teacher dies and she marries an official of the East India Company, the highly artificial and almost peremptory closure recognizes a fiction that one can entertain but that it is not as yet possible to inhabit. In an intercultural relationship, the questioning of boundaries characteristic of the feminine affirmation in a masculine culture is reconfigured as the choice of a different site.

Hamilton's *Translation of the Letters of a Hindu Rajah*[19] is a more sophisticated novel than *Hartley House, Calcutta*. Its ironic manners are in striking contrast to the lush prose of *The Missionary*, written fifteen years later. The novel is dedicated to Hastings and is in memory of Hamilton's brother, whom Hastings had assisted in gaining a position in the East India Company. He is not to be confused with that more distinguished Alexander Hamilton who, marooned in France during the Napoleonic Wars, whiled away the tedium by cataloging the Indian contents of the Bibliothèque nationale and by giving Friedrich Schlegel lessons in Sanskrit.

The word "translation" in the title is significant. Since the translator is also the author (and the editor), the multiple roles can suggest that a part of the self is sufficiently alienated from the socially constructed and acceptable self to be regarded as "foreign." It requires translation, supplemented by editorial mediation, if its now "strange" voice is to be understood. The copresence of the familiar and the unrecognized is obviously appropriate to a feminine affirmation in a masculine environment. India provides the theater for a narrative of that self-affirmation, which can be offered as history and read for what history can teach us.

A "Preliminary Dissertation" by the "editor" emphasizes by its length and care in exposition the distance that necessitates translation. As a setting for the rajah's letters, it acts in conjunction with them by specifying in a manner that is highly individual a historical and religiophilosophical context for their reading. Hamilton begins by drawing attention not simply to the antiquity of Indian civilization but also to its remarkable continuity (pp. vii–viii). She then proceeds to argue (quite unlike others who take up this subject) that this continuity must be due to the inherent stability of Indian institutions. The caste system, for instance, is perceived as socially cohesive rather than paralyzing (pp. xv–xvi). A loose federation of rajahs governed by a maharajah represents a monarchical structure that is responsive to autonomy rather than one that is inflexibly totalitarian (pp. viii–ix). This is a perception interestingly close to the "revised" view now offered by the New Cambridge History of India series.[20] Monarchs in Hamilton's presentation are governed not by unregulated caprice (the Hindu state in Hegel exists only for the freedom of the single person at the head of it) but by inherited principles, laid down in primary texts, that have gained authority by being practiced through the centuries.

A further stabilizing characteristic of Hindu civilization is the firmly marked identity that results from its being tenacious of its own doctrines "in a degree that is unexampled in the history of any other religion." This cultural cohesiveness is accompanied by an "unbounded toleration" that enables it to live in peace with others (pp. xvi–xvii).

Objections can be made to the view of Hindu India that Hamilton offers, but it deserves consideration as much as the view that overwhelmed it and that dominated discussions of India for over a century.[21] In any case, our concern here is not with the accuracy of the representation but with the forces that result in its being what it is. Hamilton's unstated intention is to argue that a civilization built on feminine principles can succeed in being just and enduring and that to say so is not to voice a pious hope; a demonstration of the proposition is to be found in India's history. When a society embodying these principles is subjugated, it is by forces superior only in strength and determined to use strength for the ends of subjugation.

Hindu India was conquered by Moslem invaders, about whom Hamilton has nothing good to say. She is less than fair to Islam, but her voice is in refreshing contrast to the chorus of voices denigrating Hindu civilization as weak, vicious, self-wounding, and largely responsible for its own fate. This is an all too familiar characterization of the feminine, and one can even argue that its export to India enables it to be displayed with a clarity and invested with an opprobrium not altogether possible in more familiar settings. Hamilton offers a different view of India as the site of an authentic femininity that calls out to be heard from rather than sequestered. Subjected to a power of oppression that is both unjustified and unrelieved, India is also presented within a theater of gender, with Islam installed as the male force. Disinterestedness may be deflected by the requirements of this theater, but the moral made available for domestication would not have been lost on an English audience.

The British, in Hamilton's scenario, cannot be successors of the Mughals. Their contribution is to produce a hero capable of playing St. George to the Moslem dragon. He must liberate an imprisoned femininity and restore it to the status it once occupied and deserves to occupy in other countries as well as India. Hastings's role in India was, to put it gently, more complex, but Hamilton takes a straightforward view of how the obligation of benevolence is to be exercised.

Her political naïveté may be in the end a reproof to those who did things differently in India and in the theater of gender in nineteenth-century England.

Hastings as liberator and dragon slayer is too much a part of the golden world to be credible in the bronze one where Philip Sidney placed the fictions that mediate our understanding of history. Like Rushdie, who blithely alters the date of Gandhi's death,[22] Hamilton places the logic of fiction and perhaps the form of romance on a higher plane than the awkwardness of fact. The correct date would not have affected Rushdie's fiction. He makes an issue of his right to be wrong simply to remind us that chronological accuracy is not the most important responsibility of a writer. With Hamilton, the investment in refusing to see what is embarrassing is heavier, and the Hastings she invents is essential to the integrity of her fiction. Her book, published the year after the impeachment ended, must proceed as if it never took place.

Hastings's treatment of the Rohillas was a prominent feature in the impeachment. Macaulay's dramatic account of the injustices perpetrated in "Rohilkund" has been found too severe by some historians, and it is true that Macaulay tends to write as if the darkest hour came before Macaulay. In Hamilton's novel, the rajah, passing through Rohilkund, finds it a place of almost idyllic bliss. The author (as editor) concedes that the account differs strikingly "from that tale of horrors which has been generally received." Eyewitnesses of the scene can best determine, she adds confidently, "which account comes closest to the truth" (1:202–3n).

The passage through Rohilkund, with its living proof of the beneficence of British administration, is a prelude to the rajah's meeting with Hamilton's idealized Hastings. It is preceded significantly by a description of an exemplary Indian monarch taken from the *Hitopadesa*, which Wilkins had translated nine years earlier. Hastings, needless to say, conforms fully to the description. The "pure and blessed spirit of humanity . . . has distinguished every act of his administration" (1:219–20). The rajah is confirmed in his desire to visit an England that can provide India with such flawless exemplifications of its own ancient texts. He undertakes the perilous voyage, arriving in an England where the impeachment ought to be in progress. No trace of it is to be found in his letters. Instead, a far less troubling event is used to establish the fictional reality of the rajah's presence in England. He attends a performance of *Zingis: A Tragedy*, which the historian Alexander Dow had published in 1769 (2:124).[23]

Cultures, precisely because of their distinctiveness, cannot be transparent to other cultures, but the vantage point of another culture can generate a critique not easily created from within the culture being viewed. As in Montesquieu's *Lettres persanes*, Hamilton's letter writer is nominally a "foreigner" but a foreigner listened to as a voice in a contested self, the exclusions of which are questioned by that foreignness, the partition of the self between two sites. Both difference and similarity are implied by the circumstances of the act of composition. Opportunities even exist for a two-way traffic that Hamilton must ignore because her vantage point is presented as an unwavering idealization, positing not only praiseworthy principles but also an implausible congruence between principles and practice. Distancing this vantage point by locating it in India allows the implausibility to be fictively entertained. Feminizing it provides an indication of the extent to which England has marginalized and psychically distanced forces that should remain important within itself.

The rajah cannot conceive of any cleavage between social philosophy and its implementation. Fortified in his innocence by the unimpeachable integrity displayed by Hastings, he proceeds on the basis that if English social behavior seems inconsistent to him, it can only be because he has not read it with sufficient care. There must be hidden significances and patterns of cohesiveness with which he, as a foreigner, cannot be familiar. If people's lives do not follow the texts of their religion, it can only be because those texts are modified by other texts that at this moment are not known to the rajah.

There is a caste system in England, but instead of being functionally aligned, it consists of people of family, people of no family, and people of style. The last category is the highest, but the principles of election to it are unclear. Nevertheless, it is more than self-proclaiming. The validity of the entire caste system, including its indeterminate upper tier, is attested to by the consensus that supports it and that must have a foundation in hidden understandings.

Poojahs exist in England, the most important among them being the poojah of cards. Its mystic dimensions are evident from the concentration and intensity of commitment displayed by participants in the poojah and by the manner in which all other concerns are put aside in deference to its imperative.

The Bible calls for equality between the sexes (the rajah's reading seems politically correct rather than textually indisputable), but this is apparently not the case in England. The inference should not be that sacred texts are being disregarded but that a secondary revelation is in place that provisionally tolerates inequality and also makes poverty not a matter for compassion but the most heinous of offenses (2:161).

The rajah's hermeneutic procedures are throughout designed to deny the existence of fissures in the social fabric of a country as exemplary as England and to see that fabric as a seamless rendering of the doctrinal patterns that are woven into it. If the procedures are extreme to the point of being comic, that is a comment on the "strangeness" of England to the idealized integrity that Hindu India has been constructed to represent. India's return to itself under Hastings is an augury of what can happen in England but only if those seeking liberation live according to standards instead of according to the casteism of style or the frivolity of the poojah of cards.

The important feature of the novel for our purposes is that Hinduism is treated as capable of yielding the paradigms of ideal behavior; that it is regarded as an oppressed and silenced voice, liberated so as to be listened to once more in the counsels of understanding; and that its restoration argues for the restoration of other voices that are in harmony with it and are not being heard. On the other hand, the contrast between Moslem tyranny and British benevolence is insensitive to the realities of dominance; the stain of power is not materially altered by the moral pretensions of those who enjoy the use of it. Even as a fable of the maiden in distress rescued from the Moslem dragon's clutches, the book is not appropriate to a more realistic era, where rescue has to be earned by the inner strength and perseverance of the oppressed. One has to read the novel to recognize that these failings are not fatal. From a vantage point that is uncontaminated, much can be seen that is quietly comic, suggesting how being uncontaminated is itself comic in an up-to-date world. There is a need for integrity, and Hindu India as the site of its realization is perceived with a sympathy and insight that are important correctives to the hostile perceptions of it that are beginning to gather force.

Both *Hartley House, Calcutta* and *Translation of the Letters of a Hindu Rajah* are cast in the epistolary form, which Owenson also uses in the best known of her novels, *The Wild Irish Girl*.[24] It is a form that is naturally conversational and indefinitely extensible. Although it can sustain a narrative and be brought to closure by it, it is not necessarily dominated by narrative requirements. Multiple correspondents can generate a crisscross of interpretations, with each interpretation weighed and sifted by the necessity of committing it to writing. The relationships between the author, the editor, a possible translator, and the writer or writers of the letters can introduce layers of commentary that do not have to culminate in judgment by a fixed standard. If our aim is a thoughtful open-mindedness, the form has advantages not easily dismissed.

It cannot be said that the authors being discussed make anything like full use of these opportunities. Owenson's novel has only one letter writer. Hamilton's has two, but the second disappears as the novel proceeds. The editorial role is used by Hamilton largely to provide us with the "Preliminary Dissertation." Owenson furnishes us with ample notes, sometimes speaking in the first person as the author and more frequently signing herself as the editor. Both figures provide documentation for what is said in the text, but the editor can sometimes differ from the text on scholarly grounds or be critical of its extravagance of style (pp. 57, 61, 100, 175).

In her introduction to *The Wild Irish Girl*, Brigid Brophy comments that "the epistolary convention, which in the course of the eighteenth century, Samuel Richardson had used with extreme emotional power and Chaderlos de Laclos had made into an ironic gallery where correspondent flashes ironic light on correspondent, is here flattened into a ribbon of first person narrative, chopped into roughly letter lengths" (p. viii). The peripheral maneuvers of editor and author make this judgment a trifle harsh, but it is true that Owenson is either unable to engage or not interested in engaging the more serious possibilities of the form. In *The Missionary*, she turned to an impetuous narrative.[25] She could have done this because the epistolary form no longer appealed to her. Alternatively, she could have made her decision because a form that may have suited the relationship between Ireland and England did not seem to her to suit the relationship between England and India. With its emphasis on closure and containment and on a dominant narrative order that its divergent constituents must not only accept but also promote, the narrative form is closer than the epistolary to the form of empire and more receptive to collaboration with the latter's coercive forces.[26]

In *The Wild Irish Girl*, a hoped-for marriage that cannot materialize is taken to be "prophetically typical of a national unity of interests and affections between those who may be factitiously severed, but who are naturally allied." In this unity, "the distinctions of English and Irish, of Protestant and Catholic," will be "for ever buried" (p. 253). The union here is between equals or at least functions as an equalizing force. Although Glorvina (cum Ireland) is seen through the eyes of a male correspondent, the male correspondent is constructed by a female author, and Glorvina is the center of attention of the novel as well as of her suitor. The marriage is presented not as the acceptance of differences that enrich each other but as the burying of distinctions. Its "unity" arises from the binding force of what is held in common.[27]

In *The Missionary*, Hilarion, who combines total dedication to his calling with an appropriately majestic Western presence, meets Luxima (a corruption of Lakshmi, significant in its elision of luxury and light) in the Kashmiri valley that ever since Bernier had been the fashionable site of Paradise. The occasion is momentous. It is the meeting of East and West, and Owenson depicts it so that its symbolic significance cannot escape even the most casual of readers:

> Silently gazing, in wonder, upon each other, they stood, finely opposed, the noblest specimens of the human species as it appears in the most opposite regions of the earth; she like the East, lovely and luxuriant; he, like the West, lofty and commanding: the one radiant in all the lustre, attractive in all the softness which distinguishes her native regions: the other, towering in all the energy, imposing in all the vigour, which marks his ruder latitudes: she, looking like a creature formed to feel and to submit; he like a being created to resist and to command: while both appeared as the ministers and representatives of the two most powerful religions of the earth; the one no less enthusiastic in her brilliant errors, than the other confident in his immutable truth. (1:149–50)

This is not simply the meeting of East and West. It is also the meeting of Adam and Eve and a meeting arranged under Miltonic auspices. In *The Wild Irish Girl*, Owenson quotes Milton frequently (pp. 39, 40, 42, 52, 82, 195), although Tasso is the poet she most often cites. In *The Missionary*, she quotes Milton almost to the exclusion of everyone else. The tableau she devises for us here vividly recalls Satan's (and the reader's) first sight of Adam and Eve in Paradise (4.288–301). In particular, it circulates obsessively around two lines delineating the difference between them: "For contemplation he and valour formed, / For softness she and sweet attractive grace." The Eastern Eve in Owenson's tableau is lovely, luxuriant, radiant in her luster, and attractive in her softness. The Western Adam is lofty, commanding, towering, and imposing. All of the epithets surrounding Hilarion are evocative of a natural right to dominance, and all of the epithets surrounding Luxima evoke a natural propensity to subjection. Owenson does not shrink from the conclusion that follows: "she, looking like a creature formed to feel and to submit; he like a being created to resist and to command." To describe Hilarion as a "being" and Luxima as a "creature" is to go beyond any hierarchical principle that Milton may have espoused. Milton, moreover, makes poetry of the principle only in a prelapsarian world. The relationship between Adam and Eve in the world we inherit from them is dialogic rather than hierarchical. In the Kashmiri Paradise, the relationship, as Owenson here formulates it, seems to proclaim itself as the engendered prologue to the imperial theme. Although Hilarion and Luxima are placed before us as "the noblest specimens of the human species" (a reminiscence of *PL* 4.321–24), the best that the East can offer seems created only to yield to the "towering" superiority of the West. It can come as no surprise that Christianity is presented as a religion of "immutable truth" and Hinduism as a religion of "brilliant errors," to which commitment is enthusiastic rather than rational.

Enthusiasm is not limited to Luxima, and Owenson can be the willing victim of her own prose, as some of her editorial comments in *The Wild Irish Girl* suggest. More persuasively, we can argue that Owenson writes for an audience (as her publisher's advertisements of her book make clear) that can be tentatively characterized as literate, affluent, and given to the fashionable. She is writing, in fact, for those people of style whom Hamilton's Hindu rajah places in the top tier of the English caste system. The set piece invokes a discourse then making its claim to dominance, endowing it with the finish of style and the blessing of voguishness. Having met the expectations of the salon, which she continues to regale with a love story, Owenson is then free to follow a route that, fortunately for the real worth of the novel, complicates as well as confirms the original tableau.

Enthusiastic cooperation with a discourse humbly endorses its fictions of self-justification, but it also offers an irreproachable way of subverting those fictions, a possibility appealing in its potential for mimicry as mockery to women writers and to subject peoples. It appears, moreover, that Owenson read *The Missionary*, as it progressed, repeatedly after dinner to "distinguished guests," who insisted on making their own contribution.[28] Subversive surrender may have been the only way to cope with the unwanted views of experts. Owenson's novel can and perhaps should be read along these lines, although, as will be suggested later, she is drawn into and does not merely adopt the discourse she both affirms and interrogates.

Compliance with the discourse is foregrounded in the emphasis on Hilarion's invincibility that is strongly announced not only in the set piece but also throughout the early pages of the novel. He displays "the heroic fortitude of the martyr" (1:28) and combines the "piety of the saint with the energy of the hero" (1:52). Yet the doctrines he preaches are later described as "rigid" (2:29). The "chill hand of religion" checks the rise of "human feelings" in him (2:7–8). Reluctant even to touch a wreath that Luxima has made part of an "idolatrous ceremony," he finds within himself "a fastidiousness which almost resembled bigotry" (1:154). He is prepared to perceive that "a pure system of natural religion" is innate in Luxima's "sublime and contemplative mind" (1:227), but he refuses to build on the common ground that this perception uncovers. Instead, he concentrates obsessively on Luxima's idolatrous practices. It becomes apparent that his repudiation of the priestess is in proportion to his attraction to the woman:

> When the Priestess disappeared, the woman stood too much confessed; and a feminine reserve, a lovely timidity, so characteristic of her sex overwhelmed the Missionary with confusion. (1:151)

> He would not submit to the analysis of his feelings, and he was determined to conquer, without understanding their nature or tendency. *Entombed* and *chained* within the most remote depths of his heart, he was deaf to their murmurs and resisted their pleadings with all the *despotism* of a great and lofty mind, created equally to command others and itself. (2:4; italics added)

Hilarion undertook to win over Luxima to Christianity because a Kashmiri pandit, displaying the opportunism that is all too characteristic of the clerisy, had assured him that Luxima's conversion would bring about mass defections from the Hindu faith. Conversion now becomes the conversion of the other within himself. Listening to Luxima is "dangerous." On the other hand, arguing with her is impossible because there is "an incoherence in her ideas" that is "not to be reconciled or replied to" (1:220).

Significantly, this finding comes after a perfectly cogent passage in which Luxima has expatiated on the difficulty of seeing God face to face and on the desirability of knowing him in his works. This is standard Christian thinking, except that it is in India, with *Paradise Lost* 5.507–12 providing the most convenient locus. Hilarion's refusal of a dialogue based on the common ground that Luxima's statement uncovers is one more erosion of the dramatic contrasts proclaimed in their original encounter. Luxima's enthusiasm includes more than a hint of rational understanding, and Hilarion is considerably less than dispassionate in protecting his immutable truths from an other who seems well on her way to sharing them.

Unfortunately, conversion is not usually a matter of building on common ground. Its drama and justification can be more compelling if common ground is minimized, if Christianity is exhibited not as the final step in a ladder being ascended but as the only means of deliverance from continuing incarceration in a prison house of error. When cultural differences are widened to this degree by the refusal to recognize shared understandings, the two cultures involved can only meet in a pattern of dominance and tutelage. That fact returns into and forces apart the gender differences with which cultural differences are intertwined.

Hilarion's invincibility is now under duress because of his "entombment" in himself in a manner ironically reminiscent of Mill-Hegel perceptions of India. It is time to turn to the lovely and luxuriant Luxima, a character truly designed to excite the wrath of Hegel. A. M. D. Hughes points to her as Shelley's archetypal heroine,[29] but at least in her interrogation of Demogorgon, Asia seems made of sterner stuff.[30] Luxima professes a religion that, as with Hamilton's Hindu India, "unites the most boundless toleration to the most obstinate faith" (1:213). She may abandon the name of Hinduism, but she clings tenaciously to its essence. Nevertheless, abandoning the name in a world largely constituted by naming is sufficient to ensure her ruin.

In a capacious generalization, the pandit tells Hilarion that "in all the religions of the East, woman has held a decided influence, either as priestess or as victim" (1:95). This is a statement as erroneous as it is comprehensive, but it defines the alternatives before Luxima, making it clear that to renounce one role is inexorably to choose the other. When she accepts Christianity and prefers a platonic life with Hilarion to a fuller one with Suleiman Shikoh (with whom she would not have done any better), she surrenders herself to victimization. Once made, the choice is irreversible. To have second thoughts is only to be placed in double jeopardy: "The unfortunate Indian was now alike condemned by the religion of truth and the superstition of error. Driven with shame and obloquy from the altar of Brahma, her life had become forfeit, by the laws of the Inquisition as a relapsed

Christian" (3:162). When truth and error concur so felicitously in their consequences, we can legitimately ask what the difference is between them.

Meanwhile, Hilarion has himself become a prisoner of the Inquisition as a result of charges brought against him by a Franciscan monk whom he had dismissed from office in an excess of "fastidiousness."[31] In an unexpected flurry of action, Luxima escapes from prison with the assistance of the pandit and audaciously rescues Hilarion from the stake. She is dangerously injured in the process, but the two are able to flee to a rocky peninsula (3:194), where Luxima expires (3:215), mistakenly believing Hilarion to be dead.

After Luxima's death, Hilarion no longer finds himself "a being created to resist and to command." He retires to an icy grotto in the fastnesses of Kashmir. His life as a *sanyasi* duly comes to a self-effacing end but not before Aurangzeb has "waded through carnage and destruction to the throne of India," seizing "a sceptre stained with a brother's blood" and wearing "the diadem torn from a priest's brow" (3:217). The destructiveness of history contrasts with the seclusion of the missionary's cave. Hilarion's dead body is discovered there by a "European *Philosopher*," a member of Aurangzeb's retinue (3:219). Beside the body is an urn holding some ashes, a significantly blood-stained crucifix, and the sacred thread of a Brahman (3:220–21).

Luxima's dying injunction to Hilarion was:

> Thou wilt say "that having gathered a *dark spotted flower in the garden of love,* she expiates her error by the loss of her life; that her disobedience to the forms of her religion and the laws of her country was punished by days of suffering and by an untimely death; yet that her *soul* was pure from sin, as when clothed in transcendent brightness, she outshone in faith, in *virtue,* all women of her nation!" (3:213)

Few writers remember Milton as vividly and thoughtfully as Owenson. Her response to *Paradise Lost* is consistently both an invocation and a critique. In her opening set piece, already discussed, she not only proclaims the hierarchical principle but also extends it to a point where it can be brought under interrogation by the rest of the novel. Her description of the banyan tree (2:8–10) washes away the Satanic propensities with which Milton's ambivalences continued to invest it and makes it resplendently emblematic of created order.[32] In using descriptions of Satan to characterize Hilarion (e.g., 3:157, 158), she locates her novel deftly in the cross play between romantic revaluations of Satan and Milton's not altogether decisive treatment of the imperial-commercial mission as Satanic. In particular, she places Hilarion's capacity for heroic resistance, his "courage never to submit or yield," in telling proximity to the closed mind of imperial self-righteousness and its inability to respond to difference. Her final statement remembers the Ludlow masque and its identification of the unspotted soul with virtue, but it also questions the exclusions of that identification by adding the contrast with the *"dark spotted flower"* gathered in *"the garden of love."* Hegel took up that last phrase with contempt.[33] Luxima puts it in tragic opposition to the forms of her religion, the laws of her country, and the womanhood of her nation.

Although the Ludlow masque is recalled in Luxima's final statement, it is Satan's recollection of Beelzebub in his unfallen glory that her last words summon most strongly into life:

> If thou beest he; but O how fallen! how changed
> From him who in the happy realms of light
> Clothed with transcendent brightness didst outshine
> Myriads though bright.
> (*PL* 1.85–88)

Luxima is a name written in light. Her disobedience consigned her to ruin, but it was disobedience only to forms and to laws. She turned away from her religion not to self-love but to the love of another. Her final statement forms an ironic end to the missionary's mission. He has, in effect, become what he beheld.

Owenson's dramatic unraveling of her novel's beginning raises troubling questions about the possibilities of relationships between cultures. Those possibilities could be considered more carefully if they were not deflected and indeed overwhelmed by a love story in which religious institutions are too readily foregrounded as the main obstacles to human relatedness. The main obstacle remains the symbiotic alliance between dominance and discourse, with gender added to the imperial family.

Owenson's tribute to this family is not without significant reservations. Like Shelley and Southey, whose work we shall discuss later, her novel is both fissured and enriched by its participation in two discourses: a literary discourse of world humanism, for which William Jones provides an Indian scholarly foundation, and an imperial discourse gendered so as to offer India the enlightenments of feminine submission to Western overlordship. Her conspicuously enthusiastic cooperation with the second discourse is partly so that she can seek out the openings in it and make use of those openings to let in the possibilities of the first discourse. But she also endorses what she resists and carries forward what she moves against. Her subversive surrender is a surrender despite its subversiveness and testifies, not for the only time, to the coercive strength of a way of viewing India that it is not possible to bypass and that must hereafter be propitiated.

The propitiation can be deemed more than sufficient in Owenson's remarkable rendering of the first meeting between Hilarion and Luxima—an encounter that the Edenic and Miltonic setting endows with an almost ancestral authority. Her styling of this encounter is extraordinarily and eloquently representative, but the very success of her composition of two essences that can only be fitted to each other hierarchically makes her the hostage of a characterization from which she must thereafter struggle to ransom herself. The sculptured antitheses so vividly prominent in her tableau rule out the possibility of any equitable relationship between their "finely opposed" polarities. An East that is totally feeling and a West that is totally intelligence can only meet on a basis that projects the regulative ordering of the psyche onto an intercultural stage.

Owenson does make evident in Hilarion the disabilities of an intelligence that shuts out feeling. Luxima is not subjected to the same critique, and her languid passivity fits a regrettable stereotype that licenses domination of the East by the West. The stereotype is also precisely that image of the feminine against which feminine protest has been consistently directed. It is striking that Owenson should choose to lavish on it so much of her undoubted skill in writing the wrong kind of prose. One might almost conclude that the stereotype is exported to India so that an identification with it can be both allowed and resisted, leaving Europe free for the emergence of a different model of womanhood. Unfortunately, several of Luxima's attributes are shipped back to England after appropriate enrichments to become incorporated into Victorian imaginings of the feminine.

A gendered relationship between cultures might be more easily negotiable if our perception of the genders were changed. The time can be judged as propitious for such changes. The recuperation of India's femininity has been attempted in nationalist counterconstructions of its history. Those in the West who have come to see its past as predatory rather than masterful may find it desirable to recognize a different tradition on a site that has been differently gendered. The question is whether the many injustices of appropriation can be successfully barred from entering the future by reenvisaging the very figures that functioned as the vehicles of those injustices. We can argue that the figures are too contaminated to serve as a basis for the difficult task of understanding between peoples. We can also argue not for a cleansing, which may no longer be possible, but for a radical reappropriation based on the distinctive ontological status that Indian philosophy gives to the feminine principle.[34]

India is not Ireland in Owenson's imagination, and if the Celt knew the Indian, as Shelley advises us,[35] that understanding is not easily to be found in her work. Glorvina has little in common with Luxima. Much is said in *The Wild Irish Girl* about British injustices in Ireland, but with *The Missionary* set in a period nearly a century prior to the battle of Plassey, not a word needs to be said about British injustices in India. England's prophetic marriage to Ireland was envisaged as a marriage between equals on the shared ground of what those equals held in common. India's marriage to England is projected as an adoring discipleship, a union of sensibility with the West's towering intelligence. India is not a real country but a contrivance, seen through the spectacles of Orientalist books that are actually projected back into an era more tolerant than the evangelicals of Hindu religious practices.

One might argue that Owenson distances evangelical constructions so that they can be disowned as Portuguese mistakes. We can allow this defense some weight. The historicizing of a current discourse is one way of suggesting that it may no longer be current. But the novel subscribes and perhaps subscribes heavily to the discourse it also interrogates. The inequality of the relationship it enshrines is not clearly seen as the root of the intercultural failure.

This is a necessary finding but need not be a final one. There is another side to it that must be taken into account and that we may even be persuaded to foreground in our engagement with the complexities of reading. If Owenson's novel falls short of what needs to be said, we can still argue that it says what circumstances permit and, in fact, strains instructively against those circumstances. Even the hierarchizing of India's femininity rescues it from more contemptuous versions of the feminine that were beginning to prevail in the dispositions of power. Questioning hierarchization is a move that the novel can only place at its horizon. Owenson's not inconsiderable achievement is to have opened the way to this placement, to have weakened the hegemonies that she herself has proclaimed so that future generations can find the real depth of the novel lying in the weakening rather than in the proclamation.

Read metafictionally, Owenson's narrative can be seen as tracking with extraordinary accuracy the narrative of the breakdown of the imperial statement. The novel's rhetorical self-entrapment, its growing anxiety with itself, its reluctance to relinquish its own inauguration, and even the use of Milton for invocations that are consistently critiques suggest more than a superficial allegory of empire. Viewed in relation to the undermining forces within imperial discourse, many of the novel's self-perplexities that might be evaluated as literary shortcomings become eloquent in mapping the disarticulation of the metafiction that they both resist and sustain.

7
Monstrous Mythologies:
Southey and *The Curse of Kehama*

∞

The extent to which Southey goes to distance himself from *The Curse of Kehama* is the most striking feature of the poem. His anxious commitment to damage control is evident from nearly everything he says about the work both formally and in the apprehensive comments of which there is no lack in his correspondence. Southey's uneasiness is particularly evident in the 1810 preface to the first edition, where proximity seems to lend vigor to the assault on what is to follow. The preface begins with a resounding dismissal of the very mythology on which the poem is based, proclaiming Hinduism to be, of all religions, "the most monstrous in its fables and the most fatal in its effects."[1]

In the history of invective against colonial peoples, monstrosity occupies an honorable place. Its origins go back to Pliny and his inheritors, who located it first at the fringes of civilization and subsequently in the margins of books.[2] The placing acknowledges both a boundary and a seepage. Using spatial distance as a response to psychological proximity, it reminds us of the monstrosity cum marginality into which we could lapse, the Circean transformations that could be our unraveling if we were to venture incautiously outside the text's borders. Readers of anti-Hindu tirades would soon find the word reassuring in its familiarity, but in 1810, it still had to be fully established in the lexicon of abuse.

"Fatal" is a less familiar word. Evoking Hinduism as a terminal ailment, it also suggests that the insidious destructiveness of the ailment lies in the nature of Hinduism's "fabling," in the quality of its religious imagination. Here Hinduism is unlike the religion of the Mexicans, which apparently surpasses the worst that India can offer. Southey finds it "beyond all doubt . . . the most diabolical that has ever existed." But the Mexican religion has been taken over by a system of priestcraft that can be eliminated, presumably without prejudice to the religion. "The Mexicans were rapidly advancing," whereas "the Brahminical system of caste . . . wherever it exists has put a total stop to the amelioration of society."[3]

Southey slips here into a convenient confusion between the institutional and the inherent, refusing to treat caste as a device of priestcraft even though he concedes that probability to the human sacrifices of the Aztecs. Possession shapes the perception of an India that cannot be redeemed and can only be converted. The problem remains of why one should write a poem of some length and ambitiousness on a subject apparently to be despised. "No figures can be imagined," Southey declares, "more anti-picturesque, and less poetical, than the mythological personages of the Bramins" (1810 preface, 117). Why, we might ask, should Southey labor at a poem on the antipoetic in which the gods and goddesses of the Hindu pantheon do not merely "supply fit machinery for an English poem" but also proceed to participate in the action instead of controlling it from an Olympian remove?

The answer to this question comprises various possibilities, not all of which are necessarily concurrent. We can begin with the proposition that the preface dismisses the poem because Southey was anxious about its reception. He had reason to be anxious. *Thalaba* had not sold well and *Madoc* had done worse, earning less than £4 in the year following its publication. Francis Jeffrey had not been kind to either poem. Southey met Jeffrey in October 1805 and was encouraged to find him lacking in stature: "Even if my temper had been more irascible, the sight of a thing not above five feet two would have quieted me."[4] A month later, Jeffrey's height had shrunk by an inch (*New Letters*, 1:407), but his stature as a critic was not to be disposed of as easily. It could be argued that *Thalaba* and *Madoc* had not sold well because they were difficult to access, but *Madoc* was about the Welsh as much as about the New World and *Thalaba*'s Orientalism was ornamental rather than structural. There were grounds for being concerned about *Kehama*. Shrouded in a mythology remote from Christianity, it could be formidably forbidding to the English reader.

The "strangeness" of *Kehama* and the difficulty of "sympathizing" with its characters became matters to which Southey returned repeatedly and apprehensively in his correspondence (*L and C*, 3:147, 180, 268, 286; *New Letters*, 1:384, 486, 527). His anxieties may have been compounded by the mixed views his friends offered on the poem. Charles Wynn may have been particularly disturbing in pointing out that although exotic machinery might be an "excellent ornament" for a poem, its function in *Kehama* seemed to be integral rather than decorative. In these circumstances, its exoticism became a handicap. Southey had to reply lamely that different valuations of the poem had been given him but that his friend Walter Savage Landor "turned the scale in its favour" (*New Letters*, 1:486).

Southey's misgivings about his poem ran deep enough to be apparent even in his remarks about its versification: "It gains by rhyme which is to passages of no inherent merit what rouge and candlelight are to ordinary faces" (*L and C*, 3:44). He was more emphatic later on the tawdriness of rhyming: "There must be quicker, wilder movements; there must be a gorgeousness of ornament also—eastern gemwork and sometimes rhyme must be rattled upon rhyme till the reader is half dizzy with the thundering echo" (*L and C*, 3:145). The harlotry of prosody fits the standard image of the Orient as courtesan, but it is not an image *Kehama* would indubitably convey if we did not have the correspondence to guide us. Southey belittles not only the poem but also his own motives in writing it, reducing it to a foray into the Oriental in which no literary capital is invested.

The phrasing of these anxieties suggests not that there was no market for writing about India but rather that Southey may have misjudged the nature of the appropriate commodity for that market. Hamilton's novel was in its fourth edition at the time *Kehama* was completed, and Owenson was about to publish a novel that would achieve both popular and literary status. Still to come was the spectacular success of *Lalla Rookh*. William Taylor made his estimate correctly in advising Southey that if he took "the Hindu superstitions" for his "machinery," the celebrity of his poem would "grow with the empire."[5]

The course of empire has indeed proceeded apace when even Hindu superstitions become commercial offerings. Perhaps Madame de Staël put the same thought more suavely in telling Byron that the public was "orientalizing" and that sticking to the East was "the only poetical policy." The policy was likely to be all the more lucrative since the East so far had nothing to offer but "Southey's unsaleables."[6] In these circumstances, it must have disturbed Southey to be advised by Taylor to "let it drop" when shown the completed text of *Kehama* (*New Letters*, 1:486). Southey's choice had responded to the literary climate, but making the wrong choice can be less frustrating than dealing with the right choice in the wrong way.

In any event, *Kehama* fared moderately well. It did not, like Byron's *Corsair*, have 10,000 copies taken up on the first day of publication, but four editions in ten years is a respectable record. Shelley recommended it to Elizabeth Hitchener as his "favourite poem" and visited Keswick to "pay homage" to its author.[7] Newman read *Kehama* as a boy and "got it well nigh by heart."[8] Coleridge described the poem as "a gallery of finished pictures in one splendid fancy piece," in which "the moral grandeur rises gradually above the brilliance of the colouring and the boldness and novelty of the machinery."[9] One might think that twenty-five years into his laureateship, and in the autumn of a collected edition, Southey's attitude to *Kehama* would relax. On the contrary, the new preface he published in the ten-volume 1837–38 edition of his poems is at war with the Indian misadventure even more aggressively than the old dismissal. Anxiety about one's literary future cannot be the reason for a hostility in which self-and-other relationships are reincarnated almost as if the poem were the other of the prefaces.

Another line of explanation might be found in the compulsions of Southey's oeuvre, as he himself chose to delineate it. The romantic oeuvre, like love in Marvell's definition of that passion, is begotten by desire upon impossibility. For Southey, the child of impossibility is an unprecedented exercise in comparative mythology, setting scholarship, historical knowledge, and imaginative power amid the widening horizons of romantic thought. It is an academic poet's dream of empire, nurtured in a library of 10,000 books.[10] A letter of March 24, 1805, to Wynn provides the details of the grand design: "You know my plan to exhibit all the fit mythologies in this form [that of *Kehama*]. After this there will remain the Runic, the old Persian, the classical—which may be considered almost as new ground so little have its recondite parts been brought forward, and perhaps the Japanese, the Jewish as romancefied by the Rabbies, and the Catholic in all its glory" (*New Letters*, 1:378). In a subsequent letter (November 4, 1812), Southey attributes the inspiration for his project to his reading, at age fifteen, Picart's *Cérémonies et coutumes de tous les peuples du monde*. Picart's book led him "to conceive a design of rendering every mythology which had ever extended itself widely, and powerfully influenced the human mind, the basis of a narrative poem" (*L and C*, 3:351; see also 1838 preface[11] and *New Letters*, 1:676).

We could argue that the necessities of his project obliged Southey to compose *Kehama*, even in the face of the distaste for Hindu mythology that the two prefaces declare so emphatically. However, romantic oeuvres are designed to welcome deferral, and gaps in their structures can sometimes be as eloquent as the poems that might conceivably fill those gaps. Moreover, the original prefaces to *Thalaba, Madoc,* and *Kehama* say nothing of their place in Southey's vast design. It is only in the second preface to *Kehama,* published twenty-eight years later, that Southey encourages us to think of the poem as written in deference to a larger commitment. "No poem," he adds, in what should be recognized by now as his favorite turn of language, "could have been more deliberately planned or carefully composed." In fact, *Madoc* took just as long to write, but the time taken is less important than how heavily the time weighed on the poet.

It is hard to escape the impression that an additional defense of the poem is being constructed. Puzzlingly, it is put into place when it no longer seems to be needed. The mythological project was very much a matter of the past by 1837, and the anticipated hostility to *Kehama* had not materialized. "I must have been very unreasonable," Southey himself tells us, "if I had not been satisfied with its reception" (1838 preface).

In seeking enlightenment from this confusion, we must hold onto a crucial fact: Southey continued to reprint *Kehama* even while repeatedly berating it. There is clearly a struggle here between the literary and the ideological selves in which neither can be allowed possession of the field. The poem can be denounced but not renounced. Southey's ambivalence toward it is not only admitted but also foregrounded in the stubborn enmity between *Kehama* and its prefaces. To subdue the contention is to slight the ambivalence. It runs too deep for facile minimization.

If we are to consider the contest between ideology and literature as it bears on Southey's poem about India, we must turn to his relationship to imperial discourse. Taylor's view that the mythology of a subjected people should be converted into cultural capital encourages such a turn. The difficulty is that the literary transaction must maximize what the imperial transaction devalues. Southey's project runs afoul of this difficulty so that the relationships between the two transactions, between the literary and the political, between the Indian other and the English self, and even between resistance and domination are written inescapably into the engagement between the delinquent poem and the disciplinary behavior of its prefaces.

Southey's troubles are compounded because even in the years of pantisocracy and Wat Tyler, when Southey might have been expected to know better, his commitment was to a view of the England-India relationship that was to come to fruition in the work of Mill and Hegel rather than to the more benign view represented by William Jones. The picture can be confusing because Southey sometimes makes statements that seem critical of imperialism, but these are meant to suggest not that imperialism is morally suspect but that it is liable to abuse when it is not practiced by the British.

"Afric's wrong and Europe's guilt" points the finger of reproach at other nations. A more gentle and docile race than the Hottentots does not exist, but it is the Boers who cruelly oppress them. Southey's next sentence starkly uncovers his rampant ethnocentrism. Since the Boers would not be easy to educate to British standards, the only practical measure he can suggest would be an importation of hangmen "for their especial benefit."[12] Hangmen were notably absent when a Hottentot woman was exhibited in a cage in London a few years after Southey's recommendation.

Southey read *The Lusiads* in Mickle's translation when he was twelve and reviewed Lord Strangford's translation in 1803. He found da Gama more atrocious than Pizarro, who is apparently a benchmark in these matters (*New Letters*, 1:337). The Portuguese conquest had "barbarised the Mahommedans." These misdeeds would be put in order when *Madoc* sang the ancestral right of the British (or more precisely the Welsh) to the New World and proclaimed the glories of colonizing in the English way.[13] The Napoleonic danger drives Southey into a frenzy of preemptive imperialism: "We ought to take the Cape and to take Egypt, for unless we have both France will. We ought to colonize both with Sepoys and Chinese—and to garrison the West Indies with Sepoys also" (*New Letters*, 1:380).

Southey is certainly in advance of others in perceiving the possibilities of Asiatic manpower in protecting the British empire from its competitors. The reference to Egypt is doubly interesting since Southey's friend, Landor, had published *Gebir* in 1798, which deals with the failure of a previous attempt to take Egypt. In 1803, after the battle of the Nile, Landor added twenty lines to the seventh book. These lines, according to him, "describe the equality which nature teaches, the absurdity of colonizing a country which is peopled, and the superior advantages of cultivating those which remain unoccupied."[14] The 1803 preface similarly refers to "the calamities which must ever attend the superfluous colonization of a peopled country."

Landor's clarification is necessary since his verse is anything but pellucid. Southey himself found it "so obscure" that he "suspected the author to be hardly sane," but he claims to have understood it "after repeated study." He cited it as "the only contemporary poem" to which he was, "as a poet, in the slightest degree indebted" (*New Letters*, 1:476).

As we have seen, the distinction between peopled and unpeopled territories owes its origin to the imagined emptiness of the New World and to the rights of occupancy that emptiness created in the minds of those determined to perceive it. It remains a distinction to be drawn only by imperialist nations according to their convenience and in keeping with standards not open to debate. Its repeated use to justify colonization makes it apparent that the "equality which nature teaches" can be much less important than the superiority that power confers. The consequence to be noted here is that the distinction, indefensible as it is, applies to India as much as it does to Egypt. Landor, writing during the Hastings impeachment, does not take the further step that British territorial expansion in India seems to invite. There is no evidence that Southey would have considered taking it.

Southey's imperialism is given its moral sustenance by a strong and persistent evangelical strain. "My own firm belief," he tells us, "is that there are but two methods of extending civilization—conquest and conversion" (*L and C*, 3:281). His preference at this stage is for conversion, but there is no evidence that he would have shrunk from conquest. It facilitates conversion, and conversion, in its turn, can protect and ennoble conquest: "In India the want of an established church is a crying evil. Nothing but missionaries can secure in that country what we have won" (*L and C*, 3:37). This is a note struck more than once in Southey's writing. He told Wynn, for instance, that unless a vigorous policy of introducing Christianity into India was adopted, there would be "more remains of the Portugueze than of the English Empire in the East."[15] "When will the East India Company be convinced," he asks in 1803, "that it is in their ultimate interest as well as their immediate duty to convert their subjects?"[16] By 1814, he is more resigned: if "we had served God with half the zeal [of the Roman Catholic Church] . . . the tree of life would long ere this have struck deep roots in Hindostan."[17] Chaos, in Southey's imagination, rages threateningly outside the frail walls of a cosmos that can only be Christian: "It is only the institutions of Christianity and the vicinity of better regulated States which prevent kingdoms, under such circumstances of misrule [as, for example, Naples], from sinking into a barbarism like that of Turkey."[18]

The main bond of companionship between conquest and conversion is the double devaluation they impose on subject peoples. Humiliation can be a fertile soil in which to plant the desire to be otherwise. It is easier to persuade a defeated nation that not just its institutions but the premises on which those institutions depend are radically at fault, that revisionary solutions will not be sufficient, that its religion and the culture that religion nourishes must be not simply modified but abandoned. This alliance of dismissive forces takes over the stage on which representations of India are paraded, coming to a climax in the work of Mill and Hegel. Southey can be seen as an early contributor to a rhetoric that the dynamics of power were to make inevitable, however differently we may choose to view it amid the retrospective realities of judgment.

Southey assigns Hinduism a distinctive place in the catalog of false religions. Islamic tales may be "metaphorical rubbish,"[19] but they are not, like those of Hinduism, monstrous, grotesque, and dangerous. The Asiatic fables may be "full of resemblances to Christianity" (L and C, 3:37), but as far as India is concerned, there is to be no building on those resemblances. The true method of converting Native Americans "is by showing them like the old blind man in Madoc, how little difference there is in the basis of our faith."[20] Hinduism similarly argues that all rivers of belief end in the same sea of understanding, but Southey, although agreeing to the proposition, apparently feels that this particular river is not to be traversed.

Hinduism is unique in its inability to sustain a society capable of progress. The Islamic world stagnated while the West advanced, even though "at one period the Mahommedan courts were the most enlightened of Europe." Southey's explanation for this stagnation is curious: "Perhaps Polygamy is the radical evil" (New Letters, 1:216). Fortunately, polygamy is permitted but not demanded by Islam, whereas caste ("class" is considered a more accurate translation) is a constituent of the creation fable as recounted in the laws of Manu. "Perhaps no religion is hostile to improvement except the Hindoo" (New Letters, 1:217), Southey concludes, putting Hinduism not at the bottom of the ladder but in a place where no ladder is available. He can be vitriolic on the evils of the caste system: "I prefer the Devil to Seeva the Destroyer. . . . The Hindu system of caste is the worst ever devised for cramping human intellect, and anything to destroy it were desirable. There are diseases where arsenic becomes medicine" (New Letters, 1:292–93).

The collective tirade against caste by Mill, Hegel, the evangelists, and Southey is remarkable in its ferocity. One has to wonder whether misgivings about English class structures and social exclusions are not being conveniently transferred to an Indian other, which can then be deafeningly upbraided. The Warrant of Precedence, which governed British protocol in India and which lays down with appalling minuteness the niceties of rank to be observed on official occasions, makes interesting reading in this context.[21] Be that as it may, the result is to define Hinduism as a religion and perhaps the only religion that the will to progress may have to eradicate. For the gathering anti-Jones majority, this conclusion cannot be less than helpful.

Unimprovable India meets its match in an England with an extraordinary capacity for improving the lot of its subjects. Christianity lays the ground for the advancement of civilization; it also lays the ground for the natural corollary of that advancement, namely, for becoming more like the English: "The converts would immediately become English in their feelings, for, like Mahomet, we ought to make our language go with our religion" (L and C, 3:37).

Macaulay's minute is on the horizon here, and Southey's anticipation of it helps direct our attention to the relationship between language and identity that is crucial in Macaulay's implicit agenda. Defenses of the minute have almost always been utilitarian defenses, leaving this relationship untouched or circumspectly minimized. Commonwealth literature, as an institution drawing together the English-speaking world and substituting cultural for imperial cohesion, returns to the submerged purpose behind the emphasis on the practical advantages of learning English. As the commonwealth era passes into the postcolonial, this implicit agenda will have to be heavily modified. The relationships between English-inheriting cultures will have to be dialogic rather than guided by a single centrality, and inheritances other than English will have to be crucial in the dialogue. A network of relationships will need to be rethought.

"We are indeed slandered about the East Indies," John Rickman wrote in correspondence with Southey. "Can anybody think," he went on to ask complacently, that "the people there are not infinitely benefited by our preponderance? . . . I see no chance of abuse of our power—when it is established." Southey concurred, adding that he was "ardent for making the world English." He was eager to review a book on military policy by C. W. Pasley that endorsed "a sort of political Islam—which teaches us to propagate freedom and good laws by the sword."[22]

"Making the world English" is a proposition that should dismiss itself by its ethnocentric absurdity. Yet it is really Hinduism's resistance to that proposition, its perception of itself as a radically different cultural site, that results in its being defined as monstrous. The monstrous is a companion to the hybrid, which, as Bacon says of the imagination, joins what nature has severed and severs what nature has joined, making unlawful matches and divorces of things. The hybrid conspires with the monstrous to change both relationships and dimensions, creating a combined excess too powerful and threatening to be brought back to the normality it ruptures. Yet both are constituents of the self, refusing to be either owned or disowned, to be safely inside or securely outside. Their violations congeal in an outrageousness that gathers to assert the double menace of their alienness and kinship. If a religion is monstrous to another religion, it is because it is the child of the other religion's exclusions.

A decade of hostile thinking about India, steadily maintained in Southey's correspondence, lies behind the opening diatribe of his preface to *Kehama*. It instructs us vehemently on how to read or perhaps how to avoid the poem. Instructions become necessary because the poem lacks them and because the reader, deprived of their guidance, may well come to an unconscionable sympathy with the monstrous. Fortitude and perseverance in the face of apparently irresistible power and the destruction of evil by the canker within itself are understandings that the poem nourishes and that are not repellent to Christianity. Indeed, Southey's enactment of that favorite romantic theme of individual goodness struggling against institutional corruption is an all-too-convincing demonstration of East-West affinities.[23]

For Southey and many of his contemporaries, Kehama was a more monstrous Napoleon, threatening not merely Europe but also the cosmos in a fantasy acclimatized to the much-proclaimed extravagances of Asia. Looking beyond the immediate parallel and back to its Western roots, we can see in Kehama's desire to be master of the universe a displacement of the Faustian urge, proclaiming a kinship between Faust and Tamburlaine of which Marlowe was decidedly conscious. A mythology that can sustain these enlightenments is not self-evidently an invention of the Devil, as Southey claims pagan mythologies to be in his second preface. He is drawing here on a tradition fathered by Augustine that comes to a climax in Milton's resounding catalog of false gods (*PL* 1.396–521) and his collective dismissal of them as abominations.

Since the Devil was having one of his best days when he invented

Hindu mythology, special precautions are needed to advise the reader on how to approach the dangerous construction that follows the preface. Vigilance is all the more important because warning devices that might have been installed in the poem seem conspicuous by their absence. A built-in European point of view might have given the reader a familiar footing in the infernal regions of the poem's mythology. A narrative voice could have provided the reader with the appropriate reorientation in the event of the reader's being surprised by sin. The very substantial body of notes that Southey provides might have addressed and placed the poem from its margins even while testifying to the authenticity of its details.

In any event, none of these safeguards are adapted. *Madoc* builds a European point of view into itself, but the poem on India is enclosed by India. The narrative voice avoids the Western intrusion that is occasionally to be found in *Thalaba:*

> So, one day may the Crescent from thy Mosques
> Be plucked by Wisdom, when the enlighten'd Arm
> Of Europe conquers to redeem the East!
> (*Thalaba* 5.6)

Indeed, on more than one occasion (e.g., 5.16, 7.4, 10.24), the narrative voice assimilates the poem to Western understandings instead of pointing reproachfully to its alienness.

Finally, the notes, drawing equally on evangelicals and on the school of Jones, do so mainly to document the poem's authenticity and to argue that when the author resorts to invention, he is no more extravagant in his inventiveness than the mythology within which he works. Condemnatory conclusions do not abound in the notes, and one can occasionally find statements that seek to moderate the revulsion against Hinduism that Southey shares with an increasing number of his countrymen. One such example is the note pointing out that suttee, although not disallowed, is not demanded by Hindu religion (8:552n).[24]

For the missionary conscience and the Mill aficionado, *Kehama* may be a poem sadly lacking in monstrosity. There is something to be said for a contemporary reviewer's suggestion that it should have been translated into Hindustani to find its proper audience.[25] It is out of synchronization with an emerging discourse to which Southey subscribed and that he may even have anticipated. The juggernaut episode may be the only part of the poem that fully satisfies the requirements of this discourse. Southey devotes a whole canto (14) to it, as if struggling to make up for lost time. It is structurally gratuitous and remains in precarious balance with a serene description of the celestial regions that relies heavily on Kalidasa (canto 7) and an account of the birth of the Ganges (canto 10) that may be the highwater mark of Southey's accomplishment as a mythological poet. "Fitter for the dotage dreams of Sir William Jones than the vision of the poet" is Southey's scathing judgment on the Hindu pantheon,[26] a judgment embarrassingly undone by the Ganges narration.

Both the celestial ascent and the descent of the Ganges are episodes that resist rather than assist imperialist devaluations of India. The same can be said of Southey's banyan tree passage (13.5), even though the writing here is routine in contrast to the élan displayed in Owenson's brilliantly flamboyant implementation of that topos.[27] The climax in Padalon, the submarine realm of Yama, god of death and judgment, is a demonstration of poetic justice, asserting the central presence of Western norms in Hindu mythology rather than an essay in an alien grotesque. Evil is incarcerated in itself in a manner that recalls the tenth book of *Paradise Lost* as well as Beckford's *Vathek*, and virtue, armed with fortitude, is given its just reward.[28]

Perhaps the principal safeguard for the errant reader of *Kehama* is the "remarkable peculiarity" of Hinduism on which its fable is built. According to Southey,

> Prayers, penances, and sacrifices are supposed to possess an inherent and actual value, in no degree depending on the disposition or motive of the person who performs them. They are drafts upon Heaven, for which the Gods cannot refuse payment. The worst men, bent upon the worst designs, have in this manner obtained power which has made them formidable to the Supreme Deities. (1810 preface)

This is a crassly commercial trivialization, confusing the gods of Hinduism with the Bank of England and assigning cash values in some celestial ledger to "prayers, penances, and sacrifices." Yet to be fair to Southey, his interpretation can be justified, given a resolutely literal reading of some of the Puranas and Vedas. To discourage such a reading, it should be sufficient merely to point to the creation hymn in the *Rigveda* (10.129), a supreme accomplishment in meditative poetry, which, as befits a meditative poem, is in the end a reading of its readers. The Vedas call for a reading that is literary rather than literal, but literal readings are less difficult and more persuasive for those seeking to devalue Hindu civilization.[29]

If we consider the religious texts of Hinduism as parts of a world rather than in isolation, the contrast between a proliferative mythology and a philosophy moving steadily in the direction of scholastic rigor culturally internalizes the self-and-other relationship in a contestation in which neither term can be privileged and in which the self can only be the other of its otherness. Here again, the readings called for by the more expansive terrain that the contestation opens have to be literary rather than literal.

In any religion mindful of its seriousness, external austerities can only be significant as the evidence of an inner purification that allows the divine selfhood within each individual to shine forth free of encumbrances. If one is "by merit more than birthright son of God" (PL 3.309), then acts of self-purification that are sufficiently sustained and resolute will enable one to be "formidable" to those gods whose possession of their places is largely titular. Power thus attained can be abused since it is in the nature of power to be abused. There is a limit to the abuse, beyond which a restorative force can and must intervene in order to keep the cosmos in being. There is also a point, according to Hindu thinking, at which the cosmos ceases to remain in being and is dissolved and withdrawn into the infinite potential.

Kehama becomes formidable to the gods not by practicing any austerity but by sacrificing as many horses as money can buy with the blessings of as many priests as he can intimidate. His career, if we insist on reading it literally, makes Hindu religion ridiculous rather than monstrous. It does say something in passing about the methods and motives of empire builders.[30] The gods who cope with Kehama by doing nothing until it is too late to do anything and who then complain that nothing can be done (7.2) also have lessons to teach us and themselves.

Southey may have felt that the "remarkable peculiarity" on which his fiction was founded was sufficient to cause loathing in the reader or at least an incredulity that would assign Hinduism to an outrageous otherness. As already indicated, he took no further steps to make his poem repellent to his audience. It would have been a paradox if he had done so, and there may be something to be gained from studying the paradox.

In an almost casual remark in the original preface, Southey tells us that the deformities in the mythological personages of the Brahmans were "easily kept out of sight." By 1838, the task of concealment had become considerably more formidable:

It appears to me that here, neither the tone of morals, nor the strain of poetry, could be pitched too high: that nothing but moral sublimity could compensate for the extravagance of the fictions, and that all the skill I might possess in the art of poetry was required to counterbalance the disadvantages of a mythology with which few readers were likely to be well acquainted, and which would appear monstrous if its deformities were not kept out of sight. (1838 preface)

To dissociate the "moral sublimity" of *Kehama* and the loftiness of its "strain of poetry" from the extravagance of its fiction and the monstrousness of the mythology through which the fiction is articulated is indeed a heroic undertaking. If accomplished, it would decisively fracture the poem. That the effort should be made at all warns us that the contamination of the Indian is to be resisted at all costs. Even the versification, once treated as ornamental, is now called on to hold the infection at bay: "The spirit of the poem was Indian but there was nothing Oriental in the style. I had learnt the language of poetry from our own great masters and the great poets of antiquity" (1838 preface).

A poem that quarantines a poem's language from its fiction and its mythology is indeed a singular construction. It also proposes a way of dealing with India that became more popular after 1857. More important, it is not clear how a poem now characterized as Indian in spirit can have its moral sublimity totally given to it by a style free of Indian infiltrations and formed exclusively on Western models.

Southey's contortions amount to saying that the poem has been Westernized to make it acceptable to a Western audience, although without prejudice to its monstrous heart. This is a difficult undertaking and one that can be called gravely misleading within the containment of the Mill-Hegel discourse. Southey is, in fact, making his apologies to that discourse by taking refuge in the proposition that the poem must give aesthetic pleasure to its readers. Unfortunately, the remainder of that Horatian tag requires the poem to instruct its readers in the course of pleasing them. Southey can only please his readers by covering up an instructional content that the Mill-Hegel discourse requires him to underline. On the other hand, not covering it up would result in a diatribe instead of a poem, designed to excite disgust rather than bring about pleasure.[31]

By 1838, the Mill-Hegel discourse, fortified by Macaulay's minute on education, was about to achieve a dominance in British perceptions of India that was to last for nearly a century. Southey had been a steady subscriber to that discourse from the inception of his career as a writer. His deference to it is entirely understandable. Unfortunately, a poem that Southey in 1810 could have passed off as a flawed experiment in an arcane mythology was now a persisting embarrassment. Part of himself had always been invested in constructions now close to attaining a monopoly of the ways in which India might be viewed. That part was waylaid by a poem he could not disown.

Retrieving the poem from the Indian contamination had also been made unnecessarily difficult. As has already been pointed out, the design could have incorporated a Western point of view. We do not know if Southey pondered this possibility. We do know that, influenced by William Jones's example, he chose a completely different approach: "I soon perceived that the best mode of treating it would be to construct a story *altogether mythological*" (1838 preface; italics added).

Jones's way of treating Indian mythology was admissible in a power relationship in which Indian culture was allowed a minor degree of attention and respect. It could be regarded as en route to Christian understanding and not as a horrifying otherness that called for root-and-branch erasure or at best for transformation rather than reform. The Mill-Hegel discourse was considerably less tolerant. Its argument was that the Indian way of imagining India condemned it to confinement within itself, to a petrifying observance of restrictions that regulated every detail of the self's response to the world. Progress called for the dismantling not only of specific institutions but also of the habits of construction that had led to them. A poem written within this discourse could not be "altogether mythological." It had to speak to Indian mythology rather than speak out of it.

In fact, *Kehama* is inside its mythology to such an extent that nearly everything it says can be said only through the mythological envelope. It is difficult under these circumstances to argue that the moral sublimity is not native to the envelopment and that it is an exterior finish laid on by the style. To make such an observation is to trivialize moral sublimity and to give style an importance it cannot possess. England's appropriation of India was not a matter of restyling it but of placing its economy in a state of dependence that included cultural accomplishments as well as physical resources. The aesthetic claim, implausible in itself, is out of alignment with the power relationship.

That power relationship, as we know, changed swiftly and drastically during the first decades of the nineteenth century, opening up huge possibilities that called out to be seized by an articulate and assertive imperial discourse. The rapidity with which political and economic discourse attached itself to the rhetoric and ideology of supremacy, formulated so tellingly by Mill and Hegel, left the development of the attendant literary discourse behind. Romantic thought had moved in the direction of a world humanism that Schwab indeed sees as the essence of the romantic project. To convert a world of thought into an empire of thought in which philosophical and poetic excellence would walk in companionship with military and political supremacy was not an enterprise for which literature was as yet ready.

The differential development of discourses that Louis Althusser has made important may provide a way of anatomizing the confusions of *Kehama*. Southey's commitment to an imperial discourse, underlined in the prose and in the two prefaces, is impeded by his involvement in a literary discourse of world humanism not yet adjusted to the imperial claim. The poem, as a result, is overdetermined by its loyalties, an overdetermination expressed at the aesthetic level by its self-troubling attempt to provide pleasure while promoting disgust. We can expect such a poem to be uneasy in its ambivalences and vacillating in its sense of priorities.

The most eloquent substantiation of the discourse of world humanism is Shelley's *Prometheus Unbound*. Southey's poem is better tuned to the imperial future. Shelley's poem can be read as if destined to speak to a more distant future, beyond that of imperialism itself. Yet Shelley's poem about the end of empires is in a relationship with the language of empire that, despite a self-awareness and a readiness to continue negotiations with its problem that Southey's poem lacks, can also be thought of as uneasily overdetermined.

Shelley's perception of India as a political actuality rather than as a site for the imagination is similar to Mill's and Southey's, even in those niceties of language that describe India as "straightjacketed" and "cramped." His simile of Asia as a golden chalice that receives the "bright wine" of Prometheus's overflowing being (1.1.809–10) is uncomfortably close to the gendered imperialism of a set piece by Owenson, discussed in chapter 6. Using the imagery of empire to assure us that empires can become irrelevant may point to the creative appropriation of an unavoidable legacy; it also points to the troubles of a poem that is written on the fault line between two discourses. Shelley and Southey locate their poems differently in relation to this fault line, but both writers are responsive to its stresses. The uneasy transcendentalism of the one and the irresolute imperialism of the other are different strategies of accommodation and avoidance.

Southey's world-mythological project is in keeping with the romantic involvement, but world projects are also designed with imperial aims in view. Knowledge and power are alike impatient of limits. Kehama's quest for dominance takes in both the celestial and the submarine. Endymion's quest for understanding explores the same expansiveness, even to the extent of following Southey's sequence. Keats's journey is, of course, by far the most probing. Wisdom is not possible without the taste of sorrow, and in the powerful blockages of the two *Hyperions*, the taste of sorrow can be no more than the promise of wisdom.

In its humanist version, a world-mythological project would proceed on the basis that every mythology that has "extended itself widely and powerfully influenced the human mind" has something to say to world understanding. In its imperialist version, such a project would seek to demonstrate that no mythology has anything significant to offer the general wisdom until it is placed in relationship to a Euro-Christian understanding that may either dismiss it altogether or raise it into acceptability by purging it of its perversions and deformities. Southey may endorse the second view officially, but his poem remains subject to the persuasions of the first one. As the discourse of empire consolidated itself, powerfully marginalizing even its imperial alternatives, his discomfort with *Kehama* became more intense. The poem on India too clearly sees "the end of the difference" and the domestication of the "wild, savage, and preposterous," to quote Emerson on the aims of historical study.[32] By 1838, *Kehama* was an embarrassment to its prefaces. Perspectives change, and a more modern reading might well find the prefaces an embarrassment to what we now make of the poem.

The Curse of Kehama is yet another instance (among several in this volume) of the capacity of literature to circumvent ideologies and to speak with a generosity that brings understanding closer to justice. The relationship between the rebellious poem and the reprimanding prefaces is remarkable for the subversive eloquence that it not only confesses to but also formalizes. It lays bare with a clarity that may be unique the quarrel between the ideological and poetic selves, between containment and proliferation, between regulatory reason and inventive fancy.

The struggle between the poem and its prefaces offers itself to many translations. The most important in this context is its transla-tion of the England-India relationship, which takes into its imperial scope and dismissive diagramming all of the other translations that have been outlined. In its individual episodes and, more persistently, in the universality of its fable, Southey's refractory undertaking both proclaims a classic imperial contrast and brings it to the verge of its humiliation.

8

Understanding Asia:
Shelley's *Prometheus Unbound*

෨

At the opening of *Prometheus Unbound*, Prometheus wishes to have his curse of Jupiter recited. It is not easy to find someone for this task. Everyone remembers the curse, preserves it as a "treasured spell," and meditates on its fulfillment in "secret joy" (1.1.210, 179–85),[1] but no one is so reckless as to pronounce it. Under a totalitarian regime, it is not wise to intone in prominent places or even in Caucasian ravines prophecies envisaging the death of the tyrant. Jupiter is the ultimate dictator, or to put it in Demogorgon's language, he is "the supreme of living things" (2.2.114) in an order by which everything living is encompassed. Hence, no one living can recite the curse, and although those who are dead can conceivably recite it, they cannot do so in the language of the living.

Fortunately, there is a third world of phantasms and shadows. Joined with their living counterparts only in death, they continue meanwhile their wraithlike existence. This is not a widely known fact. The magus Zoroaster is actually the "sole of men" to have met "his own image walking in the garden" (1.1.191–94). A denizen of the shadow world can safely recite the curse since Jupiter's vengeance would then waste itself on air, sweeping like "rainy wind through the abandoned gate / Of a fallen palace" (1.1.217–18). Earth proposes a variety of phantasms for this task, including Prometheus's own shadow (1.1.210-15). From these possibilities, the phantasm of Jupiter is chosen.

The preliminaries are complicated indeed, and more than a quarter of the first act has passed before we reach the end of the selection process. It is not easy and it should not be easy to find a voice that will foretell Jove's downfall, even in the words of someone else. But more significant than this admission of the fully inclusive grasp of the Jovian dictatorship is Prometheus's refusal to recite a curse that he intends to disown or even to have his phantasm recite it. The power of discourse and the extreme difficulty of avoiding its contamination are strikingly evident in these preliminaries. If the phantasm of Jupiter is eventually selected, it is not simply because of the nice irony of this choice or because power is destroyed by what grows in its shadow or because wreaking vengeance on one's phantasm is uncomfortably close to cutting one's nose off in order to spite one's face. Prometheus's underlying and necessarily inarticulate intention is more fundamental. It is not simply Jove who must be deposed. The Jovian discourse and the subtle knot of our participation in it have to be unraveled. We can resist the application of this discourse and still remain entangled in the proliferations of its growth not simply around but within ourselves. We can overthrow tyrants, but it is another matter to achieve the overthrow of tyranny. Jupiter's phantasm has to voice the curse because the curse itself is Jupiterian. To insist on it is only to maintain an endless will to vengeance against a power of dominance that feeds on that will.

The curse is then to be withdrawn. But there is a subtlety to its withdrawal that goes to the heart of the poem and its strikingly lucid perception of the relationship between dominance and its discourse. When the curse has been recited, Prometheus disowns it in the words "It doth repent me" (1.1.303). He might have been expected to say "I do repent it." The words fit the metrical pattern as well as those actually used, and in any case, euphony should not be the consideration foremost in Prometheus's mind at this moment. His inversion is carefully, indeed exquisitely, designed. It is not a wild exaggeration to call it the fulcrum on which the leverage of the poem, its future capacity to relocate our understandings, rests. The evident effect is to objectify the curse, to distance it from Prometheus so that it is no longer part of him. The subtler effect is to put tellingly before us the primacy of discourse and the extent to which it is constitutive of those whom it contains.[2]

The place of agency in a discourse whose hegemonic nature writes its agents has to remain profoundly problematic. Post-Reformation religious thought wrestles long and indecisively with this problem. Calvinism eliminates indeterminacy by eradicating agency, but less extreme solutions that open the divine poem to the subversive potential of free will have to find religious (and aesthetic) ways of containing and redirecting that subversiveness.

Shelley postulates a discourse sufficiently hegemonic to shape even the forms of resistance to itself. His inversion recognizes this enforced collusiveness, but it also treads on the brink of representing a totalitarian world order as consenting to its suicide by making it possible for resistance to disavow the forms of thought that have hitherto contained it. A tightrope has to be walked between hegemony and agency. Shelley's poem brings out not merely the precariousness of the tightrope but also the difficulty and the importance of finding it.

A reading based on the primacy and the constitutive power of discourse could be dismissed as highly exploitative if it had no more to work on than the relative position of four words. It is partly for this reason that the prolonged process of selecting a voice to utter the curse has been carefully gone through; the preliminaries are appropriate and called for by the climactic moment. But if no more remained to be added, the argument so far could be called only ingenious. There is, of course, more to be said. In fact, there is a series of cruxes that seem to fall into order and to open a route to our understanding of the poem if we proceed along the reading being used.

The site chosen for Prometheus's ordeal supports this reading. Aeschylus's Prometheus is pinned to a rock in a gorge in Scythia, the embodiment of barbarism in the Greek lexicon of dismissal. Shelley's Prometheus is bound to icy rocks in a ravine in the Indian Caucasus, a place where civilization may have begun rather than a place where a deep-seated barbarism lies in proximity to that abyss of Tartarus into which Prometheus is plunged to be tormented by the Furies. Shelley's insistence that we locate our minds in the Indian part of the vaguely demarcated Caucasus promises a role for Prometheus that is redemptive rather than heroically defiant. In doing so, it also responds imaginatively to the scholarship of his day. Nevertheless, it was not until 1963 that his choice became a matter of interest to our own day's scholarship.[3]

Shelley may have been encouraged in his choice by Owenson's influential novel, *The Missionary*, which he seems to have read at least three times in six months and which describes Bernier's Paradise of Kashmir as "confined within the majestic girdle of the Indian Caucasus."[4] The enclosed garden, protected by apparently impassable mountain defenses, is securely in the Miltonic tradition; that connection, taken in conjunction with the work of Jones and his colleagues, bestows on the presentation of the Indian Caucasus as a place of origins a status both scholarly and mythic. "Everything, yes, everything without exception has its origin in India" is Schlegel's excited claim, made in a letter of September 15, 1803, to Ludwig Tieck.[5] Origins include linguistic origins. If we admit the possibility that discourse began here, then Shelley's relocation of Prometheus's ordeal can be seen to go further, opening our minds to the repercussions of having discourse and dominance originate on the same site.

As Shelley composed his work, Mill's *History of British India* was coming off the presses.[6] Two years after *Prometheus Unbound* was published, Hegel was to begin his lectures on history in Berlin. The advance of humanity was an undertaking now reserved for the West. Meanwhile, the pace of territorial acquisition in India quickened. By 1818, the East India Company directly controlled 553,000 square miles of Indian territory, with an estimated population of 87 million.[7] An empire of unprecedented size was being assembled as Shelley wrote prophetically of the end of kingdoms. *Prometheus Unbound* asks to be read as a work distinctively fitted to the moment, singular in its synchronization of the ancestral and the contemporary, the primal forms of power and the prescriptive force of their continuing presence.

Aeschylus's hero claims that "all human arts are from Prometheus." In Shelley's work, it is Asia addressing Demogorgon who enumerates the gifts that Prometheus has bestowed on humanity. Aeschylus's Prometheus speaks of having taught mankind "the grouping of letters, to be a memorial and record of the past, the mistress of the arts and mother of the muses."[8] Asia, in keeping with her role as Prometheus's voice, defines the gift as speech rather than writing and endows speech with an extraordinary precedence: "He gave man speech and speech created thought / Which is the measure of the universe" (2.4.72–73).

Classical rhetoric habitually regarded language as contingent on thought, the most popular metaphor being that of a garment that thought wore in order to announce itself. When Longinus tells us that words are the pure light of thought, he is putting forward a highly refined version of this metaphor and, in doing so, moving toward the possibility that language may also illuminate what it announces. Shelley goes further and comes remarkably close to the proposition that human understanding is irretrievably linguistic, that our perceptions of the universe fall within patterns of thought that are brought into being by the dispositions and within the containment of language.

Indian religious philosophy has argued that both the cosmos and the differentiations of the language of knowing the cosmos devolved together out of the primal sound. Shelley may have been unaware of this proximity of origins, but the Caucasus in his presentation is not simply the place where language began. It becomes the site of the recognition that everything may have begun in language.

We live among representations that we make what they are and that contribute heavily to making us what we are even in our efforts to deny them. *It* must therefore repent us if *it* is to be authentically transformed. If speech created thought, thought cannot change unless discourse also changes. It can only shuffle relationships and play musical chairs within a continuing confinement.

There is a problem, and Shelley has come close to its heart. If he does not confidently proceed to a solution, it is because indeterminacy in coping with the problem lies in the nature of the problem itself. Shelley does make steadily and impressively evident the politics of representation and the extreme difficulty of emancipation from those politics.

Shelley's Asia is one of the felicities of naming, bringing her to the rescue of a nineteenth-century Asia falling increasingly under Jupiterian dominance. Mary Shelley points out that Asia is the wife of Prometheus, as she is indeed in Herodotus, although not in Hesiod.[9] Absent throughout the first act, she awaits the news of Prometheus's transformation in a "far Indian vale, / The scene of her sad exile" (1.1.826–27). It would be rash to conclude that India is perceived here as the place of exile it later became to generation after generation of raj administrators. Asia's exile is from a Jovian world to which she is alien and that must remain as it is until the curse repents Prometheus. Despite this alienation, the vale of Asia's loneliness, once desolate and frozen like the gorge in which Prometheus is imprisoned, is now "invested with fair flowers and herbs" by her "transforming presence" (1.1.828–32).

Asia's delayed appearance only after Prometheus has been cleansed of his curse ushers us into a politically charged environment. In that environment, we can imagine a captive subcontinent as awaiting the news that the principles of its liberation, retrieved from their perversion by Jovian discourse, have been made capable of entering and not simply resisting history. Critics inevitably associate Asia with the feminine[10] but not necessarily with the colonial feminine that the montage of the name, the continent, and the pointedly chosen locale of the play's action bring to the foreground of a contemporary reading. Asia's mission, significantly, is to save more than Asia. The "Celt knew the Indian" (2.4.94) before Jupiter and before the politics of divide and rule. Asia's joining of two continents is evident in her striking resemblance to Botticelli's Venus (2.4.156–60, 2.5.20–30, 3.3.64–84),[11] and as Venus-Urania, transported to a world that imperialism had made the continent of Circe, she represents a principle common to all cultures at their heart:

> Love he sent to bind
> The disunited tendrils of that vine
> Which bears the wine of life, the human heart.
> (2.4.63–65)

Love is not among the gifts of the Aeschylean Prometheus, and Asia is not mentioned in that play. Aeschylus is concerned not with revolution but with synthesis, and love is not relevant to his stark depiction of an irresistible force meeting an immovable object. Shelley is concerned not with accommodation within a discourse shaped by two polarities (the serpent and the eagle in his metaphors) but with the possible abolition of that discourse and of the principle of polarity that sustains it.

Feminine Asia, the object of Macaulay's contempt, is an interrogator of some sternness in Demogorgon's cave, the voice of a conscience not easily to be evaded. The interrogation is perplexing because Asia, far from seeking to pass beyond polarities, seems intent on inscribing them with a ferocious commitment to a rhetorical game being almost compulsively played. Some of the conventions of that game become evident when Asia, having thrice demanded that Jupiter be named, names him three times herself, after Demogorgon has thrice evaded an answer. The exchange suggests that Asia already knows what she needs to know and that verification rather than information may be the purpose of this baffling dialogue. If the bafflement persists, it is because the dialogue remains couched in a language that Asia's own self-knowledge might be expected to have made obsolete. Masters and slaves, tyrants and victims, an idyllic past set against a ravaged present, move commandingly through her angry rhetoric. Demogorgon's "I spoke but as ye speak" (2.4.112) sounds like a wearied invitation to his questioner to try a different discourse, an invitation that she sweeps aside to brandish yet once more her favorite antithesis: "Who is the master of the slave?" (2.4.114).

Yet when Demogorgon replies that the world is a passing parade, that the deep truth is imageless, and that everything except eternal love is subject to "Fate, Time, Occasion, Chance, and Change,"

Asia affirms that her heart has already known this and that "each to itself" must be the oracle of such truths (2.4.119-23). Her dialogue with Panthea has indeed made the interrogation redundant, but it remains accented by a moving authenticity. Asia represents a femininity ancestral and renascent and later to be made renascent in an India where femininity was to engender the paradigms and the philosophy of resistance. It is right that this femininity should be stern in anger against what must not be endured and gentle in sharing with Panthea the truths of the heart of which each must be the oracle. Asia speaks in two discourses that must continue to coexist uncomfortably in a world struggling not merely to inscribe but also to embed as a foundation those "beautiful idealisms of moral excellence" that become clear to Prometheus through his ordeal. It is not unfitting that she should be a different person in each of the worlds for which she speaks.

As for Demogorgon, it may be little consolation to point out that his answers are more enlightening than the "Boum, Boum" that greets the Western seeker in Forster's Marabar Caves. He is commented on almost ad infinitum, with Stuart Curran's and John Drew's remarks[12] possibly the most helpful in this context. In a world of representations, Demogorgon appears as the Maya of the moment, the representation called for by human awareness of the point it has reached in its history. Beyond these representations, the deep truth is imageless, an infinite, formless potentiality ready to flow into and animate the historically contingent forms of understanding. Shelley is aware of the relativities of representation, and if Demogorgon names himself eternity in the dethroning of Jupiter (3.1.52) and points to eternity as an ancient and tottering mother in the final lines of the poem, it is not necessarily because he does not know who he is in addition to not knowing what to say. Demogorgon represents (and to use that term is to undermine unavoidably the proposition being made) an ultimacy that is formless but that can be cognized only through forms, including the form of speech itself. In defining himself, he does so through the contingency that makes him what he momentarily is. If he names himself as eternity (and also as Jupiter's son immediately thereafter), it is to delineate the site of the naming as paradigmatic rather than historical. Shelley is not bereft of consistency in these matters. His difficulty lies in having to maintain the visionary compulsion to image finality against his own keen awareness that finality cannot be imaged.

Promethean heroism falls within a feminine gender pattern and is thus fully consonant with the choice of Asia as the emissary of that heroism. Its parent, Christian heroism as characterized by Milton, is set against the traditional masculinity of the classical heroism it replaces with its "better fortitude" (PL 9.31-33). Other relationships in *Paradise Lost* between gender patterns—between the Father and the Son in the third book and between Adam and Eve throughout the course of the poem—have their parts to play in Milton's overall view of gender relationships, which is thus too inclusive and too complex to be arranged along any single axis. In Shelley's imperial world, resistance (which, unlike rebellion, falls naturally into a feminine gender pattern) is the only recourse after the force of dominance has strengthened sufficiently to make insurrection impossible. This was not the situation in the India of Shelley's time, although it may be held to have become so after 1857. His poetry is prophetic in ways that there is no reason to believe he anticipated.

If discourse authorizes its authors and if it must repent us in order that we may repent ourselves fully, a world free of Jupiter must also be free of his discourse. The Spirit of the Hour is careful to set boundaries to that freedom by telling us that Jupiterian forms of understanding have not been destroyed; they have merely ceased to be pertinent to our identities:

> The tools
> And emblems of its last captivity
> Amid the dwellings of the peopled earth,
> Stand, not o'erthrown, but unregarded now.
> (3.4.176-79)

The word "last" is nicely ambiguous, and the passage must rank as a remarkable simulation of the status of imperial institutions in a postcolonial era. "Not o'erthrown" is a necessary reminder that the constituents of dominance remain in being, ready to be uttered once more into a discourse that must be vigilant in refusing to reinscribe them.

The Saturnian state, Asia tells us, was a state of "calm joy" but was deprived of its birthright of knowledge, power, thought, "selfempire and the majesty of love" (2.4.36-42). The imperial era is already nascent in the language or perhaps is betrayingly not erased from Asia's retrospective depiction of the Saturnian state. Prometheus gave "wisdom, which is strength to Jupiter," with the sole stipulation that "man be free" (2.4.44-45). The stipulation was predictably disregarded, and a world of dominance and subjection is the result. A return to the Saturnian state is no longer possible. We must have a new world in which the constituents of understanding are no longer centralized and thereby opened to dictatorial seizure, a world that is multivocal rather than hierarchical.

In seeking a language that does not reinscribe or at least adequately undermines what the new order repudiates, the Spirit of the Hour follows a secular *via negativa*.[13] The human identity is defined through the systematic dismissal of imperial attributes:

> The loathsome mask has fallen, the man remains
> Sceptreless, free, uncircumscribed, but man
> Equal, unclassed, tribeless, and nationless,
> Exempt from awe, worship, degree, the king
> Over himself; just, gentle, wise: but man.
> (3.4.193–97)

In a multivocal world, not all differences can be eliminated. We need a language of community, not homogeneity. The latter might let Jupiter in by the backdoor. This is a difficulty that the language of erasure cannot be expected to address. Its task is to clear away the Jupiterian debris that obscures our perception of the essentially human. Yet despite the exultation of erasure that is heard triumphantly in the Spirit of the Hour's manifesto, latent perils remain inscribed in the language. "Uncircumscribed" is a word that God in *Paradise Lost* (7.170) uses to describe himself and that has been historically secularized in the boundless scope of imperial ambition. "King / Over himself" is an idea that *Paradise Regained* made influential, but the interior hierarchization may have exterior consequences. Humanity's birthright was "self-empire"; its fate, brought on by Prometheus, was Jupiterian dominance.

An alternative to postcolonialism's *via negativa* is to use the emblems of empire to affirm the end of empire in poetry's persistent language of paradox. The icons, far from being "unregarded," are regarded in a sharply different light. Language as "a perpetual Orphic song" (4.415) in the final act has begun to threaten us with its unendingness. Demogorgon returns us to reality and the insistent claim of events. For Shelley's contemporaries, those events would have included the Peterloo massacre, which took place between the writing of the third and fourth acts of *Prometheus Unbound*.

The unbinding of Prometheus was a narrative offered in a paradigmatic realm that the human future was called on to translate. In Shelley's *Philosophical View of Reform*, developments in Spain, Germany, the United States, and France (notwithstanding the aftermath of the French Revolution) are read as indicating that this translation is beginning. With the slave uprisings in the West Indies, "the deepest stain upon civilized man is fading away."[14] Events such as Peterloo arrested the translation and threatened the emerging text of liberty with the renascence of the Jupiterian. "Gentleness, virtue, wisdom and endurance" (4.562) are addressed to a contemporary danger as well as to a paradigmatic arrangement.

Demogorgon's speech is rife with images of empire, which unexpectedly delineate not a renascent threat but the ways in which that threat is to be overcome. "Conquest is dragged captive through the deep" (4.556). Love sits on an awful throne of power, transformed only because the power is that of patience. If the serpent should make its way out of the bottomless pit from which exit is barred by the Promethean virtues, an empire is to be reassumed over the disentangled doom of a previous empire. Neither to change nor falter nor repent is the Titan's glory, even though his transformation began with "It doth repent me." Life, Joy, Empire, and Victory join together in a final concatenation that may be as appropriate for Tamburlaine as it is for Prometheus.

The accumulations of the imperial are too methodical to be purposeless. Perhaps a postcolonial language should confront the discourse of empire, appropriating it, as with Demogorgon, or dismantling it, as with the Spirit of the Hour. The language of play that Michael Scrivener sees at work in the final act up to Demogorgon's entrance is another, although intermittent, possibility.[15] The "irresponsibility" of play impedes and undermines the encodings that the usages of political and economic power entrench. Such entrenchments would reduce play to frivolity. In displaying these possibilities, Shelley may be sketching the varieties of a liberated language and may be multivocal even in his sketchings.

As Shelley's sketchings expose the possibilities and weaknesses of differing postcolonial languages, it becomes apparent that none of them are inherently free from contamination. All of them have to be safeguarded, and that safeguarding must rest on a firm connection to a subtler language more resistant to conceptualization and therefore less likely to become encoded, to petrify into the fixed positionings of discourse. The law is the letter, the book, the dogma, the institution. The gospel lives in human hearts, of which "each to itself" is the oracle (PR 1.460–64). To be uncircumscribed, to be free of divisive differentiations, is to liberate what has always been shared by the natural relatedness of the human community. The reinstatement of that relatedness, once overlaid by the directing pressures of Jupiterian discourse, does not dispense with the need for language, but it humanizes and validates that language, holding in check its propensity to tyranny.

Panthea's dream, searchingly discussed by Tilottama Rajan,[16] explores the recesses of this deeper language "orb within orb" in the depths of the eyes of the heart. "Dream" is a misnomer since, as Curran points out, there are three different dreams: "The first, narrated by Panthea, is reinterpreted by Asia, then interrupted by Panthea's account of a second dream, the interpretation of which prompts Asia's remembrance of her own corroborative dream. . . . The dream world is like Panthea's eyes into which Asia searches: 'dark, far, and measureless: / Orb within orb and line through line interwoven.'"[17] One might add that Asia does not ask that the first dream be narrated. She asks Panthea to "lift up" her eyes so that her dream can be "read" in them. Panthea's account of how she lifted up her own eyes to the "overpowering light" (2.1.67–71) of Prometheus's presence is a mirroring and validation of Asia's request. Asia's renewal of her request that Panthea lift up her eyes so that Prometheus's "written soul" can be read in them then becomes a demand for a more authentic language in comparison with which Panthea's words are "as the air," evanescent and insubstantial.

The insistence that the eyes reveal more than the "fairest shadow" (2.1.113) of the person looking into them and the persistent perception of the depth of understanding as beyond textuality yet irretrievably imaged as textuality ("read," "written") are further evidence of Shelley's extraordinary awareness of the constitutive power of language, an awareness displayed everywhere in *Prometheus Unbound*. That awareness is consistent with the knowledge that language itself may be the shadow of an understanding that can bypass it but by which it must consent to be sustained. The deep truth may be imageless, but since all perception must be imaged, the most authentic imaging is in the eyes of the dreamer "beyond their inmost depths" (2.1.119).[18] The space of that "beyond" reveals to us not merely what we are (which amounts to no more than seeing our fairest shadows) but also what we are by virtue of what we share. There is a community of feeling on which language rests and that must be *read into* as well as *entered through* the languages it nourishes and makes stable. If a text is to be protected from appropriation, it must remain anchored in the fundamental text of our humanity that all of us must learn to find and to know.

A language beyond language is desirable because *Prometheus Un-*

bound, beginning as a study of the discourse of dominance, evolves into a study of the dominance of discourse. The question of how discourse is to be freed from its own nature is one for which there can be no answer, only safeguards. Eternal vigilance is undoubtedly one of the safeguards, but even eternal vigilance can be aimless if it is unable to refer to any source beyond its own entrapment, if it can find no ground to stand on that is not penetrated by the very contamination from which it seeks to deliver itself. Shelley addresses these problems with a perceptiveness from which discourse analysis today can profit. The substratum of imaginative understanding that he posits may not be the most reassuring of deliverances, but it is preferable to the potential tyranny of an absolute or to that of its secular alternative, the progressive materialization in world history of a final cause by which history is driven forward.

Prometheus Unbound is a work that circumvents closure not because of Demogorgon's incantations over the bottomless pit but because it remains resistant to a final reading, displaying that resistance even in the diversity of its languages. Its possibilities and problematizations open it to a reading future that can stabilize its indeterminacies not simply in different ways but also in ways that can speak with the eloquence of a beginning to the place in the future from which they are viewed. To the postcolonial world, *Prometheus Unbound* is not simply a liberation text but a liberation text that richly adumbrates the opportunities and encumbrances of a liberated language. It lays down the character and technique of nonviolent resistance—"gentleness, virtue, wisdom and endurance"—in a manner that strikingly anticipates the historical development of nationalist resistance in India. It also calls on us to ensure that the revolution, when it does take place, is a revolution and not a substitution. If the true enemy is not Jupiter but Jupiterian discourse, much can remain to be done even after the elations of independence.

If we emphasize the extent to which *Prometheus Unbound* attaches itself to a contemporary, postcolonial reading, it is so that we can return less disturbingly to the knowledge that this is not how Shelley's contemporaries would have read it. Romantics, even radical romantics, were not particularly sensitive to the expansion of empire in India under their noses at a time when paradigms of liberty were in the air. Misgivings about India were voiced far less frequently than those voiced in the last quarter of the eighteenth century, already quoted in chapter 4. These misgivings came to a head in the impeachment of Hastings. Macaulay's vivid account makes clear that the impeachment was treated as the theatrical event of the decade, with ballads circulating in the street, Lady Hastings ostentatiously wearing the gaudy tiara of her ill-gotten gains, and grandes dames from high society ceremonially swooning in the aisles to the melodious thunder of Burke's periods.[19]

As Conor Cruise O'Brien convincingly argues, the impeachment needs to be seen as shifting the responsibility for managing India from the boardrooms of a private company to the more public forum of a nation's conscience. Concurring surprisingly in this shift is Adam Smith, the patron saint of free enterprise.[20] The change does not eliminate the problem of accountability; it merely elevates it, opening the way to the self-justifying fictions that characterize Victorian imperialism and that owe their origin and entanglements to that imperialism's distant yet tenaciously influential Reformation roots. Grant's atonement, Jones's restoration of India to its classical self, and the imperially assisted march of a backward people from the Saturnian to the Apollonian are competing fictions in which the final one can only prevail by overwriting rather than erasing its alternatives. It remains troubled and even fissured by residues that it cannot completely eliminate or assimilate.

Answerability to the nation may have been achieved by the impeachment, but the impeachment itself, as a highly theatrical rendering of that answerability, had a cathartic effect that diverted attention from the continuing growth of the company's possessions in India. Wellesley's talent for territorial acquisition comfortably exceeded that of his predecessors. Brian Gardner even goes to the extent of characterizing that talent as "an insatiable, unabashed, almost frenetic lust."[21] He adds that the directors of the East India Company "wrung their hands in horror" at Wellesley's conquests, but if they did so it was because of economic doubts rather than moral misgivings. It was not as yet clear to them how territory could be transformed into profits and how company dividends could survive the considerable costs of indefinitely maintaining in India a standing army larger than any in Europe. To say this is not to criticize the company's directorate but rather to point to the apparent extinction after the Hastings trial of any national conscience that might oversee that directorate. More specifically, it is difficult to find poets of the day who concerned themselves about what was happening in India, even for reasons of unenlightened self-interest.

In the earlier phase of the British attainment of dominance, the work of Jones and the members of the Asiatic Society was an important element in the perception of India. In the later phase, that perception was increasingly controlled by a utilitarian-evangelist coalition that methodically devalued India, first to create an implicit right to exploit it and then to create an explicit responsibility to take it over in the name of "improving" it or of atoning for previous excesses. With foreign competitors eliminated (the battle of the Nile in 1798 had extinguished the last possibility of a French threat to British supremacy in India), the Mahrattas remained the only power by whom this objective could be seriously contested. The Treaty of Poona marked the elimination of the Mahratta challenge. It was signed in June 1817, the year in which Shelley began *Prometheus Unbound*.

Shelley was less than responsive to the swift growth of a dominance that, despite its professed benevolence, might have been perceived as containing the germ of the Jupiterian. He was also less than sympathetic to the counterclaims of a culture that dominance was propelled into devaluing. Read in proximity to Shelley's statements, Elizabeth Hamilton's novel, discussed in chapter 6, starkly delineates the difference a decade can make to the politics of perception.

In *A Refutation of Deism*, Shelley is prepared to concede that there are "a few axioms of morality which Christianity borrowed from the philosophers of India."[22] Much of the concession is taken back by "borrowed" and "axioms." What is lent can be returned, having been improved on, and if what is lent is axiomatic, it can also be independently acquired by the natural operations of intelligence.

In *Queen Mab*, Shelley puts "Buddh" and "Seeva" on the same plane as Jehovah, as evidence that God is "Himself the creature of his worshippers" (7.28). We could take this as an example of Shelley's skepticism regarding the world's religions, an ironic reversal of the image of God in man, remaking God not simply in the image of human needs but, more coercively, in the self-justifying image of institutionalized power, with its constraints and impositions. The proposition may seek to undermine Hindu religious imagings (along with those of other religions), but it is not unfamiliar in the religion it undermines. Yeats put it to use in one of his early poems on India.[23]

Given the relativity of human forms of relationship with the divine, the saving power of a religion may well lie in the variety of constructions it is able to accommodate and among which it can continue its search for understanding. Unfortunately, Shelley was not in a position to attend to the distinctiveness of a culture that could be treated as bringing together forms of relationship as apparently divergent as "Buddh" and "Seeva." It was not until 1836, nearly a quarter of a century after *Queen Mab*, that India was established as the birthplace of Buddhism in a manner satisfactory to the West.[24]

Hinduism goes well beyond other religions in conceding the unavoidability of constructions and the provisionality of all constructions. "Maya" is the term in Hindu thought that registers this pervasive recognition and supplies it as a background for the forms of the mind. This radical skepticism is joined to a mysticism that, because of the substantial exchanges between East and West in the world of classical thought, can sometimes seem like Neoplatonism's twin sister. But the skepticism is not the ground of world abandonment, a recoil from the wilderness of forms that Hegel sees as a delirious multiplicity to be set antithetically against a transcendental nullity. The skepticism seeks not the relinquishment of all constructions or the transcendental guaranteeing of a specific construction but the principles of responsible living among constructions as they are put into place by the human project. The human project is, of course, itself a construction, but one that may be deemed necessary for human survival.

There can be more than one combination of the skeptical and the mystical, but this combination is a significant possibility among the heterogeneities of Indian thought. It raises problems that Shelley's poetry, in the development of its self-examination, seems to be equipping itself to engage. It is also distinctively Shelleyan. Shelley was not situated to recognize this overall affinity, but it deserves exploration by those who, in our time, examine Shelley's Indianness.

The passage from *Queen Mab* is followed by a brief reference to the juggernaut, which remembers the unnecessary canto that Southey gave to that "grim idol" and perhaps looks forward to Shelley's own chariot of life. Schopenhauer, engaged in a determined segregation of a Jupiterian Old Testament from a New Testament he reads as deeply informed by Indian thought, views the juggernaut, not at all disapprovingly, as a dramatic demonstration of *contemptus mundi*.[25] More typically, it was an icon for evangelical horror, the monstrous sign of an inveterate otherness.

In *A Philosophical View of Reform*, Shelley finds the country of the juggernaut so backward that even the missionaries he despises are capable of improving it. Missionary activities were legalized in India at this time, so Shelley's recommendation is not reached in the abstract. It is a finding disturbingly at odds with a novel Shelley had read and greatly admired dealing with the havoc missionaries could wreak in India. "It cannot be doubted," Shelley assures us with dismaying confidence, that "the zeal of the missionaries of what is called the Christian faith will produce beneficial results there [i.e., in India]." These benefits can be secured "even by the application of dogmas and forms of what is here an outworn incumbrance."[26]

Shelley's pages show no concern over the rapacious growth of the empire in India and register no suspicion that the intentions of empire might be other than benevolent. "The Indians," he avers in language discouragingly reminiscent of Mill, "have been enslaved and cramped in the most severe and paralysing forms which were ever devised by man." Even if "the doctrines of Jesus do not penetrate through the darkness of that which those who profess to be his followers call Christianity," a "number of social forms" modeled on "European feelings" can be substituted for the existing straitjackets. These substitutions can make future progress "less imperceptibly slow" and will facilitate "complete emancipation" when the time comes.[27]

The Eurocentric disposition is prominent here and becomes nearly overbearing in the following sentence: "Many native Indians have acquired, it is said, a competent knowledge in the arts and philosophy of Europe, and Locke and Hume and Rousseau are familiarly talked of in Brahminical society."[28] The next sentence is only just in time for the Indian reader: "But the thing to be sought is that they should as they would if they were free, attain to a system of arts and literature of their own."[29]

Little can be said in defense of this effortless digestion of the Mill-Hegel perception of India, saved only by the touch of Asiatic Society Orientalism at the end. Shelley's many affinities with Indian philosophy place themselves here in distressing contrast to his view of India's actuality, an actuality so corrupt that, at least for the moment, there can be no question of redeeming it by bringing it back to its roots in that world of thought by which Shelley's own imagination was kindled. The two levels of perception and the unbridgeable distance between them seem to point to the compulsions of a discourse so pervasive that it can be dealt with only by surrendering India to it as a historical reality in order to preserve it as a transcendental site.

"India is magnetic to Shelley," Wilson Knight tells us.[30] It is in the Indian Caucasus that Prometheus learns wisdom. It is in the Paradise of Kashmir that Asia apparently begins her redemptive action and the visionary in *Alastor* begins his self-destructive quest. India is important to Shelley but important as a territory of the imagination, a hospitable place for situating paradigms. It is not important as a place of profit and empire that rival armies fought bitterly over, as a place that the stoic and enduring figure whom Shelley placed prophetically in the Indian Caucasus was symbolically destined to free from imperial rule. The reading that liberates *Prometheus Unbound* is not quite the reading Shelley offered his contemporaries. It is the reading we learn as we look into Panthea's eyes.

9
Macaulay:
The Moment and the Minute

எஐ

Macaulay left for India in 1834. In the previous year, as the member of Parliament for Leeds, he had risen to deliver a memorable speech not simply on the reorganization of the East India Company (the nominal topic of the debate) but also on the future of the empire in India. Shelley, in a sentence struggling with itself hesitantly constructed fourteen years earlier, had written of India eventually attaining a system of laws and literature of its own. William Jones had envisaged a speedier restoration of India's cultural distinctiveness, but Shelley's embarrassments reflected the tightening grip of the Mill-Hegel view of India, even on minds with progressive dispositions. Macaulay's peroration erased even Shelley's faltering hopes. It was a resounding prophecy of the imperishable empire of England's arts and letters, to which India hereafter would inalienably belong. The cultural empire would endure even after the political one had run its course as a self-consuming artifact.[1] Macaulay's prophecy rings uncomfortably true when, fifty years after India's independence, Wordsworth is taught in the fastnesses of Gilgit, as a documentary film by David Suzuki indicates.[2]

Macaulay set sail for India as the law member of the company's governing board. Like others who departed to that country, he regarded his new position not as an opportunity but as an exile. For a writer whose historical imagination was caught up in the drama of parliamentary politics, an assignment in India could scarcely have been anything else. Macaulay accepted the appointment because he hoped he could set aside enough from his earnings to make him financially secure for his lifetime. He could then devote himself to concerns more important than India—most notably, the writing of his history of England.

Jones had gone to India a generation earlier as the company's chief justice. He too planned to live in India as modestly as the extravagances of Calcutta would permit and to save enough to sustain a life of scholarship when he returned. He remained in India until the day of his death. Macaulay stayed for no more than four years. During that brief interval, he penned the minute that is remembered as deciding India's educational future and was responsible for all of the language and nearly all of the substance of the Indian penal code. The decisions in which he was a principal participant continue to affect the lives of Indians even today far more powerfully than they seem to have affected Macaulay.

Macaulay wrote two essays on Indian history after his return, one on Clive (January 1840) and the other on Hastings (October 1841). He was secretary of war in the Melbourne administration at the time, an appointment that may account for some of his obvious relish in Clive's victories. The Indian experience may have been of no great consequence to Macaulay,[3] and Owen Edwards, in allowing it five pages in a generally admirable book,[4] could be displaying a disconcerting sense of proportion. Jane Millgate's quietly enlightening study is more generous,[5] and of course, there is a distinction to be made between what mattered to Macaulay and what in Macaulay matters to us. John Clive responds to that distinction in the 137 pages that his thorough and judicious study devotes to the minute and the Indian penal code.

The essays on Clive and Hastings appeared in the *Edinburgh Review.* Macaulay had been an established voice in that periodical from the time it published his essay on Milton, written when he was no more than twenty-five. The occasion was the unexpected discovery of *De Doctrina Christiana* in the recesses of the Public Records Office. A steady succession of essays on historical subjects followed during the next twenty years. In 1828, an essay on history appeared that would have invited reading as a preface to the other essays if Macaulay had not omitted it from the 1843 collection. In the essay, Macaulay observed that it could be "laid down as a general rule though subject to considerable exceptions and qualifications, that history begins in novel and ends in essay" (1:181).

Macaulay tells us more than once that history resembles literature, but he is usually only suggesting that the pleasures of reading history ought to be comparable to those of reading literature or that characterization and narration in the writing of histories should model themselves on literary practice. Another way of putting this proposition is offered at the outset of his essay on Henry Hallam. The province of history, we are told, has been deprived of part of itself, with literature providing the scenery and the life, while history is reduced to providing the map. The historian's task is to reunite the partitioned territory. In making these statements, Macaulay seems in no danger of approaching the more drastic recognition that the historical imagination is unavoidably fictive.

The passage quoted from the essay on history is unusual not only because it suggests two specific genres for history but also because it suggests that the very process of writing history converts one genre into another. The conversion is not a shrinkage of intentions since an essay is not a collapsed novel. It is a different form and a form, moreover, with which we do not usually associate the novel. One can understand the proposition that what begins as an epic may end as a novel. Literary history can be argued to have taken that direction, and that direction can even be discerned in the more earth-bound books of *Paradise Lost*. But the movement from the novel to the essay seems almost like the undoing of a hard-won multivocality, substituting argument for plot and the reflective for the dramatic.

In the end, Macaulay may only be saying that history is a mixed genre, programmed in one direction and pulled in another, a hybrid of the sort that purists locate in India. He can even be perceived as reading his own finding backward since his historical work began with a series of essays and proceeded to *The History of England*, which is more akin to a novel.

A more prosaic relationship between histories and novels can be found in Macaulay's review of Sir James Mackintosh's incomplete *History of the Revolution*. "We find in it," he says, "the diligence, the accuracy, and the judgment of Hallam, united to the vivacity and colouring of Southey." He adds that "a history of England, written throughout in this manner, would be the most fascinating book in the language. It would be more in request at the circulating libraries than the last novel" (3:339).

The same note is heard in a letter Macaulay wrote on November 27, 1848, to his brother, Charles, when *The History of England* was close to publication: "Everybody who has seen the book, that is to say, Lord Jeffrey, Ellis, Trevelyan, Hannah, and Longman, predict complete success and say that it is as entertaining as a novel."[6] On November 5, 1841, he had written to McVey Napier: "I shall not be satisfied unless I produce something which shall for a few days supersede the last novel on the tables of young ladies."[7]

In any event, Macaulay's history was as successful as any novel of the time. It was devoured by subscribers to circulating libraries, appeared on innumerable coffee tables, and helped to compose the Victorian frame of mind. In 1856 alone, the history earned Macaulay £20,000.

Macaulay called Mackintosh's history a fragment, providing what may be the best clue to the genre of his own work. It populates a limited space within a considerably larger space that is present to the reader but only in outline. One might say that this is the nature of writing about history—to compose fragments within apparent wholes that in turn will be perceived as fragments. It is to devise micronarratives that exemplify or seek the macronarratives with which they must be consistent.

This familiar view of coherence achieved within wider and wider boundaries and of a final inclusiveness from which nothing is shut out may carry within it the seeds of its own dismantling. If the fragment seeks the whole, if it carries the sign of the whole at its heart, the whole in turn includes and may not contain the separatist energy of the fragment. The novel splinters into the essay. The essay attempts but cannot quite attain the novel. "I cannot make it cohere" is Pound's conclusion after two generations of writing the *Cantos*, in which the will to coherence has been indefatigably exercised.

Macaulay's history, considered as a fragment, occupies a space between two great events: the Revolution of 1688, which brought the Crown into harmony with Parliament, and the Act of 1832, which brought Parliament into harmony with the nation. Not everyone saw the two events in this way, but this way of seeing them became immensely influential not simply as the initiation and conclusion of a narrative but also as a claim for progress in the popular sense or, in Hegelian terminology, for the self-realization of the idea. If a line is drawn through these two events, it can be read as pointing to a third phase in which the nation is brought not exactly into harmony with its empire but into a relationship that enables it to perceive its destiny in the image of empire it places before itself. One need not emphasize how much Victorian thinking seems to take the presence of this line for granted.

As a historian, Macaulay was in the privileged position of being able to write history into events and not merely distill it into language. He was singularly placed to contrive a text that would be seamless, that would make the future the fulfillment of the past. If we textualize power as the power to write in contrast to the helplessness of having to be written, we can see how the imperial historian is drawn irresistibly to the thematic narrative, how he can prescribe a congruence between idea and text and rely on the persuasions of uncontested power to overcome the propensities of any text to deviance. The resultant harmony offers a satisfaction that is imperially aesthetic. Other forms of history can be pleasing, including, particularly in our time, the ironic and the indeterminate; they do not solicit the imperial imagination.

India could be said to have provided Macaulay with an opportunity to extend the scope of the harmonious vision by bringing the idea of empire into relationship with the idea of progress as it was inscribed so far in the march of England. That march began at the outset of the twelfth century, when England was "in a state more miserable than the state in which the most degraded nations of the East now are" (3:358). From this discouraging starting point, England rose to heights repeatedly acclaimed in Macaulay's recitals. The peroration to the Southey essay is probably the most famous of these triumphant surveys.

Like Macaulay's essay on Bacon, the essay on Mackintosh, from which this quotation comes, was written in India. The inference waiting to be drawn was that India, with the blessing of English guidance, could be helped to proceed along the route that England had pioneered. Unfortunately, the march of progress in England was moving forward to the drumbeat of institutional change and political liberalization. It was the movement from the England "of crusaders, monks, schoolmen, astrologers, serfs, outlaws" to "the England we know and love—the classic ground of liberty and philosophy, the school of all knowledge, the mart of all trade." The milestones on this march were

> the Charter of Henry Beauclerc,—the great charter,—the first assembling of the House of Commons,—the extinction of personal slavery,—the separation from the See of Rome,—the Petition of Right,—the Habeas Corpus Act,—the Revolution,—the establishment of the liberty of unlicensed printers,—the abolition of religious disabilities—the reform of the representative system.

All of these events seemed to Macaulay "the successive stages of one great revolution," and the struggle to write them into history was "a struggle on the results of which were staked the dearest interests of the human race" (3:358–59).

Establishing English as the language of advanced understanding in

India had to be the first step in this majestic agenda, but it remained the only step as well as the first one. Beyond the removal of certain social abuses (the abolition of thuggery, suttee, and child betrothal were regularly announced to grateful Indian gatherings as typical of the lavishness of England's gifts to India), no further movement to put into effect "the dearest interests of the human race" was contemplated by Macaulay or anyone else. Regulations requiring printing presses to be licensed, introduced in Bengal in 1823, were indeed repealed in 1835, but the right to print remained subject to emergency powers. Clive finds these powers such that "five persons who may be brought together in half an hour, whose deliberations are secret, who are not shocked by any of those forms which elsewhere delay legislative measures, can in a single sitting, make a law for stopping every press in India."[8]

As for habeas corpus, preventive detention would in due course provide an antidote to the inconvenience of having to lay specific charges against those whom one would like to imprison. The "reform of the representative system" may have been the result of teaching English to Indians, but it was a consummation not devoutly sought but doggedly resisted. As one might anticipate, the history of the other has to be otherwise.

India's otherness makes it a place of exile where self-understanding is to be defended and not extended. Macaulay, in treating it as such, joins a tradition that goes back to Camões and that Shelley uses in a revolutionary version. Max Müller both recognizes and contests this tradition in imploring a group of prospective civil servants assembled at Cambridge in 1883 to treat India not as an exile but as a homecoming, a rediscovery of the West's Aryan roots:

> The ancient literature of India is not to be regarded simply
> as a curiosity and to be handed over to the good pleasure of
> Oriental scholars. . . . It can teach us lessons which nothing
> else can teach, as to the origin of our own language, the first
> formation of our own concepts, and the true natural germs
> of all that is comprehended under the name of civilization,
> at least the civilization of the Aryan race.[9]

The rampant ethnocentrism would call for underlining in another context, but here the point to be made is that Macaulay, unlike Müller, was not interested in Indian opportunities for ancestral wisdom, whether as a historian or as an ethnocentrist. His nearly total ignorance of the Indian past was not at all unavoidable in the 1830s.

It was put on and worn as a constituent of the imperial blindness that now seemed to have become obligatory if the imperial gaze was to attain its proper intensity.

The essays on Clive and Hastings concede very little to India that would make it worth the trouble of "Englishing" or justify the handsome intentions of the peroration to the 1833 speech. The remarks on Bengal are particularly severe. Edwards attributes Macaulay's adverse comments on Bacon (in an essay written during his stay in India) to "the hard intolerant heat" of the subcontinent,[10] but the Bengali psyche might be more respectable to Macaulay if it were indeed hard and intolerant. He treats it instead (characteristically and influentially) as formed by persistent wallowing in a vapor bath:

> Bengal was known through the East as the garden of Eden, as the rich kingdom. Its population multiplied exceedingly. Other provinces were nourished from the overflowing of its granaries; and the ladies of London and Paris were clothed in the delicate produce of its looms. The race by which this rich tract was peopled, enervated by a soft climate and accustomed to peaceful employments, bore the same relation to other Asiatics which the Asiatics generally bear to the bold and energetic children of Europe. The Castilians have a proverb, that in Valencia the earth is water and the men women; and the description is at least equally applicable to the vast plain of the lower Ganges. Whatever the Bengalee does he does languidly. His favourite pursuits are sedentary. He shrinks from bodily exertion; and though voluble in dispute and singularly pertinacious in the war of chicane, he seldom engages in personal conflict and hardly ever enlists as a soldier.

"There never, perhaps, existed a people," Macaulay concludes, "so thoroughly fitted by nature and by habit for a foreign yoke" (pp. 328–29).

These comments, which Brantlinger aptly characterizes as "Whig history at its most self-indulgent,"[11] come from the essay on Clive. However, it is not until the companion essay on Hastings that Macaulay allows himself to be fully carried away by the intoxications of Bengali bashing:

> What the Italian is to Englishmen, what the Hindoo is to the Italian, what the Bengalee is to other Hindoos, that was

Nuncomar to other Bengalees. The physical organisation of the Bengalee is feeble even to effeminacy. He lives in a constant vapour bath. His pursuits are sedentary, his limbs delicate, his movements languid. During many ages he has been trampled upon by men of bolder and more hardy breeds.

The weakling Macaulay presents is not altogether lacking in integrity. "His mind," we are informed, "bears a singular relationship to his body. It is weak even to helplessness for purposes of manly resistance; but its suppleness and its tact move the children of sterner climates to admiration not unmingled with contempt" (pp. 385–86).

Ethnocentrism, gendered and compounded, is a device lavishly used in the preceding passages. Valencia is distanced from Castile, Italy is further distanced spatially and ethnically from England, Asia is yet more remote from "the bold and energetic children of Europe" (including presumably Italians), India stands at a still further remove, and, in an internal differentiation matching the initial distancing between Castile and Valencia, Bengal becomes the ultimate effeminacy of effeminate India, with "Nuncomar" as the embodiment of qualities that can only prevail on the most marginal of peripheries. The pervasive conflation of spatial, moral, and gender distances sustains the invective and indeed drives it to its climax: "What the horns are to the buffalo, what the paw is to the tiger, what the sting is to the bee, what beauty according to the old Greek song, is to women, deceit is to the Bengalee" (p. 386).

It was in vain that Müller spent a whole lecture endeavoring to show his students that deceit, among all vices, was the one most sternly forbidden in the Hindu scriptures. The evidence for that assertion lay in a shelf of dusty books contemptuously swept aside by Macaulay's minute on education. Future members of the Indian civil service read Macaulay rather than Müller. Alternatively, they read Mill, who said the same thing in less flamboyant language.

Outside the imperial discourse, Macaulay can seem more progressive in his views on the status and accomplishments of women. At the end of the essay on Madame d'Arblay (Fanny Burney), for instance, he commends her for removing the stigma that had become attached to novels and for vindicating "the right of her sex to an equal share in a fair and noble province of letters. . . . The novels which we owe to English ladies form no small part of our literary glory" (6:75). The statement works hard to be generous, but there are restrictions surrounding it, focused in the indefinite article. English ladies are entitled to an equal share of only a single "fair and noble province," in which their "fine observation," "delicate wit," and "pure moral feeling" can be effectively displayed. Such commendations confer literary recognition on the "sweet attractive grace" of Milton's Eve, leaving the great game to an Adam heroically formed for contemplation and the valorous deeds of empire.

More forthright is Macaulay's rejoinder to Mill's proposal for a franchise including "all males of mature age, rich and poor, educated and ignorant." Mill stops short of extending this proposal to women, and Macaulay, in an accusation strikingly in advance of its time, charges him with placidly dogmatizing away "the interest of one half of the human race" (p. 597).

Macaulay withdrew this essay later not because he regretted his findings but because he felt he "should have refrained from using contemptuous language regarding *the* historian of British India."[12] The definite article defers to a discourse as well as to the author who is its sign. Within that discourse, elaborations of the feminine remain determined by the imperative of establishing and repudiating India's otherness. The hierarchical complementarity so prominent in Owenson's styling of the East-West encounter is not appropriate to that imperative. It must be moved back from the intercultural realm it insidiously interrogates to the safer confines of English domesticity. A more dismissive view of the feminine needs to be nurtured in the rich earth of Bengal.

A Bengali Renaissance was under way when Macaulay arrived in India and adds another layer of insensitivity to his remarks. They are of little profit to his narrative. Clive's achievement would be more heroic if a less pusillanimous people were subdued. But Macaulay has already set the stage for an achievement worthy of a second *Lusiads*, a poem he read twice on the voyage from Madras to Calcutta.[13] The heroic deeds he is about to celebrate are not only unsung but also largely unknown. Every schoolboy has learned about the conquest of Mexico, but few have been told about the conquest of India, a far more impressive feat of arms (p. 306). Ignorance about India seems unlikely in a Europe where the Orient was in vogue, where best-selling poems and novels about India were being printed, and where Queen Victoria was sitting up at night reading the galleys of *Confessions of a Thug* because she could not wait for publication.[14] Nevertheless, there can be ignorance not of the chronicle of events but of the true dimensions of a story yet to be told.

To add to the obstacles Clive faced, the British footholds in India are reduced to a toehold—"a few acres for purposes of commerce" (p. 315). The precariousness of the British position is contrasted with the exaggerated dominance of the French, expressed in the person of the "subtle and ambitious" Joseph-François Dupleix (p. 317). The enemy is a European nation, not a primitive people armed largely with bows and arrows, as Macaulay took the Aztecs to be until he read William Prescott's *History of the Conquest of Mexico* ten years later.[15] Dupleix "ruled thirty millions of people" in India "with almost absolute power" (p. 318).

Clive served three times in India. On the first occasion, he disposed of the French threat. During the second term, he won the battle "which was to decide the fate of India" (p. 338). On the third occasion, he returned as a statesman, rather than as an accountant turned soldier, to curb the excesses brought about by his conquest of Bengal. His reforms were in the right direction but did not go far enough. The nabobs became the ostentatious symbol of everything that was amiss in India: "If any of our readers will take the trouble to search in the dusty recesses of circulating libraries for some novel published sixty years ago, the chance is that the villain or subvillain of the story will prove to be a savage old Nabob, with an immense fortune, a tawny complexion, a bad liver and a worse heart" (p. 363).

In 1770, the rains failed in Bengal and the valley of the Ganges was filled with "misery and death. . . . The Hoogley every day rolled down thousands of corpses close to the porticoes and gardens of the English conquerors." We can gauge the dimensions of this tragedy from the sentence that innocently or ironically follows: "The proprietors of East India Stock were uneasy about their dividends" (p. 365). The storm broke around Clive's head, as it was to break later around that of Hastings. The mixed verdict of the House of Commons found him guilty of certain offenses but also commended him for rendering "great and meritorious services to his country" (p. 370).

In Macaulay's neatly discriminated narrative, Clive's first visit established "the renown of the English arms in the East." The second visit cemented "the political ascendancy of the English in that country." The third laid the foundations for "the purity of the administration of our Eastern Empire" (p. 372). Attached to this triumphant text is a curious subtext. In his first term at Madras, Clive twice attempted suicide. He failed and felt himself set aside for better things. In 1774, harassed by several ailments, victimized by opium, and wounded by the censure of the Commons, he tried suicide for a third time and was successful. "The pattern is almost too perfect,"

Millgate writes, and "Macaulay wisely allows it to speak for itself."[16] It does not speak very loudly. The triumphant text is not meant to be undone by the almost sotto voce counterpointing of the subtext.

If Clive laid the foundations for administrative purity, Hastings can be perceived as undermining those foundations. His life in India, as Macaulay records it, suggests not that power corrupts but that profit is the mortal enemy of principle. Apart from the vindictive pursuit of Nandakumar to his death on the gallows, all of Hastings's actions—his mercenary onslaught on the Rohillas, his relentless mulcting of Chait Singh, and his stripping away of the wealth of the Begum of Oudh—are condemned by Macaulay and then extenuated on the grounds that they were necessary to maintain the company's dividends. More than one justification has been offered for the acquisition of India. It was acquired in the service of "honour, dominion, glory and renown," because the French or the Mahrattas would have acquired it otherwise, or simply because it was available for acquisition. It may even have been acquired absentmindedly by gifted amateurs intent on the pursuit of something more important. In the face of these fictions, Macaulay's demystifying candor can seem refreshingly informative, but its underlying purpose is to provide the basis for another fiction, a richer mystification in which the *felix culpa* will be reenacted, light will emerge from darkness, and a subcontinent not altogether creditably obtained will hereafter be magnanimously governed. To confess one's failings is to put them behind one, and if profit was regrettably the motive, principle can still be the felicitous result.

It has been pointed out more than once in this book that the East India Company was a business organization and that the history and tactics of the British presence in India can only be adequately understood by bearing in mind the state of the company's balance sheets. Macaulay's deeper intention may be to sever the stubborn link between commerce and empire and to place them on different trajectories, one directed by individual self-interest and the other by imperialism's emerging moral philosophy. Yet in continuing to paint Hastings as the company's loyal and therefore unscrupulous servant, Macaulay by no means places in moral doubt the huge territorial gains that unscrupulousness brought about. Those gains are, after all, essential to his agenda.

In weighing Hastings's achievement against his failings, Macaulay finds it entirely fitting to say that Hastings added considerably to British possessions in India at a time when those possessions were shrinking elsewhere (pp. 434–35). Hastings's founding of the Asiatic Society and his encouragement of Oriental scholarship are briefly mentioned (pp. 437–38), but we can scarcely expect Macaulay to underline Hastings's attention to a culture he himself despised.

A modern scholar might make more of the curiously ambivalent relationship between possession and an understanding both opened up and closed down by possession, by the ventriloquized voice that the dominant voice creates and with which it then proceeds to place itself in dialogue. The pleasures of imperialism and of enlightened pride in marvelous possessions (which Southey found so subtly disturbing) are clearly part of Hastings's makeup but so are the satisfactions and the guilt of conquest, reassuringly contained and atoned for by the uses to which conquest is put.

It is too early in the history of understanding for us to expect exploration of such subtleties from Macaulay, and in any case, his literary temperament leans to the tale well told rather than to the tale searchingly analyzed. Nevertheless, it remains disappointing to find his estimate of Hastings's accomplishment so resolutely limited to balancing the company's books and to enlarging its holdings in real estate. We are at a less than thoughtful stage of self-glorification when the significance of a civilization is taken to be reflected in the size of its empire. Macaulay is never reluctant to make this conjunction, and military supremacy is never absent from his recitals of the splendors that make England preeminent. Walter Houghton may seem excessive in suggesting that Macaulay worshiped force, but he certainly rejoiced in the advantages that force can confer on a people.[17] Linda Colley's view that Britain was a nation whose culture largely defined itself through fighting[18] finds ample substantiation in Macaulay's essays.

It cannot be said that Macaulay's history of "British India," as recounted in the essays on Clive and Hastings, shows any sign of progress at work in that history, let alone a progress sufficiently articulate to urge its own extension into the future. Apart from Clive's alleged purifying of the company's administration, conquest is seen to have brought with it only the catastrophic concomitants of conquest. A different "turn" can be given to imperial history (by those enabled to write it into events) only when conquest is perceived as bringing responsibility in its train. Unchallengeable power cannot effectively be questioned from below. That invulnerability makes it all the more important that it should open itself to questioning from within. The acceptance and weighing of this answerability set the British empire apart from others. This is Grant's atonement put in less fervent language. We have to remember that the decision-making cluster—Bentinck, Mill, Trevelyan, and Macaulay—was not without an evangelical strain in its background.

The rhythm of progress at work in Macaulay's view of history is typically one step back for every two steps forward. We are not looking at a pause while the gains achieved are consolidated but at a regression resulting from the vulnerabilities brought into being by the nature of the advance. With lesser civilizations, there may be no recovery from the step back. Recovery depends on a capacity for self-scrutiny and the will to put the lessons learned from that scrutiny into effect.

The present is predictably the point at which the regression has ended and the requisite conditions are in place for the next advance. Frankness in admitting past errors or excesses becomes evidence that the task of self-examination has been sternly carried out. "It is true," Macaulay says in his 1833 speech on India, that "the early history of this great revolution is chequered with guilt and shame." "How should it be otherwise?," he asks. Men born in humble stations and raised rapidly to dizzy eminences are likely to be "profuse and rapacious, imperious and corrupt" (p. 704).

That situation had now been transformed. Looking at the India that in the following year would be named as the place of his exile, Macaulay saw "peace studiously preserved," "confidence gradually infused," "moderation and clemency" not to be found "in the annals of any other victorious and dominant nation," and a government "anxiously bent on the public good" (p. 705).

With the preconditions in place for India to move ahead, the next step would depend on where it stood in the march of civilization. In the year following his arrival on the subcontinent, Macaulay published an essay on Bacon that may seem as distant as possible from his Indian concerns until we remember that India's position on the Mill curve might well be on the threshold of the Baconian era. In fact, this positioning had been helpfully provided in a letter written by Rammohun Roy to Lord Amherst ten years before Macaulay's essay. Roy was protesting against the proposed establishment of a Sanskrit school in Calcutta "similar in character to those which existed in Europe before the time of Lord Bacon."[19] Such a seminary would succeed only in loading the minds of students with "grammatical niceties" and "vain and empty subtleties," adding nothing to what was known 2,000 years ago. The pre-Baconian system of the schoolmen had kept the British nation in ignorance. The Sanskrit system of education was similarly designed to keep India "in darkness."[20]

Roy can seem like a preliminary advertisement for Macaulay, but unlike Macaulay, his criticism is not directed at the Indian past. Like others in the Bengali Renaissance, he is a heavily overdetermined figure who can sometimes seem more important symptomatically than intrinsically as we thread our way among the determinations. He stands not only at the intersection of two contesting imperial discourses but also at the point of their convergence with a Hindu Renaissance, uncertainly endeavoring to take in the West without thereby assisting the West to take over India. Since the Renaissance itself is largely authorized by the status momentarily conferred on Hinduism following the West's discovery of its ancient greatness, the reform movement finds itself in the awkward position of accepting a gift that both establishes its credentials and underwrites its dependence and of making use of that gift to advance its own autonomy while at the same time implementing much of the donor's agenda.

In a theater so variously peopled, the balance of forces is indeed precarious, and the particular issues that are brought to the foreground in constituting that balance are likely to be much more than themselves. Lata Mani, in an influential article, has shown the importance of suttee as a staging ground for a debate between tradition and modernity in which both terms were given some of their crucial inflections by the site that was constructed to display them. If, in accepting this persuasive argument, we agree to treat tradition and modernity contextually rather than conceptually, we must then take account of the singularity of a context that associated modernity with dominance and tradition with failure to an extent not seen in previous stylings of this debate.[21]

Roy, who has become identified with Indian "reformist" objections to suttee, was obliged in the course of his critique[22] to respond to this situation by devaluing tradition and reinstating origins, by privileging foundational texts over subsequent interpretation, and by circumventing an alleged history of corruption in order to appeal to a pristine purity behind it. The move, irresistibly familiar to students of seventeenth-century England, reactivates within an imperial context the paradoxes of a Puritanism disabled by its own empowerment, by its endeavor to found itself upon and yet also contain the antiauthoritarian potential of the Edenic.

Colonial discourse may have flirted briefly with the figure of a contemporary India fallen from its Edenic-classical past and of Paradise regained through British intervention,[23] as in Elizabeth Hamilton's novel. But one cannot unrestrictedly license the building of progressive potentialities into the founding texts of a subject nation. A discourse that is heavily interpretative cannot sanction moves that are directed against interpretation except as a temporary tactic to secure collaboration on a highly limited agenda. The perils of such permissiveness become more evident when we recognize that the anti-interpretative move is itself deeply interpretative, embedding progressive imperatives in pristineness and bestowing on those imperatives the overriding authority of origins. In the end, it had to be argued that the failure of India lay in inherent flaws rather than historical accretions and that those flaws were entrenched not simply in a "tradition" that could be circumvented but in originating texts that it was impossible to delegitimate. V. G. Kiernan defines the Western position in one remarkable sentence that carries within it more than one metaphor this book should have made familiar: "The Indian mind had walled itself up in such a prison that only a new language could give it a ladder of escape."[24] This is another way of evoking those repeated impasses of Oriental civilizations set out so strikingly by Hegel. The Indian mind had to transcend, not reinvent, itself. It had to offer itself to an epistemological rupture, a seismic shift in the conditions of thought, for which the slow accumulation of preliminary circumstances might normally be charted over centuries. In an imperial world, a stroke of the pen could be all that was needed to initiate the work of change at this depth.

With India looking into the prospect of a new world of learning but fatally constrained from reaching forward to grasp it by the straitjacket of scholastic thought, Macaulay's essay on Bacon acquires a new relevance. Moreover, the essay is as notable for its denigration of Plato as it is for its endorsement of Bacon. Bacon's ire had been directed against the schoolmen, who are usually treated as post-Aristotelian. Macaulay prefers Plato as a negative example, ostensibly because Plato "did more than any other person towards giving the minds of speculative men that bent which they retained till they received from Bacon, a new impulse in a diametrically opposed direction" (4:117). Another reason for Macaulay's choice might be that Plato, of all Western philosophers, is the one most at home in ancient India and that his "bent" is therefore the Indian predisposition.

Given Roy's letter and Macaulay's essay, it would be easy to read the minute expansively as rejecting Plato for Bacon, particularly since so much in the minute lends itself to the contrast drawn in the essay. The minute is both less and more than such a replacement. David Kopf is on the right road in arguing that the competing proposals by Orientalists and Anglicists should be viewed not in the abstract but in the context of a cultural encounter. To proceed further along that road, we have to reflect on the suitability of the term "encounter."[25]

We are not here considering a quest for mutual enlightenment based stimulatingly on the surprise of difference but the manner in which a dominant culture puts itself into relationship with a subjected one. Understanding the subjected culture or even laying down the basis for a dialogue with it is not the primary objective of such a relationship. The dominant culture is concerned with devising managerial strategies that will maximize collaboration and minimize resistance. Making use of the subjected culture's propensities enables these strategies to be implanted in native soil. The subjected culture is concerned with placing the dynamics of reform (to use Kopf's title) in the best possible location within the varieties of acquiescence. Both can participate in and dramatize the contrast between Hinduism's golden age and its present plight, but the fictions erected on that contrast begin by being different and end by being incompatible. The indigenous narrative must be a story of the betrayal of origins. The dominant narrative may accept some of the episodes in that story, but in the end, it will have to argue that the betrayal lay in the nature of the origins. As the dominant fiction shifts into complete rejection of the indigenous version (which at one time it ambivalently sponsored), it becomes apparent that the Orientalist and Anglicist alternatives are different managerial strategies based on different evaluations of what is to be managed. The Orientalist alternative, with its reluctance to recognize that a culture once noble can be wholly beyond redemption, offers itself for elevation into the realm of the literary and the humanistic. The Anglicist view, based on imperial assumptions of superiority that in their nature cannot be dialogic, is less concerned with world understanding than with remaking the world in the Western image. Nevertheless, it cannot wholly eliminate from itself propositions that were once not without power in both Enlightenment and romantic thought.

When we speak of the Orientalist-Anglicist controversy, we think of it as a confrontation with a substantial history—a debate between alternatives that exposure over time had made familiar. This may not be an adequate representation. With three successive governors-general supporting and encouraging Oriental studies, the Orientalist alternative was entrenched in India. Kopf speaks of the Orientalist as "the man of the hour" in 1800, and by 1830, his position in India was, if anything, stronger. Orientalist views were even reflected in the Fort William curriculum, where six vernacular languages were taught and proficiency in them encouraged by prizes.[26]

After Macaulay, what remained of Fort William's functions was transferred to Haileybury, where Malthus was to be a lecturer and Mill's history a prescribed text. But in the years preceding Macaulay's arrival, the prevailing philosophy was that one governed India by becoming familiar with it and by modifying its existing institutions rather than by subjecting them to root-and-branch transformations. Even Roy, who can be quoted as if he were Macaulay, is asking for a shift in attention from the classics to the sciences and not necessarily for higher education in English.

The Anglicist alternative was an import. It had no real roots in Indian soil, not even the soil of the East India Company's premises. Adopting it was an overt act of alienation, widening difference into otherness and calling for conversion rather than cautious change. It established a philosophy of guardianship, of national responsibility for the conduct of empires until the ward came of age in the judgment of the guardian. Passed by absentee rulers, it confirmed the permanence and even the desirability of an aloofness that would make evident to a subject people the distance it still had to travel.

Yet the Anglicists carried the day and may even have carried it before Macaulay's arrival.[27] Looking at the groupings on either side, we can sagely opine that their triumph was predictable. Bentinck was the governor-general, and Trevelyan, with his reforming zeal and a dislike of the Orientalists that almost amounted to hatred, was the person to whom Bentinck listened. Mill, Bentinck's gray eminence, was not actually an Anglicist,[28] but his comprehensive devaluation of India provided a firm basis for Anglicist recommendations. With Macaulay's arrival and his appointment as chairman of the General Committee on Public Instruction, the power to make educational decisions was vested in an anti-Orientalist grouping whose local strength was difficult to challenge. But to point this out is to offer to write history as Macaulay does, building narrative suspense (as he does brilliantly) into the shifting coalescences of parliamentary power. For Macaulay to write thus is part of the literary presentation, but our interest should be in the underlying propulsions as much as in the excitements of the narrative of which individuals and alliances are the dramatis personae.

The Orientalists may have been entrenched in India, but in England and Europe, they were without a constituency. Having roots in the West mattered most in this dispute. Utilitarian and evangelical energies gave the Anglicist movement its national momentum. Behind that momentum were the enabling forces (European rather than simply English) of that discourse spoken for by Mill and Hegel, whose gathering cohesiveness we have traced in previous chapters. The Orientalists had no answer to this array of empowerments. Their own roots may have lain, as Kopf suggests, in a universalism that treated otherness as no more than a cultural differentiation and that emphasized the proximity in essence of the world's major religions. But empires are based on privilege, not universality, and on distinctive identities fashioned to claim that privilege. The now dominant idea of a chosen people destined to lead the march of civilization carried with it the imperial prerogative that is so often the suppressed agenda of the elect. It was spoken for by Hegel, not by Voltaire. The Orientalists failed because their moment was over, because in Hegelian language they were no longer in touch with the epic of the idea. The Anglicists succeeded because they rode the tide of a much larger convergence of forces than the provincialism of their name suggests.

The minute on education may well be the most important document in India's cultural history but only if it is metonymically read in proximity to an extensive complex of attitudes. There has been a remarkable consensus about reading it in this way, a consensus so effective that we need the insistences of scholarship to remind us how limited the minute was in its scope. As Gerald and Natalie Sirkin have reminded us,[29] the choice to be pondered was not between English and the Indian vernaculars but between English and Sanskrit. Moreover, the minute did not recommend that English should replace Sanskrit as the medium of higher education; it merely recommended that higher education, subsidized by the East India Company, should be conducted hereafter in the English medium.

If we (justifiably) treat this modest proposal as making English the language of all higher understanding, it is because we recognize the extent of the British hegemony and the coercive force of an ideology that has been articulated in the previous pages. The universal disposition to read the minute in this way, to discern it as a cultural watershed, to find its consequences still embedded in our attitudes, is wildly disproportionate yet instinctively correct. The minute endures in India's cultural history and haunts the aftermath of independence as a persisting name for much more than itself.

Macaulay's remarks on Indian culture have been quoted often and stand as classics of vituperation. He is not inexpert with the rapier, but in the ancient India he despised, his weapon of choice would undoubtedly have been the mace. En route to India, Egypt receives a preliminary drubbing, but India is, of course, the ideal theater for the absurdly literal reading of mythology as including "medical doctrines which would disgrace an English farrier, astronomy which would move laughter in girls at an English boarding school, history abounding with kings thirty feet high and reigns thirty thousand years long, and geography made up of seas of treacle and seas of butter" (p. 723).

Some of this is natural in a man with no taste for Plato. Some of it is understandable in a newly arrived Anglicist attacking an Orientalist faction that seemed solidly entrenched. But when every allowance has been made for the preferences of the man and the pressures of the moment, we are left with one of the most deplorable statements made by a member of one civilization about the culture of another.

Ridicule is a weapon Macaulay adds to the Mill armory, and the temptation to retaliate is strong since Western myths are not invulnerable to ridicule. But it is more useful and less unintelligent to point to the systematic program of reading about India in which Emerson was engaged and that gathered momentum as Macaulay wrote his minute. Emerson's methodical studies, fully described by Frederic Carpenter and Arthur Christy,[30] included not only the Indian texts that were available in translation but also works on India by evangelicals and others and poems such as Southey's *Curse of Kehama*. For Macaulay, "a single shelf of a good European library" was "worth the whole native literature of India and Arabia" (p. 722). He added unconvincingly that he had never found an Orientalist to deny that finding. Emerson was more generous, combining disapproval of India's current customs and practices with deep respect for its foundational philosophical and religious texts. But Emerson was seeking to understand India, whereas Macaulay was devising a way to rule it. Possession in such cases is nine-tenths of contempt.

That the real aim of the minute on education was to construct an efficient interface between India and the British administration is apparent from Macaulay's text: "We must at present do our best to form a class who may be interpreters between us and the millions who we govern; a class of persons Indian in blood and colour, but English in taste, in opinions, in morals and in intellect" (p. 729). This class was to act not only as a cadre of "interpreters" but also as a conduit for what Macaulay scholars like to call "filtration": "To that class we may leave it to refine the vernacular dialects of the country, to enrich those dialects with terms of science borrowed from the Western nomenclature, and to render them by degrees fit vehicles for conveying knowledge to the great mass of the population" (p. 729). This trickle-down theory worked as badly as trickle-down theories usually seem to do. As Gauri Viswanathan observes, it was unlikely that an anglicized elite in which a limited amount of power was invested would labor diligently at modernizing the vernaculars so as to erode its own monopoly.[31]

English was introduced as a conduit of reform, a means of keeping India in step with (although respectfully behind) the continuing advancement of the West. Ironically, it also became a gesture of removal, increasing the distance between government and the governed and establishing an Olympian bureaucracy within a steel frame of self-righteousness. It has been pointed out that entrenching English simply meant that India's lingua franca would be the language of its rulers and that this had always been so, regardless of who ruled India. But other dynasties made India their home and merged themselves with India. Their cultures were carried with their languages into the fabric of India's multivocality. The British stayed aloof, physically in the segregated world of their cantonments and psychologically on the protective heights of Western superiority and on the platform of racist theories erected later on those heights.

Two generations earlier, Burke had pointed out how the migrant character of the British administration distinguished it from others who had conquered and governed India:

> The Asiatic conquerors very soon abated of their ferocity, because they made the conquered country their own. . . . But under the English government all this order is reversed. . . . Young men, boys almost govern there, without society and without sympathy with the natives. . . . Animated with all the avarice of age and all the impetuosity of youth they roll in one after another; wave after wave, and there is nothing before the eyes of the natives but an endless, hopeless prospect, of new flights of birds of prey and passage, with appetites continually renewing for a food that is continually wasting.[32]

This distinctive alienness of the English, which Burke sees as a failure of responsibility, is seen by Karl Marx in a sharply different light: "Arabs, Turks, Tartars, Moguls who had successively overrun India, soon became Hinduised, the barbarian conquerors being by an eternal law of history, conquered themselves by the superior civilization of their subjects. The British were the first conquerors superior, and therefore inaccessible to Hindu civilization."[33]

Superiority here, as with Mill, Macaulay, and Hegel, lies in the advanced position of the West along the inevitable route of civilization. The march—that thinly disguised metaphor of intellectual fascination with the Napoleonic—may be the irresistible movement forward of the idea, of democratic institutions, or of the organization of the means of production. The underlying momentum can be differently interpreted, but the momentum, however it is interpreted, gives the West a right to leadership, to unconditional control over the marching legions, that extinguishes the nostalgia of subject peoples for institutions that in Hegel's words "do not any longer count in world history." England, Marx continues, is empowered to fulfill a double mission: "the annihilation of old Asiatic society and the laying [of] the material foundations of Western society in Asia." Spenser, Milton, and Cromwell on Ireland and Guyon in destroying the Bower of Bliss speak the same inexorable evangelical language. For Marx also the cost of transformation counts for little against the grim satisfaction that the ground has been leveled for fundamental change: "The work of regeneration hardly transpires through a heap of ruins. Nevertheless it has begun."

Philip Mason finds a "philosophic" basis for English aloofness in Plato,[34] and Plato's stately hierarchies are certainly a more elegant foundation for lofty disinterestedness than the merciless tramp of history's marching armies. There are difficulties in implementing either concept with the sad stuff of human nature, even if it is English. The superior may be inaccessible, but the inaccessible is not therefore superior.

Alienness may have been strengthened by the insulations of an imported language restricted to an interpreter class whom the British, because of the mechanism of government they had devised, had to rely on but also came to distrust. Typical Anglo-Indian novels of the period (and it is difficult to find a novel that is not typical) are suspicious of the Indian intellectual (usually a Bengali) and repose their confidence in those untainted by urban corruption, blissfully ignorant of Macaulay's minute, and hence instinctively loyal to the raj.[35] The interpreter class, brought into being as a mediating agent, becomes a primary locus of subversion. This is only one of the many examples of Aristotelian peripeteia that embellish the narrative of British power in India.

The minute and even the way in which the minute was argued were the consummation of a discourse that now seemed to have attained hegemonic status, articulating not only itself but also the permissible terms of involvement with itself. Nevertheless, the passing of the minute into policy was not accompanied by confident statements about the future of British rule over India. Trevelyan, perhaps the most fervent supporter of the minute, was among the most articulate in voicing his misgivings:

> The political feeling against us in India as foreigners and as destroyers of the independence of so many races and states is very strong.

> The existing connection, between two such distant countries as England and India, cannot in the nature of things be permanent: no effort of policy can prevent the natives from ultimately regaining their independence.

> We are, I fear, notwithstanding all our efforts for the good of the people, an unpopular domination.[36]

Emily Eden's perception is not dissimilar. "In the face of those high hills some of which have remained untrodden since the creation," she was struck by the incongruity of "105 Europeans, being surrounded by at least 3000 mountaineers, who, wrapped up in their hill blankets, looked on at what we call our polite amusements, and bowed to the ground if a European came near them. I sometimes wonder they do not cut all our heads off and say nothing more about it."[37]

What Eden sees in its immediacy is projected by Trevelyan as a narrative of the future in which popular feeling rises, the "existing connection" becomes impossible to maintain, and the Indian people regain their independence. This is a straightforward anticipation, lacking in literary depth. It is more satisfying to take up the theme of the peroration to Macaulay's 1833 speech, in which India's independence becomes England's finest hour. Philip Mason, who makes a quite notable effort to style the history of British rule in India as a self-consuming artifact, finds important precedents in Sir Thomas Munro and Mountstuart Elphinstone: "Whenever we are obliged to resign our sovereignty we should leave the natives so far improved from their connection with us, as to be capable of maintaining a free, or at least a regular government among themselves."[38] Power is yielded reluctantly here, subject to the proviso that irreparable harm should not be done by yielding it. Elphinstone's scenario is more poetic: "The most desirable death for us to die should be the improvement of natives reaching such a pitch as would render it impossible for a foreign nation to retain the government."[39]

An imperialism that can be seen as proceeding magnanimously to its own extinction would make the history of the British in India a well-wrought work of literature, morally edifying as well as aesthetically elegant. It is also a styling not without appeal to a nationalist movement whose triumph would be to have brought about the expulsion of the British by moral coercion rather than by military force. The structure of the fiction is not debated. Indeed, the idea of an imperial regime officially dedicated to its own disappearance is an open invitation to a subject people to press for evidence of a withering away that would indicate that disappearance is a real objective and not a rhetorical claim. The debate is over whether the fiction is taking the steps within itself that would prepare it for the closure it uncomfortably advocates.

Between earlier and later versions of the self-consuming artifact, a less generous view of the English mission in India intervenes. Macaulay participates in this construction as much as in the ones that bracket it. "It is by coercion, it is by the sword, and not by free stipulation with the governed, that England rules India" (14:281), he announces belligerently in replying to a suggestion by W. E. Gladstone that an implicit contract exists between England and India.[40] England's responsibilities to India are unilaterally assumed, not contractually prescribed; they are the moral claim of an advanced imperial conscience arising solely from England's answerability to its own self-image. The responsibilities to which England sees itself called can vary depending on what it wishes to think of itself and on where it chooses to place India in the space between narrowing differences and implacable otherness. After 1857, the typical location of India in that space might offer England an image of the Olympian performance of duties to an ungrateful populace, of character building at the outposts of empire, of exile endured and domestic happiness sacrificed so that the white man's burden might be shouldered. Figures of trusteeship and guardianship could be perceived as proclaiming momentous responsibilities but also as providing abundant opportunities for deferral. Much time could pass before the natives were sufficiently civilized, and in any case, the purpose of the great game was to continue playing the game and not to end it. "The sun never sets on the British Empire" was the enlightening proclamation to be found every week in the center pages of Arthur Mee's *Chil-*

dren's Newspaper. It is a fitting caption for the illusion of permanence. More persuasively, *Kim*, in the timelessness of the imperial pastoral, freezes the great game into a state of being, as the active principle placed in contestation with the contemplative one of the lama's quest.

Marian Fowler sees the history of the British in India as progressing from "crass commercialism" through "sanctimonious ideals of moral and sacred duty" to a "Late Raj period, bloated into overweening pride and arrogance."[41] The discourse to which Macaulay gave the finishing touches was able to accommodate all these forms of greatness. Like other discourses that endured, it combined cohesiveness with elasticity. As the sun sets reluctantly on it, we are able to discern its comic aspects, but the raj revival is more notable for its guilty irony, the result of an understandable desire to eat one's cake while complaining about the calories.

No discourse is totally hegemonic. If Caliban is taught language, his profit on it is not to curse but to argue, or as De Quincey puts it, to equivocate. Arguing results in requests for clarification, and continuing requests will strip a discourse of its saving opacity, its opportunities for evasion and deferral. Power is not necessarily bound by the discourse that gives it dominance. When no further spaces for maneuvering can be found, power can theoretically move to a different platform, but nations can be reluctant to relinquish their answerability to fictions that they themselves have erected and that persist in their own minds as historical and moral loyalties. The hold of an imperial fiction on the imperial mind can be extraordinarily tenacious, so that an exit maneuver within the fiction itself can be preferable to dispensing with the fiction. The turn toward the exit will take place when the assignations of discourse are sufficiently undone for Caliban to ask who really is Caliban. This is the question that Gandhi, through the civil disobedience movement, positioned himself to pose and the point at which the Furies must leave Prometheus.

Afterword:
From Center to Circumference
ॐ

At the end of a long history of misrepresentation, it is appropriate to ask how India might wish to see itself in relation to that history. The undertaking should not be avoided. To avoid it by disengaging from history and by seeking to begin de novo is a perennially attractive but not a real alternative. We cannot imagine in innocence. India is not a state of being frozen in the classical past from which paradigms for the future can be derived. India is unavoidably everything that has happened to India. It cannot eradicate its history or try to slice out of it those parts that embarrass its current definitions of nationhood. It has to find itself in relation to propositions that prevailed in the world of thought for several centuries and that now have to be worked through rather than erased.

The history of the discourse that governed India has to include not only the dominant imperial statement but also a highly articulate nationalist counterstatement. In rewriting India's femininity and in rewriting center-circumference and self-and-other distinctions as unity in diversity, the counterstatement is strikingly effective because much of its power is derived from appealing to the very history that imperial thought devalues. India's incarceration in itself, a proposition favored by evangelists, is similarly rewritten as India's reflexive recourse to its openness, and once again, the appeal is to a history that is claimed to have testified continuously to the rewriting.

Given the cohesion of the counterstatement and its foundations in Indian thought, it seems almost perverse to argue that the emancipatory effort must be directed against it as much as against the imperial statement. A critique of the counterstatement is all the more difficult because it is defensively essentialist, invoking the past not in order to admit its own contingency but in order to place itself outside a history that does no more than write out the forms of meaning of an ultimacy beyond it.

Yet an essentialist construction remains a construction, and in the aftermath of its political success, we can begin to see it as a resistance construction. A resistance construction will have to be rewritten if it is to voice the needs of an independent India. If it is not rewritten, it is likely to become involved in shadowboxing with a substituted dominance. It must then continuingly reconstruct that dominance in order to maintain its own character as a statement of resistance. India, or the Indian establishment, will become the adversary in the counterdiscourse it has itself articulated, and this tendency is not difficult to detect in recent reflections about India by progressive historians.

We might begin with India's femininity. Since the feminine includes half of the human world's diversity, the phrase "feminization of the Orient" calls on us to use it with caution. We have seen India's femininity read in Camões as signifying openness to subjugation; read in Dryden as signifying desirability and wildness; read in Hegel as a delirium of possibilities, with its evaluating center no longer a presence but a void; read subversively by Owenson as an Edenic companionship to a masculine, hierarchically superior West; and read singularly in Shelley as the generative force that bridges the distance between concept and implementation, between thought and its realization in the world.

The nationalist recuperation of India's femininity in response to these varieties of denigration (Owenson and Shelley apart) once again has deep roots in India's history. Indeed, it might be perceived as a defense against that history. The precious stone set in the silver sea and ringed on its other two sides by the world's most formidable mountains has always offered itself to a dream of self-containment, of a protected space that is the ground of a secure distinctiveness. Yet to recall John of Gaunt's speech is also to remember that the sea has not served India as a moat and that its mountains have not served it in the office of a wall. A country whose symbolic geography gathers it to itself has had to live through and survive a history of violation. The unity of India and the intactness of Indianness thus become defensive essentialisms that it is difficult to avoid. Draupadi can be humiliated but not disrobed; the legend not merely preserved in the pages of the world's longest epic but also celebrated in song and dance everywhere in India is tenacious in its hold on the imagination.

In a short story by Mahasweta Devi that Spivak translates,[1] Draupadi's disrobing is resisted by the establishment and insisted on by the victim. The real disrobing is that of the discourse itself. A cloak woven with old embroideries is thrown away to further the subversive enterprise of walking naked. The dismantling question asks how much has changed and whether inviolable India does not still continue to be violated, with the violations now concealed by the mystifications of the nationalist fable. The trope of India's femininity is tellingly unmasked, but we can argue that a different version and not a discarding of that femininity is needed, one in which Elizabeth Hamilton's recognition of feminine India's tenacity of self-knowledge and accommodative strength can be made appropriate to the realities of today. Unity in diversity is a proposition intimately linked to Hamilton's view of feminine India. Accommodative strength is called for by the distinctive cultures now flowering from India's many languages, and tenacity of self-knowledge is needed if a center no longer imperial is to maintain its contestational relationship with the margin.

As a phrase nurtured by historical circumstances, unity in diversity challenges an imperial view of India's unity in which diversity is overcome rather than respected. Like other imperial understandings, the view claims to be rooted in the ethos of the people it subjugates. "The British could not have organized India as they did," Spear observes, "if the people had not already been, as it were, apprenticed to the idea of unity."[2] If Aurangzeb was "the most implacable of annexers," the "real reason for aggression" was "the dogma of Indian indivisibility."[3] It is hard not to notice that in two pages an "idea" has graduated into a "dogma" to be written irresistibly into history by those who profited most from its implementation.

That India is a country offering itself for conquest is a proposition embodied in a memorable metaphor by Camões. We have heard its echoes in Goldsmith, Hegel, Dow, and elsewhere. That the purpose of conquest is to bestow on India a unity that it seeks but that its fragmented, natural state prevents it from attaining is a British innovation with Miltonic origins. The Miltonic presence becomes stronger if we attribute the dramatically swift expansion of British power in India to divine providence rather than to the acumen of the East India Company. There is no lack of such attributions. John William Kaye's 1853 history of the company is particularly earnest in its appreciation of the Almighty's helpfulness, and Burke writes with appropriate solemnity of Britain's "glorious empire given by an incomprehensible dispensation of Divine providence into our hands."[4] Colley even tells us that the "Probable Design of the Divine Providence in subjecting so large a portion of Asia to the British Dominion" was among the topics in an essay competition at Cambridge University, for which an appropriate prize was awarded.[5]

The gifts of an incomprehensible Providence call for exploration of the meaning of the gifts. Good works are not the basis of election, but they can be among its crucial signs. The mysterious purpose of the divine donation can only be worked out and made evident in the moral constructions that respond to that purpose. Imperialisms thus motivated will be tirelessly self-justifying; they will also be Olympian, set apart by election, accountable only to their inner voices. In a secular world, they will wear with righteousness the cloak of a transferred divinity.

Milton's God, armed with golden compasses (a printer's ornament evocative of the divine book now to be the manual of imperial discourse), sets "bounds" to a world delivered from chaos into order. Raphael, his messenger, lays down the principles of "binding" within that world's "just circumference." Lacking those principles and the strong relationship they suggest between bounding and binding, the world would sink back into the chaos from which it was rescued. Adam, professing himself well taught by Raphael's exposition, adds the spatial metaphor that has already been implied to the Archangel's hierarchical modeling:

> O favourable Spirit, propitious guest
> Well hast thou taught the way that might direct
> Our knowledge and the scale of nature set,
> From centre to circumference, whereon
> In contemplation of created things
> By steps we may ascend to God.
> (PL 5.507–12)

Raphael's treatment of the scale is an exercise in continuity. Differences on the ladder are of degree, not of kind, and body can even work up to spirit within the scale's containment. Nothing on the scale needs to be the other of anything else. In fact, the concept of otherness consorts uneasily with the monism Milton espouses in De Doctrina Christiana.

The figure is not inherently imperial, but Milton's figures pull in different directions, despite the imperiously proclaimed cohesion of his text. "God is thy law, thou mine" (4.637) is certainly a statement that an imperial power would not be reluctant to hear from subject peoples. The hierarchical modeling of geopolitical space and the Olympian elevation of the ruler above the "subjected plain" of the ruled (12.640) can be made to join with the dispositions of race, typology, and gender to provide a well-stocked grid for the migration of metaphors. The "direct" and "set" of Adam's acknowledgment to Raphael transmit the coercive force of this compounding.

Center-circumference dispositions are part of the modus operandi of imperial thought, but a city planned to display those dispositions was an innovation in imperial ordering, all the more significant because of its belatedness. Delhi replaced Calcutta as India's capital in 1911, but it took twenty years for New Delhi to be completed and to be given its crucial role in the imperial statement. Nationalist resistance was mounting at that point, and the British were to depart sixteen years later. Stressed by these anxieties, the imperial proclamation engineered by Sir Edward Lutyens was appropriately strenuous, with center-circumference relationships inscribed indelibly not simply in the vistas that led from the subjected plain to the viceregal eminence but even in the redesigning of major intersections as confusing roundabouts. Proceeding along the dominant vista of Kingsway, those devout in appreciation would ascend not by steps but by a carefully determined gradient to that imperial substitute for the house of God, the viceregal palace. The gradient as it now exists is the unsatisfactory result of a long dispute between Lutyens and Herbert Baker, his collaborator and partner. Lutyens referred to it ever after as his Bakerloo.[6] We can now read "Bakerloo" as doing more than truncating the vista of viceregal dominance that Lutyens valued so highly. The truncating also makes more imperious the north and south secretariat buildings on either side of the ramp that have become the true site of power in independent India. This is a result Baker may have foreseen.

New Delhi's relentlessly radial planning has been overgrown but not erased by India's untidiness. Erasure would not be appropriate, given the importance of the wheel in Indian iconography. But the wheel does not privilege either the hub, the spokes, or the rim. Its effective functioning as an icon depends on interdependence rather than on a centralized dominance. India, after 1947, has not moved very far in this direction. In fact, if we recall Britain's fashioning of its role in India from 1760 to 1835 as first successionist, then revisionist, and subsequently assimilationist, we might have to conclude that India today remains becalmed in the successionist phase.

It is unlikely to advance beyond it until it succeeds in engaging its often intoned commitment to secularism with a religiocultural imagining of unity that Indian nationalism once foregrounded but that it is now understandably reluctant to endorse.

Appropriations of Milton form an important presence in imperial thought. The romantics rewrote Milton. In doing so, they rewrote center-circumference relationships in a manner that approaches the Indian principle of unity in diversity. Blake casts Urizen as the first imperialist, making the Fall the totalizing and enclosing of a previous openness. Drawing the just circumference is the primal act of injustice. The Edenic state is contestational rather than hierarchical, creatively unstable, involved in continuing negotiations with itself. Likewise, Wordsworth, in the 1805 version of the Snowdon experience, finds the "imagination of the whole" residing in the turbulent but conjoined voice of many waters and not in the unchanging calm of the firmament above them. The 1850 text imperializes this language, transferring the envisioning of wholeness from the "homeless voice" of the waters to the unifying strength of the omniscience above them.[7] Both Blake and the early Wordsworth help us in annotating the Indian principle so as to open up its brevity and to wrench it away from its incantational status. The phrase is unity *in*, not unity *and* or unity *versus*, diversity. The choice of the preposition is crucial. A philosophy of immanence could be built on that slender bridge.

Center-circumference hierarchizations dominated English thinking about India, subtly nourishing the Reformation roots of that thinking by displacing the creation of the world into the creation of empire. The British wrote Milton's commanding account of the first creation into the conquest of India at the same time that the romantics were undoing that very account. It would be comforting to say that imperialism trudged behind literature in the grand march of understanding. It would be closer to the truth to conclude that the swift and decisive growth of imperial power in India snuffed out the anti-imperial tendencies in romantic literature that might otherwise have led to a different outcome. The dogma of indivisibility is Urizen's dogma, not Aurangzeb's. It is bestowed on Aurangzeb to translate a justification for territorial aggrandizement (which Blake was then energetically questioning) into a deeply felt need of the Indian people.

The omnific word bringing order into the chaos of eighteenth-century India is a submerged but potent figure in Britain's imperial rhetoric. The figure encourages us to exaggerate the self-assurance of Mughal rule. The "collapse" that followed can then be dramatized, and domination by the British can be provided with an appropriate Indian precedent. Spear, a recent historian but not one suspicious of inherited models, underlines this self-assurance by observing with some of the relish of aftersight that Mughal India thought it had the measure of its European visitors and "regarded them as pawns in the never-ending games of politics and commerce." To Mughal India's complacent confidence in its power to maintain itself against external challenges, the northern Europeans "seemed to be heavy, shrewd and dull, and in no context dangerous."[8]

Successionist thinking can be expected to attribute to the Mughals the hegemony it seeks to obtain for itself. It can then view Mughal hegemony in an ironic light as unknowingly vulnerable, as awaiting its perfecting by its inheritors. But hegemony for its own sake is less than acceptable to an imperialism blessed or harassed by a conscience. It can even be argued that previous hegemonies were made vulnerable by the thoughtless pursuit of hegemony for its own sake. A moral foundation for hegemony must be built, and that foundation is best laid (following Miltonic precedents) by stipulating anarchy as the only possible alternative to the "omnific word" of dominance.

Although British thinking about India outgrew the successionist phase, this constituent in it was preserved and even enhanced. Its persistence in Spear's work well after India attained its independence is a reminder of its stubborn vitality as a crucial part of the imperial statement. The unity of India had, of necessity, a high place in that statement, but it was a unity bestowed by a transcendent power on a fragmented India, desiring wholeness but unable to attain it.

The nationalist counterstatement invoked unity in diversity in order to retrieve the idea of unity from this imperial context. In doing so, it resorted to a defensive articulation, but one with substantial roots in Indian thought, which replaced the imperial with the immanent and the potentially contestational. The replacement converged on romantic perceptions and romantic views of the relationship between the fragment and the whole. It also went further, laying the basis for its own deconstruction. The transition from the early romantic view of the fragment as seeking wholeness to the later perception of it as resisting wholeness charts a movement that applies itself with disconcerting relevance to the problems of contemporary India. It also prefigures the movement from modern to postmodern modes of understanding, reminding us that the Indian nationalist poem was high modernist, even to the extent of reaching its maximum articulation at the same historical point as the literary movement it paralleled.[9]

Yet unity in diversity does more than prewrite romantic thought and rescue the idea of unity from imperial contamination. Modern historians can find in the phrase a more accurate description of eighteenth-century India than the central dominance and circumferential anarchy written into earlier stereotypes. The thirty-one-volume New Cambridge History of India, loosely federated like the eighteenth-century India it perceives, may even provide, when it is completed, an oeuvre obtaining unity from diversity, avoiding grand narratives and espousing *petits récits*. C. A. Bayly can now position his contribution to this project so as to put it to us that the Mughal empire was a "much less substantial hegemony" and the society of eighteenth-century India was "more varied" than the "stereotype of decline and anarchy" that was the "unwritten emblem" of the authors of the old Cambridge history.[10] Bayly can even concede that "the presumption that the decline of a powerful, extractive, all-India state in the form of the Mughal Empire brought misery seems a curious reflexive shadow thrown by the imperialists of the following century."[11] Nevertheless, the perspective of the older history "seems now, for all its drama, not so much wrong as manifestly inadequate as a theme."[12]

How the theme will be made adequate is not clear. World pictures are anathema today, but if we insist too much on the density and thickness of the actual, we may be left not with translucence but with an opacity that forbids interpretation instead of stimulatingly resisting it. The more persuasive theme might include a less hegemonic center, a circumference no longer thought of as intrinsically wayward, and the possibility of center-circumference relationships that are cooperative rather than resistant to each other. These sophistications might bring the model up to date and could also locate it within the space of "practical" politics in contemporary India. Unity in diversity goes beyond these refinements and presents itself as a more audacious exercise in risk taking that empowers the margin and inscribes center-circumference relationships as contestational rather than cooperative. We can say that the principle belongs to poetics rather than to politics, but the poetics of politics have a paradigmatic force, substantiated in this case by an Indian political tradition that is as much populist as it is authoritarian.[13]

The contemporary prestige of the margin makes it important that the center should not be lost in the circumference and that diversity should recognize rather than submerge its contestational opposite. When Rushdie writes of the "lust for centrality" and the "Indian longing for form,"[14] he acknowledges a force of consolidation in Indian thought that the word "lust" both intensifies and subverts. "Longing for form" is a phrase that needs to be reinscribed as we recall complaints about Hinduism's formlessness; Lowes Dickinson cowering before the proliferations of temple sculpture;[15] Forster's Fielding returning with relief to "the Mediterranean harmony";[16] Yeats's contrast between "calculation, number, measurement," and "Asiatic vague immensities";[17] and Pound's ugly invective about the "obnubilations" of Indian art.[18] The longing for form is surely most intense when the pressure of multitudinousness bears in on its fragility, when the proliferation of the temple facade and the "complete simplicity / Costing not less than everything" of the temple's inner sanctum are brought together in the interplay of contraries. Rushdie typically and justly questions the "lust for centrality" even as he concedes it, disclaiming the center not as a location but as an exclusive point of reference. As a point of reference, it is parodied by the novel's exuberant paranoia.[19] Likewise, the linearity of Padma's "what happens nextism" is eddied around by the narrator's digressions and dilations, by the refusal of the "squirming facts" (as they are called by Wallace Stevens)[20] to offer themselves to the sequential imperative. But the linearity is significantly not dismantled. The novel's movement to its climax through its own distractions and the devastatingly comprehensive peripeteia of its unraveling testify to a longing for form, manifest even in the forms of undoing.

The point here is not to savor Rushdie's complexities, which would call for much more than limited space in an afterword, but to indicate the degree to which he writes the principle of unity in diversity into the poetics of his novel. Because Rushdie's treatment of the principle is contestational and because of his repeated references to the foremost poet of contestation, Blake,[21] his work nourishes the convergence of Indian and romantic understandings along lines already discussed in these pages.

One far-reaching consequence of placing unity and diversity in a contestational relationship is that center-circumference and center-margin mappings, as well as the typological and progressive readings of history that are annexed to these geopolitical dispositions, will have to be fundamentally rethought. An interesting preface to this rethinking is provided unexpectedly in Paul Scott's *Raj Quartet* and specifically in the many interpretations it offers of Queen Victoria's picture, interpretations carefully placed both in historical time and in the progress of the novel.[22] At first, the picture is a means of teaching Indian schoolchildren the English language, which carries with it the considerable benefit of imparting the meaning of empire through its visual grammar. Outside the picture is the space of uncreatedness. Inside, all is significant, with the scale of nature leading us by steps from the frame's just circumference to the queen's central presence. At the end of Scott's novel, in a grimly comic hyphenation, the picture is described as an "alle-gory." But the most radically destabilizing reading is offered by Barbara Batchelor, who sees the picture more than once as unfinished because the "unknown Indian" is absent from it.

If we carry our reflections on this statement well beyond any point Barbara Batchelor could have intended, it will be apparent that there will have to be unknown Indians as long as we persist in composing pictures. A dangerous consanguinity may exist between spatial forms and political understanding. One virtue of contestational thinking is that it frees us from forms with built-in dispositions of privilege that must then be painstakingly undermined in the very process of inscribing them. Moreover, insofar as the contestational forces are thought of as open rather than adversarial to each other, the dynamic and continuingly changing states of equilibrium at which they arrive may be closer to the turbulence and complexity of the actual than to the current simplifications of political and social mechanics.

It is not customary to read the *Mahābhārata* contestationally, but as the palimpsest of the nation's narration, it is forced into contention with its own overwriting. The torsional forces engendered by its layerings persuade us to find its enlightenments in its entanglements. Its stresses and strains may be specific to itself, but they are also evocative of the founding dubieties that underlie the text of any nationhood. To read it is to carry its problematics into the space that contemporaneity occupies and to add another layer to the palimpsest, rewriting it in response to and in extension of the text's own troubled process of self-formation.

Rigveda 10.129[23] is a more ultimate scene of writing, imagining cosmic beginnings behind the mythohistorical beginnings that are encompassed by the *Mahābhārata*'s overlayings. As befits a poem of the source, it is also a poem of irreducible belatedness. The Shining Ones who are the creation's first witnesses come into being only after previous and unknowable events have set a scene capable of being witnessed. Like Shelley's *Triumph of Life*, *Rigveda* 10.129 ends with a query, but its waterfall of questions following questions descends not into an abyss of indeterminacy but into the peace of the mind's happiness at the possibilities that it has urged into its own life and that it is now unceasingly called on to explore.

It is distressing to do no more than point a passing finger at two works, one exquisitely brief and the other hugely encompassing, that can be crucial to Indian ways of self-understanding. The stringently limited and highly preliminary concern here is to suggest that these works be considered as scenes of writing that bear on our future writing of ourselves.

The disquieting paradox of the *Mahābhārata* as a scene of writing is that it asks not to be rewritten but unwritten. It is the poem of the original trauma and of an ancestral, fratricidal holocaust, of a long, inexorable march toward disaster that enlightened counsel tried vainly to avoid. Strikingly, the poet in the poem is a participant as well as a narrator, a biological parent within the fable as well as an imaginative parent outside it. He is both the voice and the victim of the poem's momentum, an author committed to bringing into being an epic that is struggling not to be. Confronting an independent India at every turn in the road of the nation's life, the *Mahābhārata* calls on us to abort its reincarnation.

Blurring the line between the actual and the imagined is an accusation frequently brought against Indian modes of thought. Literature, in its nature, can place itself outside the accusation. The *Mahābhārata* disturbs us because it is so much more than literature, because the threat of its realization bears so powerfully on the actual, because we must learn to avoid its outcome without altogether disavowing its poetics.[24]

As the previous paragraphs have suggested, it may be impossible not to imagine India, even among those who have identified and reproached those forms of imagining that have served imperial aims. Nevertheless, the imagining must proceed within restraints if we are to circumvent the accusation that the main distinctiveness of the site called India is its endless rhapsodizing of itself. To expose constructions of India by Western dominance and the essentialist counterconstructions of a defensive nationalism is not thereby to mark out a terrain free from the hazards of constructions. The best we can do is minimize those hazards by seeking to define the conditions of our imagining.

The main effort has to be to join the distinctiveness of India's past to the desirabilities of a human project that is itself a construction, sustained but also interrogated by the forms of understanding that enter its composition. Placing ourselves along this line of connection, we can benefit from the perception of India's beginnings as lying not in a single source but in a mixed origination. Such a commencement locates us from the outset amid the instabilities and accommodative stresses of dialogue and prescribes an inaugurating openness that we must struggle continually to disentangle from the institutional closures to which it has repeatedly been subjected.

These closures have often been emphatic enough for many to feel that modern India must turn away from a history in which it is unable to find a foundation or even a precedent. Such a maneuver may be momentarily reassuring because of its disavowals, but it also comes uncomfortably close to conceding the otherness of Indian thought to any progressive agenda. By depriving classical India of any presence in world understanding, it reduces modern India to an epiphenomenon of the West. More insidiously, it entrenches one history by neutralizing another, by implicitly accepting the West's view of the India it appropriated, and by being content to claim limply that an independent India can implement more successfully than a subjected one a program to which it has subscribed but not contributed.

The alternative is not easy to construct (or even imagine), but an India that wishes to write itself into and not merely to be written by world understanding has to fall back on the powerful ambivalences that characterize its founding texts and has to find within their invitations to openness the sustenance it can carry into the present moment. The familiar saying that Hinduism is not a religion but a way of life is too easily appropriated by collective coercions that can prescribe not merely the nature but also the nuances of the way. We need to urge the saying back into the deeper recognition that founding texts should be treated not as prescribing a way of life but as offering a way for the life of thought. The creation hymn in the *Rigveda* is an exemplary charting of this way. We should see it as prefacing and entering into the problem-ridden, multilayered nature of India's two founding epics and as manifest in the extraordinary range of metaphysical possibilities that are embraced by Hindu religiophilosophical texts. Even the Sanskrit language of these texts is creatively many-sided in its floating syntax, in its propensity for indeterminate compounding (the word like the world is pulled apart by what it consolidates), and in the divergent etymological roots of its conceptual vocabulary.[25]

An India stripped of its differences is a subscriber, not a contributor, to world understanding. An India disrespectful of the accommodative strength that has characterized its history will be assimilated rather than accommodated to principles it will be unable to revise or even resist. To set aside or to ignore rather than to reinvigorate India's past is to deny it any distinctive entry into the future. On the other hand, to demand that a modern India, often unreceptive to its past, accommodate a culture now uncertainly located, to filiations and affiliations that seem to resist each other is to set down a compounded difficulty in India's revisionary thinking about itself. It is a difficulty India must confront. In doing so, it must succeed in not confusing the space given to it by Western revisionary thinking with the space its own articulacy is able to find for itself.

India and the West are enormous simplifications, and one cannot be deaf to the irony of using the homogenizing language of imperialism to mark out a terrain for a distinctive postimperial gathering of voices. If the irony is not to become an embarrassment, we need to admit that major coalescences of diversity such as "India," with a long and stubborn history of self-imagining, have a place that is vital in the tissue of cultural thought. They have to be received as opportunities for understanding and not merely as occasions for vigilance. We need to place these compendious namings under the suspicion generated by a long and destructive history of the tyranny of absolutes. We also need to see them as validated by their own persistence, by the place they have earned in our envisioning of ourselves. Perhaps we should proceed to the recognition that essentialist and relativist ways of thinking coexist, constitute each other, and even communicate with each other in the tensions of scholarly language.

These tensions become manifest when we assert that India, a land of many languages and of cultures often vociferous in their differences, is held together by much deeper bonds than a simple community of economic interests. It would be an exaggeration to say that one is driven to this proposition; one is also called to it by what Rushdie describes as the Indian longing for form. That longing must now face the stubborn difficulties of its implementation in a world that cries out, with all the peremptoriness of the actual, for forms of imagining that are answerable rather than Edenic. It must hold itself in place by continually obtaining its legitimacy from a diversity it must not only countenance but also embrace. Essential India was a name withheld from history and was endowed with a mystique by that withholding. In seeking control of its future, the name's meaning must change and its implications must be rewritten. Imagined communities are most potent in exile. They are more credible, although less compelling, amid the abrasions of their reinstatement.

Notes

Introduction: Preliminary Navigations

1 Klaus E. Knorr's important but neglected study, *British Colonial Theories, 1570–1850* (Toronto: University of Toronto Press, 1944), esp. pp. 50–59, examines the significance of mercantilism in the relationship between commerce and conquest.

2 Jan P. Coen, quoted in Brian Gardner, *The East India Company: A History* (New York: McCall, 1972), p. 31.

3 Antonio van Diemen, quoted in ibid.

4 Joshua Child, quoted in Philip Mason, *The Men Who Ruled India* (London: Pan Books, 1987), p. 20. See p. 44 for the East India Company's view that it had to become a "nation in India." Mason's work was originally published in two-volume form under the pseudonym of Philip Woodruff. The two works differ; both are cited.

5 Ramakrishna Mukherjee, *The Rise and Fall of the East India Company* (Bombay: Popular Prakashan, 1973), p. 75. Charles accepted loans from the East India Company to the extent of £170,000 over sixteen years. The company also had to resort to large-scale bribing in the endeavor to protect its monopoly. James Mill estimates these bribes at £90,000 in 1693 (ibid., p. 84). Nevertheless, the New or English East India Company was recognized by Parliament in 1658, having offered incentives superior to the old one. The contest between the two was settled in 1702 by an Instrument of Union.

6 See Mason, *Men Who Ruled India*, p. 19, on the difficulties of balancing the Mahratta presence with the trading relationships being established with the Mughals. The boredom and "amusements" of social life in Bombay during this period are vividly conveyed in Dennis Kincaid's *British Social Life in India, 1608–1937* (London: George Routledge, 1938), pp. 33–53.

7 The senior factor at Surat was William Methwold. In Salman Rushdie's *Midnight's Children* (London: Pan Books, 1982), Methwold is associated with the last British footprint just as his namesake was with the first.

Methwold's bequeathing of his estate on condition that it be left intact reflects the safeguards surrounding Britain's departure from India.

8 For Child's War, which led to the acquisition of Calcutta, see John Keay, *The Honourable Company: A History of the English East India Company* (London: Harper Collins, 1991), pp. 148–68. There are several other accounts, but this is the most judicious.

9 Charnock is described by Brian Gardner as "a singularly ruthless individual—who became a legend in Anglo-Indian history" (*The East India Company*, p. 63). On the other hand, John Keay characterizes Charnock as "an old and respected servant of the East India Company" (*The Honourable Company*, p. 148).

10 For Calcutta in its heyday, see Philip Davies, *Splendours of the Raj: British Architecture in India, 1660–1947* (Harmondsworth: Penguin Books, 1987), pp. 47–76; John Keay, *India Discovered* (London: William Collins and Sons, 1988), pp. 20–22; and John Pemble, ed., *Miss Fane in India* (London: Headline, 1985), pp. 19–21. The best evocation of Calcutta's Palladian elegance is provided in the striking illustrations in Jagmohan Mahajan's chapter on the city in *The Raj Landscape: British Views of Indian Cities* (New Delhi: Spantech, 1988), pp. 39–56.

11 Lucy Hughes-Hallett examines this feminization at work in Dio Cassius's *Roman History* in *Cleopatra, Histories, Dreams, and Distortions* (London: Bloomsbury Books, 1990), p. 49. In the depiction of the battle of Actium on Aeneas's shield (*Aeneid* 8.675–728), Egypt is not only feminized but also animalized and India is associated with the monstrous and the demonic. The shield and its many contrasts between Rome and the Orient are examined in detail in David Quint, *Epic and Empire* (Princeton: Princeton University Press, 1993), pp. 21–31. Ironically, Aeneas as a Trojan and therefore an Asian does not escape feminization by his opponents, who seem particularly offended by his hairstyling. He is described by a rejected suitor of Dido as a second Paris with his greasy hair bound up beneath a bonnet and by Turnus as an Asian renegade curling his hair with heated irons and drenching it with myrrh.

12 Angus Calder's *Revolutionary Empire: The Rise of the English-Speaking Empires from the Fifteenth Century to the 1780's* (New York: E. P. Dutton, 1981) is notable for its recognition of Ireland's place in the formation of English imperialism. R. F. Foster's *Modern Ireland, 1600–1972* (London: Penguin Books, 1988) is of crucial importance. However, neither deals with the potentially embarrassing relationship between England's rejection of Spanish imperialism and its cultivation of imperialism in Ireland. Scholarship on early modern English constructions of Ireland has expanded formidably after Calder. The range of this scholarship is well brought out in Brendan Bradshaw, Andrew Hatfield, and Willy Maley, eds., *Representing Ireland: Literature and the Origins of Conflict, 1534–1660* (Cambridge: Cambridge University Press, 1993). Connections

between imperial perceptions of Ireland and of India remain almost un-examined by the expansion.

13 Stephen Greenblatt's chapter on Spenser in *Renaissance Self-Fashioning from More to Shakespeare* (Chicago: University of Chicago Press, 1980), pp. 157–93, remains the classical examination of this propensity in rela-tion to otherness. Macaulay in his essay on Sir William Temple is strik-ingly clear on the root-and-branch compulsion. (*Critical and Historical Essays and Lays of Ancient Rome* [London: Routledge, 1898], pp. 449–50). When Mountjoy received his appointment in 1600, his plan, according to Foster, "was to make Ireland 'a razed table' upon which the Elizabe-than state could inscribe a neat pattern" (*Modern Ireland*, p. 36).

14 Edmund Spenser, *The Faerie Queene*, ed. Thomas P. Roche Jr. (Harmonds-worth: Penguin Books, 1978), p. 1196n. References to *The Faerie Queene* are to this edition.

15 Ibid., p. 1187n.

16 References to Milton's poetry are to John Carey and Alastair Fowler, eds., *The Poems of John Milton* (London: Longmans, Green, 1968). *Paradise Lost* is hereafter cited as *PL*.

17 Foster writes of Ireland in 1600 as presenting English observers with a "constant conundrum. How could the Irish be both savage and subtle? Both warlike and lazy? At once evidently 'inferior' yet possessed of un-governable pride? Cowardly, yet of legendary fortitude in the face of death? Socially primitive, but capable of complex litigation?" (*Modern Ireland*, p. 25). All these paradoxes (with the exception of that in the sec-ond question) are applicable to British constructions of India and are in fact used by Macaulay in his essays on Clive and on Hastings (*Critical and Historical Essays*, pp. 524–71, 627–92).

18 Sir John Temple, *The Irish Rebellion* (London, 1641), p. 2; Edmund Spen-ser, *A View of the Present State of Ireland*, ed. W. L. Renwick (Oxford: Clarendon Press, 1970). Foster adds Fynes Moryson and William Cam-den and finds Ireland's alleged Scythian ancestry "a particular favourite" (*Modern Ireland*, p. 32). In "Constructing the *View of the Present State of Ireland*," *Spenser Studies* 11 (1994): 216–23, Jean R. Brink argues that Spenser may not have written the *View*. So far, this possibility has not been widely accepted.

19 Lord Byron, dedication to *The Corsair*, in Frederick Page, ed., *Byron Poetical Works* (Oxford: Oxford University Press, 1970), p. 277. "Wild-ness," used approvingly by Byron, can have completely different con-notations in an imperial discourse with a strong religious constituent. Milton's repeated employment of the word invests it heavily with infer-nal associations. Hegel uses the term routinely in pointing to India as a site of passion and extravagance.

20 *Prometheus Unbound* 2.4.94, in Thomas Hutchinson, ed., *The Complete Poetical Works of Percy Bysshe Shelley* (London: Humphrey Milford,

Oxford University Press, 1907). References to Shelley's poetry are to this edition.

21 M. M. Kaye, *The Shadow of the Moon* (1957, rptd. Harmondsworth: Penguin Books, 1979), pp. 79, 37. Elsewhere, Lucknow is described as a "beautiful, barbaric city" and as an "evil, beautiful, fantastic city" (pp. 379, 28).

22 Oliver Goldsmith, *Goldsmith's History of Man and Quadrupeds with Numerous Original Notes* (London: Smith Elder and T. Tess, 1838), 2:23. Goldsmith's remarks are original only as reflection. The description, as the editors note, is taken largely from Georges Buffon's *Histoire Naturelle*.

23 Percival Spear, *India: A Modern History*, rev. ed. (Ann Arbor: University of Michigan Press, 1972), p. 226.

24 Schlegel's openness to otherness is well brought out by Gary Handwerk: "Envisioning India: Friedrich Schlegel's Sanskrit Studies and the Emergence of Romantic Historiography," *European Romantic Review* 9, 2 (Spring, 1998), pp. 231–42. Other scholars have drawn attention to Schlegel's subsequent disillusionment with India. Handwerk argues that Schlegel saw founding Sanskrit texts as envisioning an India that was not fully realized even in classical India and from which India's subsequent history made it more distant. The ideal remains in being for assimilation into a world understanding that is implicitly Germanic.

25 *Prometheus Unbound* 3.4.179.

26 Ibid., 3.4.577–78.

27 Partha Chatterjee, *The Nation and Its Fragments: Colonial and Postcolonial Histories* (Princeton: Princeton University Press, 1993).

28 Benedict Anderson, *Imagined Communities: Reflections on the Origin and Spread of Nationalism* (London: Verso Books, 1983).

29 Quint, *Epic and Empire*, esp. pp. 8–9.

30 Said does say that the Orient is one of Europe's "deepest and most recurring images of the other," but the same sentence also characterizes the Orient as Europe's "cultural contestant." The next sentence adds that "the Orient has helped to define Europe (or the West) as its contrasting image, idea, personality, experience" (Edward W. Said, *Orientalism* [New York: Vintage Books, 1979], pp. 1–2). The language is more qualified than the reports of it that are offered. It is notable that Said does not even mention the other in his index.

31 Edward W. Said, *Beginnings: Intention and Method* (New York: Basic Books, 1975), esp. pp. 5–6, 50–51.

32 Edward W. Said, "Representing the Colonized: Anthropology's Interlocutors," *Critical Inquiry* 15 (Winter 1989): 223.

33 Greenblatt, *Renaissance Self-Fashioning*, esp. chapter 4 on Spenser; Stephen Greenblatt, *Learning to Curse: Essays in Early Modern Culture* (London: Routledge, 1990) and *Marvelous Possessions: The Wonder of the New World* (Chicago: University of Chicago Press, 1991); Michel de Cer-

teau, *Heterologies: Discourse on the Other*, trans. Brian Massumi (Minneapolis: University of Minnesota Press, 1986) and *The Writing of History*, trans. Tom Conley (New York: Columbia University Press, 1988).

34 Tzvetan Todorov, *The Conquest of America: The Question of the Other* (New York: Harper Perennial, 1992).

35 Ibid., p. 247.

36 Ibid., p. 87.

37 Todorov's formulation of this recognition is extraordinary: "The cultural model in effect since the Renaissance, even if borne and assumed by men, glorifies what we might call the feminine side of culture: improvisation rather than ritual, words rather than weapons" (ibid., p. 92). These remarks are unlikely to convince many feminists and will not move those who think that superior weaponry had something to do with the British conquest of India.

38 Ibid., pp. 248-49.

39 David Spurr, *The Rhetoric of Empire: Colonial Discourse in Journalism, Travel Writing, and Imperial Administration* (Durham: Duke University Press, 1993).

40 Gayatri Chakravorty Spivak, *In Other Worlds: Essays in Cultural Politics* (London: Routledge, 1988) and *Outside in the Teaching Machine* (London: Routledge, 1993); Homi Bhabha, *The Location of Culture* (London: Routledge, 1994); Lisa Lowe, *Critical Terrains* (Ithaca: Cornell University Press, 1991); Sara Suleri, *The Rhetoric of English India* (Chicago: University of Chicago Press, 1992). To these should be added Kate Teltscher's *India Inscribed: European and British Writing on India, 1600-1800* (Delhi: Oxford University Press, 1995). For further discussion, see my review article, "Excess of India," *Modern Philology* 95, no. 4 (May 1998): 490-500. Jyotsna G. Singh's *Colonial Narratives/Cultural Dialogues: Discoveries of India in the Language of Colonialism* (London: Routledge, 1996) is more hospitable than the above to Said's overall statements. S. P. Mohanty's "Us and Them: On the Philosophical Bases of Political Criticism," *Yale Journal of Criticism* 2, no. 2 (1989): 1-31, is not a study in the undoing of discourse, but by positing a minimal rationality that self and other must share, it lays open to interrogation within imperial discourse itself the extreme versions of otherness that discourse can generate.

41 Bhabha, *Location of Culture*, p. 174.

42 W. B. Yeats, "Per Amica Silentia Lunae," in W. B. Yeats, *Mythologies* (London: Macmillan, 1959), p. 340.

43 Suleri, *Rhetoric of English India*, pp. 16-17, 272.

44 Raleigh Trevelyan, *The Golden Oriole: A 200 Year History of an English Family in India* (New York: Simon and Schuster, 1987), pp. 202-3. The phrase encapsulates a notorious remark in E. M. Forster, *A Passage to India*, ed. Oliver Stallybrass (London: Penguin Books, 1985), p. 34. The remark is antedated in a novel by G. A. Henty, who pushes the memsahib

factor as far back as 1857 in *Rujub the Juggler* (New York: Hurst, 1901), pp. 29, 33. Discussion of the issue has been extensive and vigorous.

45 Yeats's thinking about the mask is in effect a claim that one must inhabit the other in order to know the self. There is a distinction (based on Blake's distinction between specter and emanation) between a true mask that leads back into the self and a false mask that leads away from it. The nature of true and false masks is determined by the system rather than by the individual or the collective. Yeats's formulation acknowledges a necessary collusion between the self and the other that is brought out clearly in "Ego Dominus Tuus": "I call to the mysterious one who yet / Shall walk the wet sands by the edge of the stream / And looks most like me, being indeed my double / And prove of all imaginable things / The most unlike, being my anti-self" (in Richard J. Finneran, ed., *W. B. Yeats: The Poems* [New York: Macmillan, 1983], p. 162).

46 Bhabha, "Articulating the Archaic: Cultural Difference and Colonial Nonsense," in Bhabha, *Location of Culture*, pp. 123–38. Bhabha's specific example is the "Boum, Boum" of Forster's Marabar Caves. The noise parodies the sacred word "Om" and does indeed reduce ultimate origination to self-reproducing nonsense. Nevertheless, the point made is not simply about incomprehensible India but also about the manner in which the word is heard differently within the limitations of those who listen to it. This is a proposition familiar in Indian philosophy, with Sankara as its most notable exponent. Forster prepares us for this realization in the opening pages of his book, and Eliot in the final section of *The Waste Land* (published two years before *A Passage to India*), as well as in the epigraphs to *Four Quartets*, is advising us similarly of the relativities of understanding. As Cleo Kearns notes, the Upanishadic glosses of the sound "da" emitted by the thunder "are the products or projections of three communities of interpretation . . . each of whom have listened to the original sound and heard in it their particular word or message" (Cleo Kearns, *T. S. Eliot and Indic Traditions: A Study in Poetry and Belief* [Cambridge: Cambridge University Press, 1987], p. 221). It is, of course, impossible to decide whether the same word is being heard differently or whether different words are being heard, but the possibilities of communication between cultures will depend on the presupposition adopted. Imperial power and its view of the nature of otherness seem committed to the second presupposition. The other is untranslatable and yet paradoxically kept in place by being translated. Both transparency and inaccessibility to the imperial gaze are involved in a conundrum of power that thrives on the success and feeds on the failure of that gaze. With some simplification, we could treat *Kim* as a novel of transparency and *A Passage to India* as a study in the opaque.

47 Suleri, *Rhetoric of English India*, pp. 2–6, 21, 28, 112.

48 Edward W. Said remarks that *Kim*'s "picture of India exists in a deeply antithetical relationship with the development of the movement for

Indian independence," *Culture and Imperialism* (New York: Knopf, 1993),
p. 32. See also Jon Thompson, *Fiction, Crime, and Empire* (Urbana: University of Illinois Press, 1993), pp. 89–90. The postcolonial cult of *Kim* calls for examination. It is remarkable that the exclusions of a novel should be treated as adding to its charm and not as questioning its depth of understanding.

49 Said, *Culture and Imperialism*, pp. xii–xiii, 69–71. See also Said's "Representing the Colonized," p. 221, for narrative as "a major cultural convergence" that has "resonated with echoes from the imperial context."

50 See Balachandra Rajan, *The Form of the Unfinished* (Princeton: Princeton University Press, 1985), where this argument is developed at length.

51 In the nineteenth-century deification of history, the march of mind is a crucial metaphor for the conquest of the world by the idea. Keats is responsive to this tide of thought to the extent that he agrees that "there really is a grand march of intellect." He adds that in promoting that march "a mighty providence subdues the mightiest minds to the service of the time being" (Hyder Edward Rollins, ed., *The Letters of John Keats* [Cambridge: Harvard University Press, 1958], 1:282). It is this "general and gregarious advance of intellect" that enables Wordsworth to see farther into the "dark passages" of the mind than Milton. There is a potential contention here between the intellect and the emotions that Keats intensifies by promising that in *Hyperion* the march of passion and endeavor will be undeviating (p. 207). When he moves later to the conclusion that the heart is the "Mind's Bible," the "Mind's experience," and the "teat from which the mind or intelligence sucks its identity" (2:102–3), he has powerfully modified his original commitment to the march.

52 Jawaharlal Nehru's *Discovery of India* (New York: John Day, 1946) and his speech proclaiming India's independence are the classic articulations of this counterpoem. It is instructive to note that a scholarly statement by professional historians such as Bipan Chandra, Mridula Mukherjee, Aditya Mukherjee, K. N. Panikkar, and Sucheta Mahajan in *India's Struggle for Independence, 1857–1947* (New Delhi: Penguin Books, 1989) also sees form emerging from fragmentation, with the gathering cohesion and widening inclusiveness of the Indian nationalist movement speaking in the end not only for India but also for all subjected peoples.

53 Greenblatt, *Learning to Curse*, pp. 179–80. The semiemancipation that Greenblatt characterizes with adroitness is "by no means autonomous" but is also "not reducible to the institutional and economic forces by which it is shaped."

54 The study of imperial relationships offers a dimension to gender studies that has yet to be adequately explored. The suggestions for exploration made so far refer to traffic from the theater of gender to the imperial world. Movement in the reverse direction may be as important and has scarcely been examined.

55 Said, *Culture and Imperialism*, pp. 161, 132.

56 Barbara Johnson, *A World of Difference*, 2d ed. (Baltimore: Johns Hopkins University Press, 1989).

57 The secret name is linked to Adamic naming, which is part of Adam's assumption of "dominion absolute" over "beast, fish, fowl" (*PL* 12.67–68). The names are given to Mowgli by the serpent Ka, the oldest inhabitant of the jungle, who is therefore the jungle's memory. Ka, not accidentally, means "who." The second part of Mowgli's claim to leadership is that he can outstare any creature in the jungle in eyeball-to-eyeball confrontations. The imperial gaze is transparently evoked, but we are also made aware that superior knowledge gives the gaze its power. As Ronald Inden points out in *Imagining India* (Oxford: Basil Blackwell, 1991), pp. 86–87, the jungle is a familiar metaphor for India.

58 Forster, *Passage to India*, p. 178.

59 I do not seek to evade the possibility that indeterminacies may be not residual but central (as the Draupadi legend disturbingly suggests), that spaces of indeterminacy resist determination of their limits, and that the underground proliferation of these spaces makes it impossible to cordon them off. I merely raise the question here and elsewhere of whether readings of historical events are entirely coincident with these readings of textual behavior.

60 Hyperbolic acceptance that draws on the general reliance on hyperbole of court poetry, Eastern and Western, can also be discomfiting by pressing hegemonic claims to the boundaries of absurdity. Thus Keshub Chander Sen's encomium of Queen Victoria (in Stephen Hay and I. H. Quereshi, comps., *Sources of Indian Tradition* [New York: Columbia University Press, 1958], 2:66–67) can be read according to taste as either wittily subversive or grovelingly servile.

61 Edward W. Said, "Orientalism Reconsidered," in *Literature, Politics, and Theory*, ed. Francis Barker, Peter Hulme, Margaret Iversen, and Diana Loxley (Colchester: University of Essex Press, 1985), p. 215.

62 Postmodernism was seen initially as a conspicuously male movement, with feminism perceived largely as an image of the movement's self-marginalization (Susan Rubin Suleiman, *Subversive Intent: Gender Politics and the Avant-Garde* [Cambridge: Harvard University Press, 1990], pp. 186–89; Linda Hutcheon, *A Poetics of Postmodernism: History, Theory, Fiction* [London: Routledge, 1988], pp. 61–71). Matters have now advanced to the point where Sara Suleri can warn us against "the dangerous democracy accorded the coalition between postcolonial and feminist theories in which each term serves to reify the potential pietism of the other" (Sara Suleri, "Women Skin Deep: Feminism and the Postcolonial Condition," *Critical Inquiry* 18 [Summer 1992]: 759). The coalition between the postmodern and the postcolonial is subject to the same cautions, particularly when we take into account the traditional feminizing of subjected peoples. The two movements do indeed share (and share

with feminism) a considerable range of metatactics, but the method should not be taken as all of the message. Kwame Anthony Appiah's "Is the Post- in Postmodernism the Post- in Postcolonial?" *Critical Inquiry* 17 (Winter 1991): 336–57 suggests some desirable distinctions. See also Linda Hutcheon, " 'Circling the Downspout of Empire,' " in *Past the Last Post: Theorizing Post-Colonialism and Post-Modernism*, ed. Ian Adam and Helen Tiffin (Calgary: University of Calgary Press, 1990), pp. 167–89.

63   Jean François Lyotard, *The Postmodern Condition: A Report on Knowledge*, trans. Geoff Bennington and Brian Massumi (Minneapolis: University of Minnesota Press, 1981). "The form of the unfinishable" is not Lyotard's phrase. For Said's objections to Lyotard, see "Representing the Colonized," pp. 222–23. Jameson continues to be committed to a grand narrative and to a cultural logic that responds to the logic of that narrative. Since the grand narrative is embedded in the political unconscious, the response to it will be complicated by the patterns of behavior that the unconscious exhibits. *Petits récits* can be treated as avoidances of a grand narrative that will nevertheless manifest itself intermittently and sometimes eruptively through those avoidances.

64   There is a latent absolutism in this kind of almost metaphysical resistance to totalization that must guard against being tainted by what it opposes.

65   See Masao Miyoshi, "A Borderless World? From Colonialism to Transnationalism and the Decline of the Nation-State," *Critical Inquiry* 19 (Summer 1993): 726–51. Describing postcoloniality as a condition that is "safely distant and inert," Miyoshi goes on to argue that by dedicating our attention to it or even to post-Marxism, "we are fully collaborating" with the "hegemonic ideology" of transnational corporations, "which looks, as usual, as if it were no ideology at all" (p. 751). Colonialism (in the forms it has hitherto assumed) may be safely distant and inert, but postcoloniality, in seeking to erase or relocate the cultural and psychological legacies of colonialism, has not by any means laid those problems to rest. Miyoshi is, of course, right in pointing to a more immediate and menacing agenda to which attention must be given.

66   It should be apparent from this paragraph that I do not endow discourse with the kind of sovereignty to which Aijaz Ahmad objects in *In Theory: Nations, Classes, Literatures* (London: Verso Books, 1992). Nevertheless, I treat discourse as exercising a constitutive force and not as merely offering a mediating facility.

1. The Lusiads and the Asian Reader

1   Luis Vaz de Camões, *The Lusiads*, trans. Leonard Bacon (New York: Hispanic Society of America, 1950), p. xix. References to *The Lusiads* are to this translation.

2　James H. Sims, "The Epic Narrator's Mortal Voice in Camões and Milton," *Revue de Littérature Comparée* 51 (1977): 374–84; L. Martz Louis, "Camoens and Milton," *Ocidente: Revista Portuguesa de Cultura*, special issue (November 1972): 45–59.

3　*The Lusiads*, p. xxv.

4　*PL* 4.172–77.

5　William Julius Mickle, *The Lusiad; or The Discovery of India: An Epic Poem* (Oxford: Jackman and Lister, 1776), p. cxlvii. Mickle was by no means a responsible translator. For an account of his inventions and omissions, see George S. West, "W. J. Mickle's Translation of *Os Lusiads*," *Revue de Littérature Comparée* 18 (1938): 184–95.

6　Afonso de Albuquerque, quoted in Mukherjee, *Rise and Fall of the East India Company*, p. 100.

7　William C. Atkinson, *A History of Spain and Portugal* (Harmondsworth: Penguin Books, 1960), p. 148; G. V. Scammell, *The First Imperial Age: European Overseas Expansion, c. 1400–1715* (London: Unwin Hyman, 1989), pp. 97, 14.

8　This paragraph draws on Scammell, *First Imperial Age*, pp. 12–17, 67–101; G. V. Scammell, *The World Encompassed: The First European Maritime Empires, c. 800–1650* (Berkeley: University of California Press, 1981), pp. 275–30; Fernand Braudel, *The Mediterranean and the Mediterranean World in the Age of Phillip II*, illus. ed., trans. Sian Reynolds (New York: Harper Collins, 1992), pp. 383–406; and C. R. Boxer, *The Portuguese Seaborne Empire, 1415–1825* (London: Hutchinson, 1969), pp. 39–64. John Dos Passos's *The Portugal Story: Three Centuries of Exploration and Discovery* (London: Robert Hale, 1970) is rich in evidence but suffers from heroic idealization.

9　In 1647, Fletcher's *Island Princess* describes itself as set in India, whereas its setting is the Spice Islands of Ternate and Tidore. The habit persists into the nineteenth century. India proper is referred to as West India and the East Indies as the other India. See, e.g., Emily Hahn, *Raffles of Singapore: A Biography* (New York: Doubleday, 1966), pp. 89, 163, 202.

10　K. M. Panikkar, *A Survey of Indian History* (Bombay: National Information and Publications, 1947), p. 116.

11　Heinrich Zimmer, *The Art of Indian Asia*, ed. Joseph Campbell (Princeton: Princeton University Press, 1988), 1:363. For a more problematized account, see K. N. Chaudhuri, *Asia before Europe: Economy and Civilization of the Indian Ocean from the Rise of Islam to 1750* (Cambridge: Cambridge University Press, 1990), pp. 58–61.

12　*The Lusiads*, p. 395n.

13　Christopher Ricks, ed., *The Poems of Tennyson* (London: Longmans, Green, 1969), pp. 1441–49. Ricks's headnote indicates the extent of Tennyson's research. On the Portuguese mission to Akbar's court, see Bamber Gascoigne, *The Great Moghuls* (London: Jonathan Cape, 1971), pp. 110–15; on Akbar's "religion," see pp. 115–19. Tennyson's poem makes British rule over India a fulfillment of Akbar's vision, which Aurangzeb all but destroyed. British rule is thus domesticated by being placed in succession to enlightened Mughal intentions. The canonical contrast between Akbar and Aurangzeb can then be presented as a regression that British power is fortunately able not only to reverse but also to consummate in the triumph of Christianity, as the religion into which other religions must flow.

14 R. H. Major, "Journey of Abd-Er-Razzak," in *India in the Fifteenth Century: Being a Collection of Narratives of Voyages to India*, ed. R. H. Major (1858; reprint, New Delhi: Asian Educational Services, 1992), p. 23.

15 Robert Sewell, *A Forgotten Empire (Vijayanagar): A Contribution to the History of India* (reprint, New Delhi: Asian Educational Services, 1982), p. 257. Paes's narrative is reprinted on pp. 236–90.

16 Scammell, *First Imperial Age*, p. 81.

17 Panikkar, *Survey of Indian History*, p. 176.

18 Ibid., p. 226.

19 Burton Stein's *Vijayanagar* (Cambridge: Cambridge University Press, 1990) is the most up-to-date and scholarly account available of the Vijayanagar kingdom. I have also drawn on the following for this paragraph: Sewell, *Forgotten Empire*; R. C. Majumdar, H. C. Raychaudhari, and Kalinkar Datta, *An Advanced History of India*, 4th ed. (Madras: Macmillan, 1978), pp. 359–74; Romila Thapar, *A History of India* (1965; reprint, London: Penguin Group, 1990), 1:324–36; and K. A. Nilakanta Sastri, *A History of South India*, 4th ed. (Madras: Oxford University Press, 1966), pp. 264–312.

20 Sewell, *Forgotten Empire*, p. 128.

21 One should contrast this with Paes's observation that Vijayanagar's standing army (which he estimated at 1 million) consisted of "the finest young men possible to be seen or that ever could be seen, for in all this army I did not see a man that would act the coward" (ibid., pp. 279, 281).

22 Ibid., p. 208.

23 Kenneth Curry, ed., *New Letters of Robert Southey* (New York: Columbia University Press, 1971), 1:337.

24 See Bailey W. Diffey and George D. Winius, *Foundations of the Portuguese Empire, 1415–1580* (Minneapolis: University of Minnesota Press, 1977), pp. 181–83, 186. This misunderstanding is amusingly developed in E. G. Ravenstein, ed., *A Journal of the First Voyage of Vasco da Gama, 1497–1499* (1898; reprint, New Delhi: Asian Educational Services, 1995), p. 49.

25 Sir Walter Raleigh, *The History of the World*, ed. C. A. Patrides (Philadelphia: Temple University Press, 1971), p. 173.

26 Said, *Culture and Imperialism*, p. 9. The soliciting of Western domination is carried extraordinarily far back into Indian history by Jonathan Fast in his novel *Golden Fire* (New York: Arbor House, 1986). Here we

meet a princess with skin "white as rice flower," hair "like burnished gold," and eyes "blue as the sky" (p. 15), a Goth from the "Land of Ice" (p. 17) whose father was a general in the Roman army and who is now one of the wives of the emperor, Samudra Gupta. She gives birth to a son, conspicuously blond haired, who defeats Rama, the villainous and perverted claimant to the throne, marries the beauteous Dhruvadevi, and brings India an era of prosperity.

27 Greenblatt, *Renaissance Self-Fashioning*, pp. 172–92.

28 See chapter 4.

29 Richard Helgerson, *Forms of Nationhood: The Elizabethan Writing of England* (Chicago: University of Chicago Press, 1992), pp. 155–76, 189–90.

30 C. M. Bowra, *From Virgil to Milton* (London: Macmillan, 1945), p. 138.

31 Thomas Greene, *The Descent from Heaven: A Study in Epic Continuity* (New Haven: Yale University Press, 1963), p. 225.

32 Gerald M. Moser, "What Did the Old Man of the Restelo Mean?," *Luso-Brazilian Review* 17 (1980): 149. The old man's harangue is also considered by Jack E. Tomlins, who argues that two playlets written by Gil Vicente in 1509 and 1520 are echoed in the episode. He concludes that the opening dedication, the old man's rebuke, and the disillusioned envoi of the epic were all composed after the poet's return from India. The poem "flies apart at three junctures," thus undoing "the very business of the epic." Before *The Lusiads* was published, Camões "saw the Oriental conquest—with India the brightest diamond in the crown—as mere vanity and total ruin" (Jack E. Tomlins, "Gil Vicente's Vision of India and Its Ironic Echo in Camões's 'Velho do Restelo,' " in *Empire in Transition: The Portuguese World in the Time of Camões*, ed. Alfred Hower and Richard A. Preto-Rodas [Gainesville: University of Florida Press, Center for Latin American Studies, 1985], pp. 170–76). Tomlins in effect confirms my view of the marginal location of the poem's misgivings about itself. His argument is that these recantations came too late to enter a central space already occupied by a previous poem. The recuperation via chronology can only be conjectural and is not supported by any evidence except the desirability of the recuperative arrangement, but that desirability makes a statement that will be becoming familiar.

33 Alexander A. Parker, "The Age of Camões," *Texas Quarterly* 15, no. 4 (1972): 11.

34 Kenneth David Jackson, "Alabaster and Gold: A Study of Dialectics in *Os Lusiados*," *Luso-Brazilian Review* 17 (1980): 203.

35 *The Lusiads*, pp. 411–23.

36 Quint, *Epic and Empire*, p. 117.

37 Ibid., p. 120. In genre terms, epic *could* be deflected into romance by the Adamastor episode but maintains its status as epic by fully containing that episode.

38 Ibid., p. 118.

39 Thetis is not to be confused with Tethys.

40 Quint, *Epic and Empire*, p. 124. Quint's reading is disputed or perhaps "balanced" by Lawrence Lipking's in "The Genius of the Shore: *Lycidas*, Adamastor, and the Poetics of Nationalism," *PMLA* 111, no. 2 (March 1996): 218. See also the ensuing correspondence in *PMLA* 112, no. 1 (January 1997): 123–24.

41 Helgerson, *Forms of Nationhood*, p. 190. Mickle's reading is described as a "bizarre twist" in this spiral. Commerce and its relationship to national identity are "central to *The Lusiads*," but Camões worked to suppress what Mickle strove to exalt.

42 The integral relationship between commerce and empire is underlined in Knorr, *British Colonial Theories*, pp. 19–22.

43 C. A. Patrides, ed., *The Complete English Poems of John Donne* (London: J. M. Dent and Sons, 1985), p. 184. The highly male sexual imperialism of this passage is crossed by the uneasiness of submission to a female monarch who lays down the terms of the license, receives the bond for its execution, and imprints both with the royal seal of approval. The appropriately distant site for this uneasiness is Amazonia, which, as Louis Montrose observes, cries out to be invented (Louis Montrose, "The Work of Gender in the Discourse of Discovery," in *New World Encounters*, ed. Stephen Greenblatt [Berkeley: University of California Press, 1993], p. 202). The remoteness of Amazonia makes possible lessons on the perils of role reversal that it would be less than tactful to intone in England. Reducing the monarch's body to colonial status (albeit with her approval) is among the passage's subversive satisfactions. In the process, the seal that was the monarch's property becomes the property of her subject in a restoration of sexual-political normalcy sufficiently peripheral to be discounted even while it continues to be imagined.

2. Banyan Trees and Fig Leaves: Some Thoughts on Milton's India

1 Dryden's play *Aureng-Zebe*, first performed at Drury Lane on November 17, 1675, the year after the second edition of *Paradise Lost* was published, seems to offer a different view of the Orient. Appearances can be wittily misleading, as chapter 3 attempts to show.

2 J. B. Broadbent, *Some Graver Subject* (London: Chatto and Windus, 1960), pp. 101–2.

3 India's association with the land of Faerie is picked up in Keats's "The Cap and Bells or The Jealousies."

4 See James H. Sims, "Camoens' *Lusiads* and Milton's *Paradise Lost*: Satan's Voyage to Eden," in *Papers on Milton*, ed. Philip Mahone Griffith and Lester F. Zimmerman (Tulsa: University of Tulsa Press, 1969), pp. 38–39.

5 Sir Thomas Roe, *The Embassy of Sir Thomas Roe to the Court of the*

Great Mogul 1615-19, ed. William Foster (London: Hakluyt Society, 1899). For Hawkins, see *Early Travels in India, 1583-1619*, ed. William Foster (London: Humphrey Milford, Oxford University Press, 1921), pp. 70-121; for Coryat, see ibid., p. 269. A typically lively account of Roe's embassy is provided in Gascoigne's *Great Moghuls*, pp. 141-50.

6 The phrase is used by Shakespeare in *Love's Labour's Lost* 4.3.218-21, although not with the associations with which Milton invests it. Its most famous and possibly final use is in Wordsworth's sonnet on the extinction of the Venetian republic.

7 As translated in Waldemar Hansen, *The Peacock Throne* (Delhi: Banarsidass, 1972), p. 68.

8 On Milton's revisionary treatment of Camões, see James H. Sims, "A Greater Than Rome: The Inversion of a Virgilian Symbol from Camoens to Milton," in *Rome in the Renaissance: The City and the Myth*, ed. P. A. Ramsey (Binghamton, N.Y.: Center for Medieval and Early Renaissance Studies, 1982), pp. 334-44.

9 Scammell, *World Encompassed*, pp. 101-2.

10 John Milton, *A Mask Presented at Ludlow Castle* 705-35.

11 Adam Smith, *The Wealth of Nations*, ed. Edwin Cannan (New York: Random House, 1994), p. 235.

12 *Complete Prose Works of John Milton* (New Haven: Yale University Press, 1973), 6:352.

13 The view put forward here is consistent with that offered in Sims, "Camoens' *Lusiads* and Milton's *Paradise Lost*," pp. 43-44. See also Quint, *Epic and Empire*, pp. 253-67. Quint rightly observes that "Milton in keeping with his general criticism of the earlier epic tradition exposes as false the distinction which that tradition draws between martial heroism and mercantile activity" (p. 264).

14 Pope Alexander IV, quoted in R. E. Latham, trans., *Marco Polo: The Travels* (London: Penguin Books, 1958), p. 11.

15 See John Drew, *India and the Romantic Imagination* (Delhi: Oxford University Press, 1987), p. 166. Compare *PL* 9.76-82 and the comment in Carey and Fowler, *Poems of John Milton*, p. 860n. Joseph E. Duncan observes that the association of Paradise with India was strongest during the Middle Ages when Prester John was reputed to have established himself in the Far East. With his relocation to Ethiopia, interest in India as the site of Paradise waned (Joseph E. Duncan, *Milton's Earthly Paradise: A Historical Study of Eden* [Minneapolis: University of Minnesota Press, 1972], pp. 76, 195). The most extensive discussion is in Stephen G. Darian, *The Ganges in Myth and History* (Honolulu: University of Hawaii Press, 1978), pp. 172-82.

16 Carey and Fowler, *Poems of John Milton*, p. 695n.

17 Raleigh, *History of the World*, pp. 136-39. Patrides (Intro. p. 38) sees Raleigh as a possible source for this passage, but it should be remem-

bered that Raleigh seems to distance himself from the identification he discusses (p. 38).

18 Carey and Fowler, *Poems of John Milton*, p. 920n.

19 Robert Southey, *The Curse of Kehama* 13.5.

20 Thomas Moore, *Lalla Rookh*, in A. D. Godley, ed., *The Poetical Works of Thomas Moore* (London: Humphrey Milford, Oxford University Press, 1915), p. 42. In an even more fervent commendation of the banyan tree, Sydney Owenson describes it as "the most stupendous and beautiful production of the vegetable world" and as a "symbol of eternity" whose "great and splendid order the Architect of the universe himself designed." Defying "the decay of time, it stands alone and bold, reproducing its own existence and multiplying its own form" (Lady Morgan [Sydney Owenson], *The Missionary*, 2d ed. [London: J. J. Stockwell, 1811], 2:9–10). See also the compendious entry in Henry Yule and A. C. Burnell, *Hobson-Jobson: A Glossary of Colloquial Anglo-Indian Words and Phrases and of Kindred Terms, Etymological, Historical, Geographical, and Discursive,* ed. William Crooke (New Delhi: Munshiram Manoharlal, 1994), pp. 65–67. Milton's lines on the tree were known sufficiently to be quoted by a Bengali Moslem, Dean Mahomed, in a 1794 account (published in Ireland) of his travels in India and departure from it. See Michael H. Fisher, *The First Indian Author in English: Dean Mahomed (1769–1851) in India, Ireland, and England* (Delhi: Oxford University Press, 1996), p. 82.

21 Quoted in Carey and Fowler, *Poems of John Milton*, p. 920n. Although Renaissance herbalists resemble each other markedly in their descriptions of the banyan tree, Gerard's language here is striking in suggesting the essential similarity between the proliferating wood and the barren desert. Both are places of temptation in Milton's work. Gerard's infernalizing of the tree, which romantic writers reverse, should be contrasted with Milton's ambivalences. R. R. Cawley in *Milton and the Literature of Travel* (Princeton: Princeton University Press, 1951) cautions us against searching for single sources of passages in Milton, who usually amalgamates more than one source. S. Viswanathan, "Milton and Purchas's Linschoten: An Additional Source for Milton's Indian Figtree," *Milton Newsletter* 2, no. 3 (October 1968): 43–45, puts forward a case for this ingredient in the conflation. The case is disputed by James Patrick McHenry in "A Milton Herbal," *Milton Quarterly* 30, no. 2 (May 1996): 69.

22 Kester Svendsen, *Milton and Science* (Cambridge: Harvard University Press, 1956), p. 135.

23 Pliny makes the comparison to Amazonian shields, but Raleigh, who claims to have actually seen banyan trees in the New World, disagrees (*History of the World*, pp. 137–39).

24 These crucial lines are as follows: "Such of late / Columbus found the American so girt / With feathered cincture, naked else and wild / Among the trees on isles and woody shores" (*PL* 9.1115–18). The "of late," which

seems to advise us of the up-to-dateness of Milton's scholarship, refers to discoveries that took place 170 years before *Paradise Lost* was published. The distant event is also misperceived. Columbus did not find the American girt at all but clad in "native honour," as Adam and Eve were before taking refuge in the banyan tree. The "featured cincture" in which Milton chooses to attire the "American" refers to much later encounters on the mainland. The confusions of time and place seem to be made with one overriding purpose. If first nations can be identified with the original shame rather than with the original innocence, their distance from a redeemed Christian state can be made more important than their proximity to the Edenic. Western encounters with the New World were initially beguiled by that proximity. As the need to devalue subjected civilizations took over, the depth of distance inevitably prevailed. Milton seems to provide a microenactment of this historical change in perception, as his language passes from a nakedness associated in the fourth book with majesty and innocence to a nakedness now associated with wildness. Paradise can be a "wilderness of sweets" and "wild above rule or art" (5.294-97), but these Edenic connotations are heavily overlaid by the infernal associations that surround wildness in its fallen state. So pressing are these associations that Adam sees the luxuriance of Paradise as a wilderness, even as he decides to partake of the fruit with Eve (9.910).

25 Carey and Fowler, *Poems of John Milton*, p. 920n.

26 This is the mandate given by the shade of Anchises to Aeneas in the sixth book of the *Aeneid*. The excellence of others (presumably the Greeks) may lie in astronomy, philosophy, literature, and the fine arts; the Roman accomplishment will be to govern other nations with the firmness and justice those nations are unable to find within themselves.

27 Camões (*The Lusiads* 1.54) mentions Mombasa, Quiloa, and Sofala. Milton repeats all three names in 11.399-400 and inserts Melind, not simply for the alliterative effect but because Melind was crucial to the outcome of da Gama's voyage. See E. M. W. Tillyard, *The English Epic and Its Background* (London: Chatto and Windus, 1959), p. 241, and Bowra, *From Virgil to Milton*, p. 238.

28 Scammell identifies the pilot as Ibn Majid, "the most distinguished navigator of the time" (*World Encompassed*, p. 235). Ravenstein, in his edition of *First Voyage of Vasco da Gama*, identifies the pilot as "a native of Gujarat" (pp. 45-46n).

29 Carey and Fowler do not capitalize "great mogul" (*Poems of John Milton*). Other editions capitalize and underline it. I retain the capitalization elsewhere. In coupling Agra and Lahore, Milton follows early travelers such as William Finch, Thomas Coryat, and Edward Terry, the last of whom describes Agra and Lahore as "the two choice cities of this Empire." The tree-lined boulevard connecting the two cities is admired by all (*Early Travels in India*, ed. W. Foster, pp. 155-67, 243-44, 293).

30 *Paradise Regained* is hereafter cited as *PR*. Carey and Fowler note that G. W. Whiting (*Review of English Studies* 13 [1937]: 209-12) has produced evidence to indicate that Taprobane usually meant Sumatra (*Poems of John Milton*, p. 1139). However, *The Lusiads* (10.107) identifies Taprobane with Sri Lanka. Since Taprobane is mentioned by Milton in conjunction with the Malay Peninsula ("golden Chersoness"), Sumatra is indicated, particularly since *The Lusiads* (10.124) suggests that Sumatra was once joined to the Malay Peninsula. "Indian isle" may seem to suggest Sri Lanka, but Sumatra was part of "further India," and "utmost" would be less effective if Sri Lanka were intended. According to Major, the identification of Taprobane with Sumatra "was maintained throughout the maps, almost all of them Italian, of the sixteenth century and was continued by Mercator" (*India in the Fifteenth Century*, p. lxii).

31 Since contemporary Rome was the other of Protestantism, it is fitting that classical Rome in its decadence should provide this other with its ancestry. But Rome's story is also England's and is a clear warning of how the reformed collective self can slide back into the other if it is wanting in vigilance.

32 Don M. Wolfe et al., eds., *Complete Prose Works of Milton* (New Haven: Yale University Press, 1953-), 4:684.

33 Milton may be alluding to the passage in the *Aeneid* discussed in note 26.

34 English imperialist and Protestant poetics are never very far from each other. Barbara Lewalski's *Protestant Poetics and the Seventeenth Century Religious Lyric* (Princeton: Princeton University Press, 1979) has demonstrated how heavily the religious poetics of seventeenth-century England depended on the image of God in the self. Within imperialist poetics, the presence of the image confers the right to dominion, but the right can be argued to be contingent on a standard of behavior that testifies convincingly to that presence. Gandhi's achievement was to have brought the interrogative pressure of the civil disobedience movement to bear decisively on this moral linchpin, displaying in the process a degree of Christian heroism that the dominant power was requested to find in itself.

3. Appropriating India: Dryden's Great Mogul

1 Dedication to the Earl of Mulgrave, quoted in L. A. Beaurline and Fredson Bowers, eds., *John Dryden: Four Tragedies* (Chicago: University of Chicago Press, 1967), p. 107. References to *Aureng-Zebe* are to this edition.

2 Samuel Johnson, *Rasselas and Other Tales*, in *The Works of Samuel Johnson*, ed. Gwen J. Kolb (New Haven: Yale University Press, 1990), 16:37.

3 Michael Wood's *Legacy: A Search for the Origins of Civilization* (London: Network Books, 1992), p. 87, reproduces a painting by Benjamin West of Clive receiving the revenue grant from Shah Alam II. It can be

contrasted with the reproduction of a religious debate held at Akbar's *ibadat-khana* (p. 74). (See Gascoigne, *Great Moghuls*, p. 116, for another depiction of the same event.) In both paintings, the Mughal monarch occupies the traditional center position and the Portuguese priests are kneeling in the circle around Akbar, whereas Clive and his entourage are stiffly erect. Those nearest Akbar's throne are the Islamic mullahs and not the Portuguese Jesuits; in West's painting, Clive's left leg all but brushes against the throne and his right hand extends over it to receive the grant. Akbar inclines slightly toward his Moslem counselors as if in debate with them; Shah Alam bends forward as if offering a concession to Clive from a throne of which he is now only the nominal occupant.

4   The Akbar-Aurangzeb contrast is needed to provide the British, as successors to the Mughals, both with an example to avoid and with a precedent on which to improve. It is explicit in eighteenth-century British histories of India (see chapter 4) and in Tennyson (see chapter 1, n. 13) and lies behind the severely adverse comments on Aurangzeb by William Jones and Sydney Owenson (see chapters 4 and 6). Rammohun Roy endorses this contrast in affirming that Akbar's "memory is still adored" whereas Aurangzeb's name "is now held in abhorrence" (Shashi Ahluwalia and Meenakshi Ahluwalia, eds., *Raja Rammohun Roy and the Indian Renaissance* [New Delhi: Mittal Publications, 1991], p. 125). Most Indians would find little to like in Aurangzeb, but not everyone would wish to subscribe to a polarity that glorifies Akbar as a consequence. Aziz's nostalgia for the days of Mughal glory, his preference for Aurangzeb over Akbar, and his critical remarks on Akbar's universalism need to be viewed against this background (Forster, *Passage to India*, pp. 83, 155–56, 266).

5   Beaurline and Bowers, *Dryden: Four Tragedies*, p. 108.

6   James Anderson Winn, *John Dryden and His World* (New Haven: Yale University Press, 1987), p. 273.

7   François Bernier, *Travels in the Mogul Empire, A.D. 1656–1668*, 2d ed., trans. Archibald Constable (Oxford: Oxford University Press, 1914).

8   Hansen, *Peacock Throne*, pp. 352–53.

9   Spear, *India*, p. 147. For a brief and helpful account of Bernier's ideas on India and their influence, see S. N. Mukherjee, *Sir William Jones: A Study in Eighteenth Century British Attitudes to India* (Cambridge: Cambridge University Press, 1968), pp. 11–15.

10 Beaurline and Bowers, *Dryden: Four Tragedies*, p. 108; Winn, *John Dryden and His World*, p. 273; George McFadden, *Dryden the Public Writer, 1660–1685* (Princeton: Princeton University Press, 1978), p. 185.

11 Hansen, *Peacock Throne*, p. 353.

12 McFadden, *Dryden the Public Writer*, p. 185.

13 Samuel Johnson, *Lives of the English Poets* (London: J. M. Dent and Sons, 1925), 1:198.

14 In the prologue to *Aureng-Zebe*, Dryden describes himself as grown weary of "his long-lov'd Mistris, Rhyme" (Beaurline and Bowers, *Dryden: Four Tragedies*, pp. 8–9). Passion is too fierce to be bound in fetters. But rhyme can be a protection as well as a bondage. Thus in the prologue to *All for Love*, first performed on December 12, 1677, Dryden describes himself defensively as "without his Rhyme" and as fighting "this day unarm'd." He is also under the disadvantage of recounting a well-worn tale almost as old as Dido's (ibid., p. 207). The prologue is mystifyingly titled as a prologue to *Antony and Cleopatra*.

15 McFadden, *Dryden the Public Writer*, p. 185.

16 Dedication to the Earl of Mulgrave, in Beaurline and Bowers, *Dryden: Four Tragedies*, p. 108.

17 Michael Alssid, "The Design of Dryden's *Aureng-Zebe*," *Journal of English and Germanic Philology* 64 (1965): 464.

18 These lines do not attain the impassioned brilliance of Donne's conflation of the imperial, the commercial, and the sexual in the nineteenth elegy. Nevertheless, the underlying insinuation asks to be pursued. The East India Company's venture is the acquisition of India (Indamora). Its shareholders, seeking the "double gains" of commerce and possession, have laid out all their stock to make this climactic "purchase." Thus the acquiring of India is foreseen even at a time when the British position in India (see introduction) was precarious. This reading would not have been esoteric in a London where the East India Company was already one of the city's largest employers, where Bombay had been leased to the company by the Crown, and where Charles (who had read Dryden's play in draft form) was, it will be remembered, accepting substantial loans from the company.

   Laura Brown's exploration of the representation of women in the context of mercantile capitalism from 1688 to 1730 would have benefited considerably from an examination of *Aureng-Zebe*. "The female figure," Brown argues, "through its simultaneous connections with commodification and trade on the one hand and violence and difference on the other, plays a central role" in constituting the "mercantile capitalist ideology" (Laura Brown, *Ends of Empire: Women and Ideology in Early Eighteenth-Century English Literature* [Ithaca: Cornell University Press, 1993], p. 11). One might plausibly suggest that Indamora and Nourmahal exemplify between them the "simultaneous connections" that Brown delineates. It could further be argued that the two representations in their hidden complementarity testify to the intimate link between commercial satisfactions and the exercise of an imperial power by which "violence and difference" can be held in check.

19 Harold Lamb, *Nur Mahal* (Garden City: Doubleday, Doran, 1935). Lamb argues interestingly that "women who lived behind the veil can never find their way into the pages of scholars except as names" and that it

is fiction rather than history or biography that can bring such women "from the silence" (Author's note).

20 T. J. Murari, *Taj: A Story of Mughal India* (Sevenoaks, England: New English Library, 1987).

21 Hansen, *Peacock Throne*, pp. 37, 43.

22 McFadden, *Dryden the Public Writer*, p. 200.

4. James Mill and the Case of the Hottentot Venus

1 Robert Orme, *A History of the Military Transactions of the British Nation in Indostan from the year MDCCXLV* (London, 1763). For a more sophisticated exercise in the genre (and one more appreciative of the Sepoy contribution to British victories in India), see Philip Mason, *A Matter of Honour: An Account of the Indian Army, Its Officers and Men* (London: Peregrine Books, 1976). Pages 29–109 deal with events up to Buxar. Mason's narrative supports the melancholy conclusion that "Afro-Asia was taught to conquer itself for foreign pay, most of it taken out of Afro-Asian pockets" (Victor G. Kiernan, *European Empires from Conquest to Collapse, 1815–1960* [London: Fontana Paperbacks, 1982], p. 16).

2 Alexander Dow, *The History of Hindostan,* 3 vols. (London: S. A. Bechert and P. A. De Hontd, 1768–72); Francis Gladwin, *The History of Hindostan during the Reigns of Jehangir, Shah Jehan, and Aurangzebe* (Calcutta, 1788); Thomas Maurice, *The History of Hindostan, Sanscreet and Classical,* 7 vols. (London, 1800); Maurice Thomas, *The Modern History of Hindostan* (London, 1802–10); Mark Wilks, *Historical Sketches of the South of India,* 3 vols. (London, 1810–17). These histories and others are discussed by J. S. Grewal, *Muslim Rule in India: The Assessments of British Historians* (Calcutta: Oxford University Press, 1970).

3 Wilks asked Sir James Mackintosh if it was true that Moore had never been in the East. When Mackintosh confirmed that he had not, Wilks replied that that showed him that "reading over D'Herbelot" was "as good as riding on the back of a camel." Moore took pleasure in this sally (Thomas Moore, *Lalla Rookh* [Chicago: Henneberry, n.d.], p. 16).

4 See Keay's *India Discovered,* pp. 176–91, for an account of the survey. A fuller but less involving narration is provided in Clements R. Markham, *A Memoir of the Indian Survey* (1878; reprint, Amsterdam: Meridian, 1968), pp. 66–147. The survey's climax was the locating of India's highest peak, named appropriately after one of the surveyors.

5 Dow, *History of Hindostan,* 3:xxxv–xxxvii.

6 Goldsmith, *History of Man,* 1:114–15. At a time when little that was positive was being said about India's self-respect, Thomas Moore's note provides a much-needed corrective in referring to "That national independence, that freedom from the interference and dictation of foreigners, without which, indeed, no liberty of any kind can exist; and for which

both Hindoos and Persians fought against their Mussulman invaders with, in many cases, a bravery that deserved much better success" (*The Poetical Works of Thomas Moore, with Memoir by David Herbert M. A.* [London: Charles Griffin, 1872], p. 82n). This note is not in Godley's edition.

7 C. R. Boxer, *The Dutch Seaborne Empire, 1600-1800* (London: Hutchinson, 1977), pp. 199-202; Gertrude Z. Thomas, *Richer Than Spices* (New York: Alfred A. Knopf, 1965), pp. 93-115; Smith, *Wealth of Nations*, pp. 235-38. Entrepôt trade could have grimmer consequences, with Indian textiles exchanged for African slaves acquired for labor in the New World (Lawrence James, *The Rise and Fall of the British Empire* [London: Little, Brown, 1994], p. 26).

8 Samuel Foote, *The Nabob*, in Paula Backscheider and Robert Howard, eds., *The Plays of Samuel Foote* (New York: Garland Press, 1983), pp. 39-40. Literature on the nabobs includes *The Nabob: A Novel in a Series of Letters* (London, 1785) and *The Disinherited Nabob: A Novel, Interspersed with Genuine Descriptions of India* (Dublin, 1787). Book 2, chapter 7, of Benjamin Disraeli's *Sybil* (1845) recounts the story of a "Nawab" who began life as a waiter in an exclusive club on St. James's Street and rose to become a member of the House of Lords. The last nabob is Jos Sedley in William Thackeray's *Vanity Fair* (1847). Foote's play is perceptively discussed in Singh, *Colonial Narratives*, pp. 53-78. More than Singh (esp. on p. 59), I see the furor over the nabobs as helping to open a transitory space during which the idea of empire was not altogether unquestionable.

9 Foote, *The Nabob*, p. 65.

10 Roger Williams, quoted in Calder, *Revolutionary Empire*, p. 90.

11 Henry Mackenzie, *The Man of Feeling*, ed. Hamish Miles (London: Scholartis Press, 1928), p. 170.

12 William Cowper, *The Task*, 4.28-30, in *The Poetical Works of William Cowper*, 4th ed., ed. H. S. Milford (London: Oxford University Press, 1934), p. 183.

13 Kirkpatrick Sale, *The Conquest of Paradise: Christopher Columbus and the Columbian Legacy* (New York: Plume Books, 1992), pp. 169-72.

14 Samuel Johnson, *The Works of Samuel Johnson*, ed. Donald J. Greene (New Haven: Yale University Press, 1977), 10:421-22. Some years earlier, Cornelius de Pauw had described the discovery of the New World as the most calamitous event in human history. See J. H. Elliott, *The Old World and the New* (Cambridge: Cambridge University Press, 1970; Canto edition, 1992), p. 1.

15 Johnson, *Works*, 10:421. The most powerful indictment of empire was in the Abbé Raynal's *Philosophical and Political History of the Settlements and Trade of the Europeans in the East and West Indies*. It was published in 1770 or 1772 (the date is indeterminate) in four volumes, subsequently expanded to eight and then to twelve. It went through twenty authorized

and a considerably larger number of pirated editions. Henry Steele Commager describes it as preaching the immorality of war and the iniquity of colonies and as the first history "to do justice to the colored races" and "to fit together politics and economics and religion and society into a single pattern" (Henry Steele Commager, "Was America a Mistake?," *Horizon* 9, no. 4 [Autumn 1967]: 30–33).

16 Beaurline and Bowers, *Dryden: Four Tragedies*, p. 30. The editors are elaborating on a comment by John Loftis.

17 Smith, *Wealth of Nations*, p. 675. Smith's remark is in a tradition outlined by Elliott (*The Old World and the New*, pp. 9–10) and only briefly challenged by eighteenth-century misgivings.

18 Jesuits such as Thomas Stevens and De Nobili acquired some knowledge of Sanskrit, and an unpublished Sanskrit grammar by Heinrich Roth may have been used by Paulinus for a Sanskrit grammar published at Rome in 1790. Abraham Rogers published at Leyden in 1651 a work incorporating 200 stanzas of Bhartrhari. This version of the Proverbs is generally accepted as the first direct translation of a Sanskrit text into a European language. It seems to have stood alone for more than a century.

19 Wendy Doniger, *Hindu Myths: A Sourcebook Translated from the Sanskrit* (Harmondsworth: Penguin Books, 1975), pp. 12–14.

20 It is important to see the movement from the proliferative abundance of the facade to the bareness of the inner sanctum as a metaphor for the progress of understanding as well as an architectural binding of contraries. "A condition of complete simplicity / costing not less than everything" is the end of the journey in Eliot's *Four Quartets*. But the end does not erase the beginning. Each is contained in the other, as the opening line of Eliot's "East Coker" and its inversion in the final line of the poem indicate and as is made evident in the metaphysical statement that the movement through the temple asks us to experience. Repeated references in the Upanishads to the deep cavern of the heart and to the small space within the lotus of the heart establish the inner sanctum as a retreat from multiplicity but also as the germ of that multiplicity. The statement made by the architecture of the Hindu temple goes beyond reconciling the real and the phenomenal; it situates us within their necessary coexistence.

21 William Beckford, *Vathek*, ed. Roger Lonsdale (Oxford: Oxford University Press, 1970), p. 123n.

22 Ibid., p. 145n. The editor describes this as a "more complex and derisive version" of the note to Samuel Henley's 1786 translation of *Vathek* from the French. Beckford disowned Henley's edition.

23 In a letter to Hastings on October 23, 1786, Jones states that the Gita "owes its appearance" to Hastings's patronage (Garland Cannon, ed., *The Letters of Sir William Jones* [Oxford: Clarendon Press, 1970], II:718). The editor's notes point out that Wilkins had shown Hastings his translation

and that Hastings's introduction, written on the spot, had led to publication by the company (pp. 660–61). A drawing by Blake, of which "the subject is, Mr. Wilkin translating the Geeta," has unfortunately not survived (Martin Jarrett-Kerr, "Indian Religion in English Literature, 1675–1967," in *Essays and Studies of the English Association, 1984* [London: Humanities Press, 1984], p. 89).

24 Raymond Schwab, *The Oriental Renaissance: Europe's Rediscovery of India and the East*, trans. Gene Patterson-Black and Victor Reinkins; foreword by Edward W. Said (New York: Columbia University Press, 1984).

25 Percy Bysshe Shelley, *The Triumph of Life* 211.

26 Lord Teignmouth, ed., *Memoirs of the Life, Writings, and Correspondence of Sir William Jones* (London: Hatchard, 1807), p. 288. John Shore (Lord Teignmouth) later became a governor-general of India.

27 Mukherjee finds that Jones's career "shows more than anything else, the dichotomy of the attitudes of some of the British in India" who were "radicals at home, attracted to India's past, and yet committed to authoritarian rule over her peoples" (*Sir William Jones*, p. 3; see also pp. 125–28).

28 Warren Hastings, quoted in P. J. Marshall, *The British Discovery of Hinduism in the Eighteenth Century* (Cambridge: Cambridge University Press, 1970), p. 189.

29 P. J. Marshall, ed., *The Writings and Speeches of Edmund Burke* (Oxford: Clarendon Press, 1981), 5:386. The difference between Fox's East India Bill and the Magna Carta is that one was bestowed by Parliament and the other exacted from the monarch. That difference can become crucial given Burke's treatment of human rights as inherited rather than inherent, as a "patrimony" derived from one's "forefathers," and even as an "*entailed inheritance*" (Edmund Burke, *Reflections on the Revolution in France*, ed. Conor Cruise O'Brien [Harmondsworth: Penguin Books, 1968], pp. 117–20; Burke's italics). If rights are historically constituted, some diffusion of power is necessary to constitute them. A totally disempowered people cannot set up a patrimony to be bequeathed. The history of a people can bestow on its rights an articulation distinctive to that people, but it is a dangerous proposition to say that those rights exist only insofar as they can be traced to a historical beginning.

30 Jones described Milton as the "most perfect scholar" and "sublimest poet that our country has ever produced" (letter to Lady Georgiana, September 7, 1769, in Cannon, *Letters of Sir William Jones*, 1:39). Elsewhere he described Milton as one of the greatest men "who ever adorned this island" (Mukherjee, *Sir William Jones*, p. 51).

31 Teignmouth, *Memoirs of the Life, Writings, and Correspondence of Sir William Jones*, pp. 588–89.

32 Ibid., p. 592.

33 Satya S. Pachori, ed., *Sir William Jones: A Reader* (Delhi: Oxford Univer-

sity Press, 1993), pp. 59, 61. I have cited this compilation rather than to the six-volume 1799 edition or the thirteen-volume 1807 edition, both of which are difficult of access.

34 Ibid., p. 58 (Jones's italics).

35 Ibid., p. 62.

36 The pages on Mill that follow have to be placed in contestation with Javed Majeed's *Ungoverned Imaginings: James Mill's "The History of British India" and Orientalism* (Oxford: Clarendon Press, 1992), the most thoughtful and intelligent study so far of Mill's work. Majeed sees Mill as a more complex figure than I do, working within boundaries that are less clear-cut and more indeterminate than my reading suggests. Part of the assertiveness of my characterization may be the result of my placing Mill within imperial history and proceeding to read him as a decisive contributor to that history. Some of the complexities of a mind can be rubbed away when it is put into position as the mainspring of a discourse. Paradoxes worthy of attention can and do arise when writers are appropriated by a discourse that they themselves have been indispensable in articulating. Thus Macaulay would not have been possible without Mill, even though Mill was no supporter of Macaulay's minute. Both utilitarians and evangelists tended to be interventionists in India, whereas Mill leaned toward a more restricted interface between subjected peoples and those responsible for governing them. We can take note of these divergences and still continue to urge that Mill's work be pondered in an environment that the title of Majeed's book is not backward in invoking.

37 Percival Spear, *A History of India* (1965; reprint, London: Penguin Books, 1978), 2:47.

38 Calder, *Revolutionary Empire*, p. 158.

39 Patrick Brantlinger, *Rule of Darkness: British Literature and Imperialism, 1830–1914* (Ithaca: Cornell University Press, 1988), p. 78.

40 Trevelyan, *Golden Oriole*, p. 212.

41 Calder, *Revolutionary Empire*, p. 775.

42 See chapter 7.

43 Paul Johnson, *The Birth of the Modern: World Society, 1815–30* (London: Weidenfeld and Nicolson, 1991), p. 253.

44 John Barrell, *The Infection of Thomas De Quincey: A Psychopathology of Imperialism* (New Haven: Yale University Press, 1991), p. 192. De Quincey found more than this in Kant. Section 4 of Kant's *Observations on the Beautiful and Sublime* ("Of National Characteristics") contains remarks on blacks' inferiority and on the Hindu addiction to the grotesque. De Quincey's translation of this chapter appeared in the *London Magazine* of April 1824. John T. Goldthwait in his edition and translation of *Observations* draws attention to a precedent in Hume ([Berkeley: University of California Press, 1965], p. 123n).

45 The primary study of the Hottentot Venus is Sander L. Gilman's "Black

Bodies, White Bodies: Toward an Iconography of Female Sexuality in Late Nineteenth Century Art, Medicine, and Literature," *Critical Inquiry* 12 (1985): 204–41. See also Johnson, *Birth of the Modern*, pp. 242–43; Suvendrinal Perera, *Reaches of Empire* (New York: Columbia University Press, 1991), pp. 98–99; and Stephen Jay Gould, *The Flamingo's Smile: Reflections on Natural History* (New York: Norton, 1987), pp. 291–306.

46 David Masson, ed., *The Collected Writings of De Quincey*, rev. ed., 14 vols. (Edinburgh: Adam and Charles Black, 1889), 1:89–98. References to De Quincey's writings are to this edition. Barrell's fine book on De Quincey, *Infection of Thomas De Quincey*, pays little attention to these games. Nigel Leask's brief remarks are telling in pointing out how De Quincey's strategy is "the product of an extreme anxiety of empire, which identifies with the pariah-victim the better to condemn him to subservience" (Nigel Leask, *British Romantic Writers and the East: Anxieties of Empire* [Cambridge: Cambridge University Press, 1992], p. 5).

47 Gombroon, situated on the Persian Gulf and mentioned by Moore (Godley, *Poetical Works of Thomas Moore*, pp. 405n, 407n), was later named Bandar 'Abbas. De Quincey relocates it south of the equator, encouraging a conflation between Gambia and the Cameroons.

48 James Mill, *The History of British India*, abridged by William Thomas (Chicago: University of Chicago Press, 1975), pp. 157–58. Where possible, references are to this edition rather than to one of the many editions published in the nineteenth century. The most compendious of these is the nine-volume fourth edition with notes and continuations by Horace Hayman Wilson (London: James Madden, 1880). Wilson's note on this passage points out that Mill confuses the mythology of Hinduism with its philosophy. Absurdity resides almost exclusively in the former. Hindu philosophy's "disregard of all external and merely temporal existence" and its "exclusive direction of the power of the mind to a man's own soul" may be "unwise and ill-directed" but "can scarcely be termed with justice mean and degrading" (1:384). Wilson subscribes here to the proposition (often and perhaps overwhelmingly reiterated) of Hinduism as a religion of world abandonment. The best response might be to ask how dharma can be a significant and even crucial concept in a religion unable to generate a social philosophy. Nevertheless, the practical consequences of the Western view should be obvious. A civilization incapable of social thought will need to have its social engineering done for it.

49 Mill, *History of British India*, p. 197.

50 Ibid., pp. xix, xii.

51 Ibid., pp. 299–329.

52 Percival Spear, *The Nabobs: A Study of the Social Life of the English in Eighteenth Century India* (Gloucester, Mass.: Peter Smith, 1971), appendix D.

53 *Blackwoods Edinburgh Magazine* 6 (1805): 617. The high esteem in which

Jones held Indian literature and philosophy was acquired only after his arrival in India and his "discovery" of the Indian past. As Mukherjee indicates, Jones prior to that point had regarded Indian poetic accomplishment as no more than imitative of the Persians (*Sir William Jones*, p. 47).

54 John Carnac, quoted in O. P. Kejariwal, *The Asiatic Society of Bengal* (Delhi: Oxford University Press, 1988), p. 81.

55 Mill, *History of British India*, p. 13.

56 Philip Mason (pseud. Philip Woodruff), *The Men Who Ruled India*, vol. 2, *The Guardians* (New York: Schocken Books, 1984), p. 360. In a curious and commendable footnote, Mason seems to completely recant his book, but the recantation remains his, leaving intact the views of Jowett and his disciples and their material consequences for India (p. 368).

57 Ibid.

58 Forster, *Passage to India*, pp. 31–32. Barbara Rosencrance's fine analysis of these opening paragraphs stops short of my findings in this chapter (Barbara Rosencrance, *Forster's Narrative Vision* [Ithaca: Cornell University Press, 1982], pp. 184–94).

59 Michael Edwardes, *The Orchid House: Splendours and Miseries of the Kingdom of Oudh, 1827–1857* (London: Cassell, 1960), pp. 32–33.

60 S. Radhakrishnan, *Indian Philosophy*, 2d ed. (London: George Allen and Unwin, 1929–30), 1:186–87, and *Eastern Religions and Western Thought*, 2d ed. (London: Humphrey Milford, Oxford University Press, 1940), pp. 84–90. Mistranslations of the Indian philosophical and moral vocabulary are not difficult, and it can even be argued that the vocabulary is locked into Indian civilization to such an extent that any translation will be a mistranslation. Among mistranslations, the rendering of Maya as illusion is the most destructive because it establishes an illusion-reality binary that makes Indian civilization either totally world denying or committed to the irresponsible cultivation of a world of pleasure and fancy in which reason cannot claim a controlling status.

5. Hegel's India and the Surprise of Sin

1 *The Faerie Queene*, in particular book 6, places the pastoral and the purposeful in a relationship of contestation in which neither term is privileged. Hegel proposes a relationship in which the purposeful repudiates the pastoral.

2 Georg Wilhelm Friedrich Hegel, *The Philosophy of History*, trans. J. Sibree (1899; reprint, New York: Dover, 1956), pp. 40–41. References in the text are to this edition of *The Philosophy of History* unless otherwise indicated. References to Hegel's *Lectures on the Philosophy of Religion* are to the three-volume translation of the 1840 second German edition by E. B. Speirs and J. Burton Sanderson (New York: Humanities Press, 1962). The edition by Peter C. Hodgson of the translation by R. F. Brown, P. C.

Hodgson, and J. M. Stewart, with the assistance of H. S. Harris (Berkeley: University of California Press, 1988), is more scholarly. It reconstructs the 1827 lectures rather than those delivered in 1831, reconstruction of which, according to the editor, would involve a substantial degree of conjecture. After 1827, Hegel revised and substantially enlarged the section on India. The revisions and additional material can be found as variants in the notes to the Hodgson edition, but I have preferred to quote from a translation that incorporates these changes. I am reassured in doing this by Hodgson's characterization of the 1831 lectures as "representative of Hegel's religious thought at its best and clearest" (p. 24). Hegel's changes and augmentations after 1827 dispose of the view that his opinions on India may have matured as he reflected on them further and as more material on India became available. The later text (insofar as it can be reconstructed) is more hostile to India than the earlier.

3   Stanley Fish, *Surprised by Sin: The Reader in "Paradise Lost"* (London: Macmillan, 1967).

4   See Hegel, *Philosophy of Religion* (Hodgson edition), p. 46, for Hegel's negative response to the German vogue for India. The rhetorical dramatization studied here has so far escaped notice.

5   Despite Greenblatt's persuasive juxtaposition of the Bower of Bliss with the ravaging of Hispaniola, the Oriental associations of the Bower remain strong, particularly in reflecting a sophisticated decadence stereotyped as Oriental, which the Western psyche was learning to expel from itself (*Renaissance Self-Fashioning*, pp. 179–84).

6   Nirad C. Chaudhari, *The Continent of Circe: An Essay on the Peoples of India* (London: Chatto and Windus, 1965).

7   These remarks have not escaped comment, but the comments have been recent and their belatedness reflects the extent to which a Eurocentric text has been Eurocentrically read. This Eurocentrism is reflected in the negligible attention given to the representation of India in the world scheme of *The Philosophy of History* and *The Philosophy of Religion*. The most specific and instructive comments on Hegel's India are offered by Inden in *Imagining India* (esp. pp. 45–52), but much more needs to be said.

8   Estimates of depopulation in the New World vary considerably, as might be expected, but have tended to rise as it became clear that the original population was underestimated in the interests of perceiving the New World as "empty" and as therefore calling out for colonization. Scammell puts the population of Mexico at 27 million in 1500 and perhaps only half a million a century later (*First Imperial Age*, p. 182). Peru's population fell from 7 million in 1500 to little over a half million in 1620. According to Greenblatt, the population of Hispaniola fell from 7–8 million in 1492 to 28,000 by 1512 (*Renaissance Self-Fashioning*, p. 226).

9   Hegel's racism is examined by Darrel Moellendorf in "Racism and Ratio-

nality in Hegel's *Philosophy of Subjective Spirit," History of Political Thought* 13, no. 2 (Summer 1992): 243–55. Moellendorf argues that although Hegel's philosophy of spirit is "tainted by the unusual (for Hegel) causal role which he gives to a biological category, namely race," his racism "can be traced to the general ideology of the nineteenth century" and "does not follow from any of his fundamental claims about spirit" (p. 243).

10 Hegel, quoted in ibid., p. 246.

11 Hegel, quoted in ibid., p. 248.

12 T. M. Knox, trans., *Hegel's Philosophy of Right* (Oxford: Oxford University Press, 1967), p. 218. References to *The Philosophy of Right* are to this edition.

13 Hegel's obsession with the wildness of India is carried into *The Philosophy of Religion*, which refers to "an endless breaking-up of the One into the Many, and an unstable reeling to and fro of all content" (2:9); a "wild play of begetting and destroying" and "a wild whirl of delirium" (2:24); a "wild, extravagant disorder" (2:44) and "a wild extravagance" of "desire" (2:45).

14 This is the "dispersive vacillation between extremes" that Hegel makes part of a pattern of bondage from which only the Caucasian race has freed itself. *The Philosophy of Religion* develops this perception more fully. One extreme of the "dispersive vacillation" is the union with God that consists of the annihilation and "stupefaction of self-consciousness" (2:34). The other extreme is a "wild, extravagant disorder" (2:44) in which "everything is squandered on imagination and nothing reserved for life" (2:45). The "people of India are sunk in the most complete immorality" because they are the victims of a contingency that is total and that can look to nothing outside its endless mutations except the "stupefaction" of union with the ultimate.

15 The German enthusiasm for Kalidasa's *Śakuntalā* is perhaps being contrasted here with the cooler reception of the play in England. Hegel's opinion is in harmony with Mill's findings in *The History of British India*, published the year before Hegel began his Berlin lectures. For the German response to *Śakuntalā*, see Dorothy M. Figueira, *Translating the Orient: The Reception of "Sakuntala" in Nineteenth Century Europe* (Albany: State University of New York Press, 1991). Figueira seeks to show how translations of *Śakuntalā* reflect the agendas of their translators. They are not agendas that Hegel would have endorsed.

16 Hegel's recognition of India's propensity for military defeats is in an established tradition. His actual comments are less abusive than Goldsmith's (see chapter 4) but may be potentially more threatening: "The important thing here is not personal mettle but aligning oneself with the universal. In India five hundred men conquered twenty thousand who were not cowards but who lacked only this disposition to work in close

co-operation with others" (*Philosophy of Right*, p. 296). Lack of heroic fiber is a humiliating reason for failure, but it is perhaps a less dangerous one than misalignment with the universal.

17 Max Müller, *India: What It Can Teach Us—A Course of Lectures Delivered before the University of Cambridge* (New York: Funk and Wagnalls, 1883).

18 Hodgson notes that "most of the secondary sources available to him [Hegel] were prejudiced or ill informed, reflecting the attitudes of the British East India Company" (Hegel, *Philosophy of Religion* [Hodgson edition], p. 46). European scholarship on India was also available to Hegel, but since his aim was to correct the German infatuation, the British denigration came naturally to hand. Among the secondary sources "reflecting the attitudes of the British East India Company," we might list Alexander Fraser Tytler's *Considerations on the Political State of India* (London: Black, Perry, Booksellers to the Honourable East India Company, 1815). Tytler's extensive remarks on Brahman depravity approximate Hegel instructively, notably in the comment that the "day of a Brahmin is passed in eating and sleeping" (p. 274). Tytler does not find it inconsistent to observe elsewhere that "in India, from the effects of the climate, no European ever walks" (p. 38).

Vituperation against Brahmans as the custodians of Hinduism's petrified practices is routine during the Mill-Hegel era. The Jones era was more sympathetic to Hinduism, but Burke is still unusual in referring to Brahmans in his remarkable speech on Fox's East India Bill as "an ancient and venerable priesthood, the depository of their [the Indian people's] laws, learning and history, the guides of the people whilst living, and their consolation in death" (Marshall, *Writings and Speeches of Edmund Burke*, 5:389–90). In *An Historical Disquisition concerning the Knowledge Which the Ancients Had of India* (London, 1791), William Robertson takes a view of Hinduism that approaches Burke's. Hegel shows no evidence of having read Burke or Robertson. See Karen O'Brien, *Narratives of Enlightenment: Cosmopolitan History from Voltaire to Gibbon* (Cambridge: Cambridge University Press, 1995), for comment on Robertson's views.

19 The significant but less than obvious relationship between Hegel's views on civil society and the views current among members of the Scottish Enlightenment is studied in Norbert Waszek, "The Division of Labour: From the Scottish Enlightenment to Hegel," *Owl of Minerva* 15 (Fall 1983).

20 Hayden White in "Rhetoric and History," in *Theories of History: Papers Read at a Clark Library Seminar* (Los Angeles: William Andrews Clark Memorial Library, 1976), pp. 13-14, argues that even Hegelian logic cannot provide the form and syntax of historical discourse. It is "the enthymeme rather than the syllogism which is the structural principle" of

this discourse, and "rhetoric rather than logic" is its "organon" (p. 16). In his much fuller examination of the genre of *The Philosophy of History*, White sees Hegel as proceeding through potential tragedy and beyond irony to a comedic vision (Hayden White, *Metahistory* [Baltimore: Johns Hopkins University Press, 1973], pp. 81–131). But any progress beyond irony may remain vulnerable to further ironies. Irony can become its own perpetuation.

21 John Milton, "Of Education," in Wolfe et al., *Prose Works of Milton*, 11:402–3.

22 Robert Young, *White Mythologies: Writing History and the West* (London: Routledge, 1990), p. 3.

23 Panikkar, *Survey of Indian History*, pp. 58–59. The guru in Gita Mehta's novel, *Raj* (New York: Ballantine Books, 1989), p. 137, is making a statement that is historically justified.

24 S. Radhakrishnan, ed. and trans., *The Principal Upanisads* (New York: Harper, 1953), pp. 69, 73.

25 Kurt F. Leidecker suggests some of the ways in which Hindu thought might be regarded as Hegelian ("Hegel and the Orientals," *New Studies in Hegel's Philosophy*, ed. Warren E. Steinkraus [New York: Holt Rinehart and Winston, 1991], pp. 156–66).

26 The supersession of fancy by reason in the advance of history may seem reflected on a literary level by Thomas Peacock's *Four Ages of Poetry* (1820). But Peacock was entertained by rather than obsessed with his argument.

27 Herbert Marcuse, *Reason and Revolution: Hegel and the Rise of Social Theory* (Boston: Beacon Press, 1970), p. xii; see also pp. ix, 39, 45, 47–49, 69, 153–54.

28 Hans-Georg Gadamer, *Hegel's Dialectic: Five Hermeneutical Studies*, trans. P. Christopher Smith (New Haven: Yale University Press, 1976), pp. 67–69.

29 Theodor Adorno, *Hegel: Three Studies*, trans. Shierry Weber Nicholsen (Cambridge: MIT Press, 1994), pp. 89–148.

30 Gustav Emil Mueller, ed. and trans., *Encyclopedia of Philosophy* (New York: Philosophical Library, 1959), p. 107.

31 Ibid., p. 118.

32 Ibid., p. 217.

33 A. V. Miller, trans., *Hegel's Phenomenology of Spirit*, with a foreword by J. N. Findlay (New York: Oxford University Press, 1977), p. 19.

34 John Milton, *Areopagitica*, in *Prose Works of Milton*, 11:553.

35 Hegel's italics. Translation of paragraph 347 of *The Philosophy of Right*, in Walter Kaufmann, *From Shakespeare to Existentialism* (New York: Doubleday, Anchor Books, 1960), p. 117.

36 Ernst Cassirer, *The Myth of the State* (New Haven: Yale University Press, 1946), p. 274.

37 The nakedly imperial implications of Hegel's thinking in *The Philoso-*

phy of Right are examined by Tsenay Serequeberhan in "The Idea of Colonialism in Hegel's Philosophy of Right," International Philosophical Quarterly 29, no. 3 (September 1989): 302–17.

38 Kaufmann, From Shakespeare to Existentialism, p. 123.

39 Finneran, W. B. Yeats: The Poems, pp. 336–37.

40 Clark Butler, ed. and trans., Hegel: The Letters (Bloomington: Indiana University Press, 1984), p. 116.

41 Ibid., p. 325.

42 Edward Mendelson, ed., The English Auden: Poems, Essays, and Dramatic Writings, 1927-39 (New York: Random House, 1967), p. 151.

6. Feminizing the Feminine: Early Women Writers on India

1 India as a laboratory for canon formation and for the pedagogical practices surrounding the canon is studied by Gauri Viswanathan in Masks of Conquest (New York: Columbia University Press, 1989), esp. p. 65. As Viswanathan notes, the idea of India as a testing ground was originally explored by Eric Stokes in The English Utilitarians and India (Oxford: Oxford University Press, 1959).

2 See chapter 4 and Marshall, British Discovery of Hinduism, p. 185.

3 Francis G. Hutchins, The Illusion of Permanence (Princeton: Princeton University Press, 1967), p. 5.

4 Charles Grant, quoted in Majeed, Ungoverned Imaginings, p. 80.

5 Ibid.

6 The subversiveness of mimicry is addressed by Homi K. Bhabha in "Of Mimicry and Man: The Ambivalence of Colonial Discourse," in Bhabha, Location of Culture, pp. 85–92. Although imperial discourse is both subtended and subverted by the mimicry it calls for, the feminization of subjected peoples rests on a hierarchical relationship that discourages mimicry. Thus, even in its primary figurations, imperial discourse can be found at odds with itself.

7 For the different modelings of Chandrapore, see Forster, Passage to India, pp. 31–32; for the promise and the appeal, see pp. 148–49. One could say that the paragraph on pp. 148–49 puts to work yet once more the much-used trope of India's femininity. The observation would be correct but worse than worthless. Forster's rendering of a figure too familiar to call for attentiveness is deeply eloquent in its immediacy but also in its evasiveness. "How can the mind take hold of such a country?" suggests at once exasperation with colonial nonsense, fortification of the mind against that nonsense, and the mind's need for an incomprehensibility in which it seeks to find yet fears to lose itself. India's hundred mouths are a multiplied invitation, a monstrous polyvalency, the embodiment of the voracious feminine and at the same time the multitude of forms that infinity requires to make itself manifest. The mouths speak through objects "ridiculous and august," inviting us to reflect on a separation that

becomes no longer easy to maintain. Their "promise" was historically opulence and the seduction of the exotic. Their "appeal" can be India's vulnerability, a claim on the exploitative conscience, proffered under the cloak of a contiguous naming that calls for the imperial burden to be shouldered. India is what is beheld in India, the terrain of the gaze, the discovery that changes as we grasp it, the unveiling of the knower in the knowing. These recognitions, which do not merely traverse an imperial trope but open up its possibilities even as they encapsulate its history, give substance to Suleri's caution against crude transpositions of gender into empire (*Rhetoric of English India*, p. 15). At the same time, we have to take into account Brown's justified finding that the discursive intertwinings of the sexual, the commercial, and the imperial have yet to be adequately explored (*Ends of Empire*). Works such as this, cognizant of both warnings, must come to rest along a line that only tact and attentiveness are capable of drawing convincingly.

8 Inden, *Imagining India*. Inden convincingly brings out the extent to which Western scholarship on India was ideologically inflected.

9 These characterizations are all offered by Inden in ibid. Inden stops short of calling them different names for India's femininity.

10 Ibid., pp. 4, 45–48.

11 Benita Parry, *Delusions and Discoveries: Studies on India in the British Imagination, 1880–1930* (Berkeley: University of California Press, 1972).

12 Brantlinger, *Rule of Darkness*, pp. 199–224.

13 Jenny Sharpe, *Allegories of Empire: The Figure of Woman in the Colonial Text* (Minneapolis: University of Minnesota Press, 1993), p. 96; see also pp. 93–94.

14 Suleri's consideration of this matter is appropriately complex but does not deny that subjugation in the domestic order, limited dominance in the imperial one, and the valorizing of empire by the sacrifice of family life required to maintain it constitute a configuration too tightly interlocked to be easily pried open and one in which the opportunities for maneuvering are restricted (*Rhetoric of English India*, pp. 75–110). Most forthright of all is Antoinette M. Burton in "The White Woman's Burden," in *Western Women and Imperialism: Complicity and Resistance,* ed. Napur Chandur and Margaret Strobel (Bloomington: Indiana University Press, 1992), pp. 151–52.

15 Anne K. Mellor, "Romanticism, Gender, and the Anxieties of Empire: An Introduction," *European Romantic Review* 8, no. 2 (Spring 1997): 152.

16 A. L. Basham, ed., *A Cultural History of India* (Oxford: Clarendon Press, 1975), pp. 373–74. Basham describes the work as the first novel about India written in English. Mrs. Francis Sheridan's *History of Nourjahan* (1767) can be regarded as belonging to another genre.

17 Schwab, *Oriental Renaissance*, p. 102.

18 Mill's derogatory comparison of Hinduism with Islam puts an end to the Jonesian interregnum, that brief period during which Hindu religion

and culture could be sympathetically viewed. Before the interregnum, Islam was seen as India's official religion. After the interregnum, it became India's preferred religion, and a Hinduism first merely colorful and then inconveniently invested with classical authority was increasingly perceived as chaotic and dangerous.

19 References to *Translation of the Letters of a Hindu Rajah* are to Elizabeth Hamilton, *Translation of the Letters of a Hindu Rajah*, 5th ed. (London, 1811), 2 vols.

20 See, in particular, C. A. Bayly, *Indian Society and the Making of the British Empire* (Cambridge: Cambridge University Press, 1988).

21 Hamilton's novel was written in the middle of the Jonesian interregnum, but one should not forget that only eleven years earlier, Beckford's *Vathek* had treated Hinduism as the infernal circumference of an Islam already circumferential to Christianity. The interregnum was a fragile affair, with evangelical imaginings of India luridly at work during its span. As has already been suggested, the quarter century after 1785 provided a narrow time frame of opportunity during which Hindu culture could be sympathetically examined. Hamilton may go further than anyone else in endorsing that culture and in urging its reinstatement. We can attribute the strength of her commitment not solely to a detached esteem for things Hindu but also to a desire to idealize Hindu India as a site of the culturally feminine; but although this explanation is plausible, it is perplexed by her defense of caste hierarchies to which gender hierarchies can be deemed analogous. The forces at work during the interregnum are examined in an important study by Rosane Rocher, "British Orientalism in the Eighteenth Century: The Dialectics of Knowledge and Government," in *Orientalism and the Postcolonial Predicament: Perspectives on South Asia*, ed. Carol A. Breckenridge and Peter van der Veer (Philadelphia: University of Pennsylvania Press, 1993), pp. 215–49.

22 Rushdie, *Midnight's Children*, p. 166.

23 Fisher notes that "thousands of Indians made the trip to Europe" over the years up to the publication of Hamilton's novel. "Most were sailors, servants, wives or mistresses of Europeans. A few were travellers or visiting dignitaries" (*First Indian Author in English*, pp. 191–92). Fisher's book reprints the text of *The Travels of Dean Mahomed*, published by subscription at Cork in 1794. Mahomed emigrated to Ireland in 1784 and married an Irish student, Jane Daly, in 1786. His book, cast in the epistolary form, is in interesting proximity to Hamilton's novel. It is the first book by an Indian author presenting India to a Western public.

24 References to *The Wild Irish Girl* are to Lady Morgan (Sydney Owenson), *The Wild Irish Girl*, with an introduction by Brigid Brophy (London: Pandora Press, 1986).

25 References to *The Missionary* are to Lady Morgan (Sydney Owenson), *The Missionary*, 3 vols. (1811; reprint, Delmar: Scholar's Facsimiles, 1981).

26 In *Revolution and the Form of the British Novel, 1790–1825: Intercepted*

Letters, Interrupted Seductions (New York: Oxford University Press, 1994), Nicola J. Watson connects the decline of the epistolary novel and the rise of more authoritarian third-person narratives to the remodeling of British national identity during the Napoleonic period. Fisher estimates that "England had produced some 800 epistolary novels by 1790" and that during the 1750–1800 period "approximately one out of every six works of English fiction used it" (*First Indian Author in English*, p. 222).

27 In one of the few articles of note on Owenson's ideology, Joseph W. Lew argues that "*The Wild Irish Girl, Ida of Athens* and *The Missionary*, different in technique as they may be, form an imaginative unit. In these three novels, Owenson explores the range of possible 'outcomes' to imperialism: from euphoric union to dysphoric mutual destruction" (Joseph W. Lew, "Sydney Owenson and the Fate of Empire," *Keats-Shelley Journal* 39 [1990]: 43–44). The problem remains of why Ireland should be the site of the euphoric and India of the dysphoric construction. Insofar as India is a surrogate for Ireland, *The Missionary* can be read as reassuringly distancing the uneasy possibility of a dysphoric text that might still be written about Ireland. Yet as Katie Trumpener argues, the "central political tendency" of the national tale "shifts gradually from a celebratory nationalist politics, which both recognizes cultural distinctiveness and believes in the possibility of trans-cultural unions, towards another, more separatist politics, in which a history of cultural oppression makes rapprochement and reconciliation more and more inconceivable. The national tale's marriage plot and its national characters are deeply affected by these shifts" (Katie Trumpener, "National Character, Nationalist Plots: National Tale and Historical Novel in the Age of *Waverley*, 1806–1830," *English Literary History* 60 [1993]: 703). If we are witnessing an ideological shift rather than the composing of an "imaginative unit," the unfortunate outcome of *The Missionary* becomes a less distant intimation of what the future could hold in store for Ireland.

28 Mary Campbell, *Lady Morgan: The Life and Times of Sydney Owenson* (London: Pandora Press, 1986), p. 108.

29 A. M. D. Hughes, *The Nascent Mind of Shelley* (Oxford: Clarendon Press, 1947), pp. 90–92. Leask finds Luxima a character type to which Shelley "returned obsessively in his Oriental poems." Offsetting this obsession is Shelley's "radical scepticism regarding Hindu culture" (*British Romantic Writers and the East*, p. 192).

30 Echoes of *The Missionary* in Shelley's poetry are considered in S. R. Swaminathan, "Possible Indian Influence on Shelley," *Keats-Shelley Memorial Bulletin* (1958): 30–45, in the context of the writings of William Jones and of Moor's *Hindu Pantheon* (1801), a work Shelley owned. John Drew carries the study considerably further in his extensive examination of the presence of *The Missionary* in Shelley's *Prometheus Unbound in India and the Romantic Imagination* (Delhi: Oxford University Press, 1987), pp. 240–82. There are iconographic similarities between

Shelley's Asia, Botticelli's Venus, and traditional depictions of Lakshmi that, taken together, might make Asia a statement of the romantic movement toward a world humanism enlarged beyond Greco-Roman boundaries. If Asia is in herself the marriage of East and West, and if she is that world conscience she seems ardently to be in her strongly phrased encounter with Demogorgon, she has to be distinguished from Luxima, who represents only one side of that marriage and who represents it, moreover, in a hierarchical relationship for which Milton's prelapsarian Eve clearly provides the model.

31 The Goan Inquisition, established in 1560, was not abolished until 1812, the year after the publication of Owenson's novel. Its special objects of hatred were Portuguese who, like Hilarion, Indianized themselves excessively and converts who, like Luxima, reverted to Hinduism or never really renounced it. For a graphic account of the Inquisition's cruelties, see Paul William Roberts, *Empire of the Soul: Some Journeys in India* (Toronto: Stoddard, 1994), pp. 85–89. See also Boxer, *Portuguese Seaborne Empire*, pp. 269–70.

32 See chapter 2, n. 20, for Owenson's rendering of this set piece.

33 Hegel, *Philosophy of History*, p. 140. Hegel may well have been aware of *The Missionary* and could be alluding to it in this passage. Luxima might be India incarnate, a temptation to be sternly rejected, and the marriage of East and West even in its hierarchical modeling, a proposition to be resoundingly denounced.

34 The functional division between male and female in Hindu thought is between concept and implementation and not between *natura naturans* and *natura naturata*. The relationship between Prometheus and Asia seems to approximate this functional division, as does the relationship between the Father and the Son in *Paradise Lost*.

35 *Prometheus Unbound* 2.4.94.

7. Monstrous Mythologies: Southey and The Curse of Kehama

1 Robert Southey, Preface to *The Curse of Kehama*, in *Poems*, ed. Maurice H. Fitzgerald (Oxford: Oxford University Press, 1909), pp. 117–18. This edition reprints the 1810 and not the later preface.

2 Antony Grafton, *New Worlds, Ancient Texts: The Power of Tradition and the Shock of Discovery* (Cambridge: Belknap Press of Harvard University Press, 1992), pp. 45–47. The world, Grafton suggests, was still read, according to Pliny, by discoverers more concerned with accommodating their findings to the book than with rewriting the book according to their findings. See also Greenblatt, *Marvelous Possessions*, pp. 21–22. Elliott is particularly thought provoking in his comments on a Renaissance conservatism that should be only momentarily surprising (*The Old World and the New*, pp. 13–17). For a bibliography of the monstrous directed toward the interests of this book, see Greenblatt, *Marvelous Possessions*,

p. 159n. Sir Thomas Browne's witty comments in *Religio Medici* (1.15–16) deserve attention (Norman J. Endicott, ed., *The Prose of Sir Thomas Browne* [New York: Doubleday, 1967], pp. 20–23). Physical monstrosities of the kind that Othello relates to Desdemona recede into the background as Indian civilization and Indian art in particular become the habitat of the monstrous. See Partha Mitter, *Much Maligned Monsters* (Chicago: University of Chicago Press, 1992), for further investigation of the expanding scope of monstrosity.

3 *The Life and Correspondence of Robert Southey,* ed. Charles Cuthbert Southey, 6 vols. (London: Longman, 1849–50), 3:18; hereafter cited as *L and C.*

4 Kenneth Curry, ed., *New Letters of Robert Southey,* 2 vols. (New York: Columbia University Press, 1965), 1:406; hereafter cited as *New Letters.*

5 J. W. Robberds, ed., *Memoirs of the Life and Writings of the Late William Taylor,* 2 vols. (London: John Murray, 1843), 1:375. In an unsigned review of *The Curse of Kehama* published in two installments (*Eclectic Review,* March 1811, pp. 185–205; April 1811, pp. 334–50), John Foster carries the thought further. The most important passages of the review are printed in Lionel Madden, ed., *Robert Southey: The Critical Heritage* (London: Routledge and Kegan Paul, 1975), pp. 138–45. "It was a thing not to be endured," Foster writes, "that, while we are as proud as Kehama of possessing India, we should not be able to bring to the augmentation of our national splendour that which India itself deems its highest glory, its mythology." The failure of a poet of Southey's status to achieve this "augmentation" proves "the utter desperateness of the undertaking." It is as if a "fine British fleet" were dispatched to India "for the purpose of bringing back, each ship, a basket of the gods of crockery" (p. 144).

6 Lord Byron, letter to Thomas Moore, August 28, 1813, in Leslie A. Marchand, ed., *Byron's Letters and Journals* (Cambridge: Belknap Press of Harvard University Press, 1974), 3:100–101. See also Rupert Christiansen, *Romantic Affinities: Portraits from an Age, 1780–1830* (New York: G. P. Putnam's Sons, 1988), p. 195. Madame de Staël's advice, reported by Byron three years after *Kehama* was published, indicates that Southey's apprehensions about his audience were not unfounded.

7 Drew, *India and the Romantic Imagination,* p. 236. See also Leask, *British Romantic Writers and the East,* p. 96.

8 Madden, *Robert Southey: The Critical Heritage,* p. 332.

9 James Engell and Walter Jackson Bate, eds., *Biographia Literaria* (Princeton: Princeton University Press, 1983), p. 64.

10 A firsthand description of Southey's library can be found in the section on Southey in De Quincey's *Literary Reminiscences* in Masson, *Collected Writings of De Quincey,* 11:337–38. Casaubon in George Eliot's *Middlemarch* is engaged in a mythological project similar to Southey's but disclaims any interest in recent poets.

11 Robert Southey, 1838 preface to *The Curse of Kehama*, in *The Poetical Works of Robert Southey*, 10 vols. (London: Longmans, 1837–38).

12 Geoffrey Carnall, *Robert Southey and His Age: The Development of a Conservative Mind* (Oxford: Clarendon Press, 1960), p. 79.

13 Ernest Bernhardt-Kabisch, *Robert Southey* (Boston: Twayne Publishers, 1977), p. 111.

14 Stephen Wheeler, ed., *The Complete Works of Walter Savage Landor*, vol. 13, *Poems* (New York: Barnes and Noble, 1969), 1803 preface, p. 344.

15 Robert Southey, quoted in Carnall, *Robert Southey and His Age*, pp. 78–79. For Portuguese methods of conversion, see Boxer, *Portuguese Seaborne Empire*, pp. 65–83.

16 Robert Southey, quoted in Majeed, *Ungoverned Imaginings*, p. 82.

17 Ibid.

18 Robert Southey, *The Life of Nelson* (London: Bell and Daldy, 1861), p. 162.

19 Bernhardt-Kabisch, *Robert Southey*, p. 93.

20 *Annual Review for 1806*, p. 593. Quoted in Carnall, *Robert Southey and His Age*, p. 78.

21 For the protocol of the warrant, see Geoffrey Moorhouse, *India Britannica* (New York: Harper and Row, 1983), pp. 131–36; Davies, *Splendours of the Raj*, pp. 224–25.

22 Carnall, *Robert Southey and His Age*, pp. 124–27.

23 In *Literature as a Heritage* (Cambridge: Cambridge University Press, 1987), pp. 18–19, Marilyn Butler draws attention to the manner in which Byron and Shelley transfer Southey's anti-Hindu scenes to anti-Christian contexts. She adds that "Southey's representation of society within India might be construed as humanitarian, egalitarian and radical." This latent populism makes the poem subversive of a discourse the accuracy of which it also seeks to certify and is one more complication of the extraordinary antipathy between the poem and its prefaces.

24 References to the notes to *The Curse of Kehama* and to the 1838 preface are to the *Poetical Works of Robert Southey*. Modern editions print the 1810 preface and do not reprint the notes.

25 Madden, *Robert Southey: The Critical Heritage*, p. 131.

26 Bernhardt-Kabisch, *Robert Southey*, p. 83.

27 See chapter 2, n. 20.

28 Southey improves on his predecessors with the resemblance between Kehama's eternal incarceration in himself and the curse he inflicts on Ladurlad. No such name as Ladurlad is to be found in Hindu literature. The Anglicizing, along with the conversion of Gandharva to Glendoveer — a tribute perhaps to Scottish valor — is faintly comic at this point in time. Nevertheless, Westernized names point to more substantial discoveries of the West in India that are not conducive to a discourse of estrangement.

29 Drew is taking a literal reading for granted when he finds Southey's nar-

rative "firmly based on what he had (rightly) gathered was the essential, as also the peculiar feature of Hinduism" (*India and the Romantic Imagination*, p. 237). Drew then quotes the passage from the 1810 preface we are now considering. No one could be less inclined to hostile judgments against Hindu civilization than Drew, but the literal reading of Puranic and Vedic texts must be as methodologically suspect as those naturalistic (rather than semiotic) readings of Indian art that Mitter rightly criticizes in *Much Maligned Monsters*. The year 1987 may seem late in the day for resistance to figural readings, but Drew's view becomes far more justifiable when we find a philosopher of the status of Surendrenath Dasgupta resorting to similar readings of the Vedas in *Indian Idealism* (Cambridge: Cambridge University Press, 1933), pp. 1–19. Dasgupta is concerned with putting forward an evolutionary view of Hindu religious thought in which the "primitive" Vedas pave the way for the more "advanced" Upanishads. If we adopt this line of interpretation, there is no need to recuperate early texts by attempting to read them figurally. In any case, figural readings are not to be expected from philosophers, although Sri Aurobindo points us in the right direction by endeavoring to read the Gita as a philosophical allegory of the soul. My endeavor is to site Indian religiophilosophical texts on a literary terrain and to request that they be examined through the hermeneutics appropriate to such sites. The request is not extraordinary: if the Old Testament were read with stubborn literalism, the results might well be, to use Southey's word, "peculiar."

30 In the *Eclectic Review* (March 1811, p. 186), John Foster caustically observes that Clive would have had no difficulty in seeing Kehama off the premises. Unfortunately, it is not impossible for the modern reader to discern resemblances between Kehama and Clive.

31 Foster sharply focuses Southey's dilemma: "We may wonder in very serious simplicity, why the poet should choose deliberately to excite at once the two opposite sentiments of pleasure and disgust, with the knowledge, too, that any attempt to prolong them both is infallibly certain to end in the ascendancy of the latter" (Madden, *Robert Southey: The Critical Heritage*, p. 140). In characterizing Foster's review as a "very suggestive misreading," Leask points to the problematics that surround the question of a correct or even an appropriate reading (*British Romantic Writers and the East*, p. 96). Southey's own reading of his poem is, as we have seen, highly indeterminate, partitioned irretrievably between the poem and its prefaces. A more modern reading situated on the poem and marginalizing the prefaces could still find the poem arguing indecisively, although productively, with itself.

32 In his essay on history, Emerson argues that the driving force behind inquiry into the past is to domesticate the monstrous to "see the end of the difference," to do away with the "wild, savage, and preposterous There or Then and to introduce in its place the Here and the Now" (*The Col-

lected Works of Ralph Waldo Emerson, vol. 2: *Essays: First Series,* text established by Alfred R. Ferguson and Jean Ferguson Carr [Cambridge, Mass.: Belknap Press, 1979], p. 7).

8. *Understanding Asia: Shelley's* Prometheus Unbound

1 References to Shelley's poetry are to Hutchinson, *Complete Poetical Works of Percy Bysshe Shelley.*

2 A similar turn of language takes place in Genesis 6:6: "And it repented the LORD that he had made man on the earth, and it grieved him at his heart." I am grateful to Lorenzo Minnelli for drawing my attention to this inversion. The antecedent of "it" is more specific in *Prometheus Unbound,* but it is entirely possible that the direction of Genesis 6:6 is being reversed so that the repenting in Shelley deconstructs not only man as constituted by the curse but also God as "the creature of his worshippers" (*Queen Mab* 7.28).

3 Joseph Raben, "Shelley's *Prometheus Unbound:* Why the Indian Caucasus?," *Keats-Shelley Journal* 12 (1963): 95–106; Stuart Curran, *Shelley's Annus Mirabilis: The Maturing of an Epic Vision* (San Marino, Calif.: Huntington Library, 1975), pp. 61–70. Vague demarcations are exemplified by Burke, who speaks (perhaps recalling *PL* 3.431–32) of "Mount Imaus (or whatever else you call that large range of mountains that walls the northern frontiers of India)" (Marshall, *Writings and Speeches of Edmund Burke,* 5:394).

4 Lady Morgan, *The Missionary,* 1:130, 2:107.

5 Schwab, *Oriental Renaissance,* p. 71.

6 It was not until 1821 that Shelley placed an order for Mill's history. Yet in *A Philosophic View of Reform,* published two years earlier and discussed later in this chapter, he displays his commitment not only to Mill's view of India but also to the rhetoric in which that view is drenched.

7 Spear, *India,* p. 226.

8 Whitney J. Oates and Eugene O'Neill Jr., eds., *The Complete Greek Drama* (New York: Random House, 1938), 1:140.

9 Curran, *Shelley's Annus Mirabilis,* pp. 45–47; Kenneth N. Cameron, *Shelley: The Golden Years* (Cambridge: Harvard University Press, 1974), p. 479.

10 Lawrence J. Zillman, ed., *Shelley's "Prometheus Unbound": A Variorum Edition* (Seattle: University of Washington Press, 1959), p. 330.

11 See also Stuart M. Sperry, *Shelley's Major Verse: The Narrative and Dramatic Poetry* (Cambridge: Harvard University Press, 1988), p. 215n.

12 Curran, *Shelley's Annus Mirabilis,* pp. 51–53; Drew, *India and the Romantic Imagination,* pp. 265–68. Leask points persuasively to the presence of the *Kena* Upanishad in the exchange between Asia and Demogorgon (*British Romantic Writers and the East,* pp. 149–50). Rammohun

Roy had translated this Upanishad shortly before the appearance of Shelley's poem.

13 See Leask, *British Romantic Writers and the East*, pp. 146–47. Analogies with Indian turns of language are not particularly striking here, given the universality of the *via negativa* as a mystical procedure. The secularizing of the language strategy in the passage quoted is unusual and can cumulatively convey the discarded impositions of a previous discourse.

14 David Lee Clark, ed., *Shelley's Prose, or the Trumpet of a Prophecy* (Albuquerque: University of New Mexico Press, 1954), p. 239.

15 Michael Henry Scrivener, *Radical Shelley: The Philosophical Anarchism and Utopian Thought of Percy Bysshe Shelley* (Princeton: Princeton University Press, 1982), pp. 240–45. Play is an important element of Hindu thought, entering into the activities of a cosmos that can be seen as self-delighting as much as it is purpose dedicated. Dedication to a purpose can be accepted as a form, but not the only form, of self-delight.

16 Tilottama Rajan, *The Supplement of Reading: Figures of Understanding in Romantic Theory and Practice* (Ithaca: Cornell University Press, 1990), pp. 306–10.

17 Curran, *Shelley's Annus Mirabilis*, p. 100.

18 The traditional difference between intuitive and discursive reason (which Milton in *PL* 5.487–90 makes into a difference of degree rather than kind) points to a more immediate, nondiscursive "language" in which presence is less corrupted by the linguistic screen.

19 An account of the impeachment as theater, less theatrical and more analytical than Macaulay's, can be found in Suleri, *Rhetoric of English India*, pp. 49–74. Teltscher offers a different analysis in *India Inscribed*, pp. 157–91.

20 Conor Cruise O'Brien, *The Great Melody: A Thematic Biography and Commented Anthology of Edmund Burke* (London: Minerva Books, 1993), pp. 257–384; Smith, *Wealth of Nations*, p. 84.

21 Gardner, *East India Company*, p. 146.

22 Roger Ingpen and Walter E. Peck, eds., *The Complete Works of Percy Bysshe Shelley*, 10 vols. (London: Ernest Benn, 1926–30), 6:38–39.

23 W. B. Yeats, "The Indian upon God," in Finneran, *W. B. Yeats: The Poems*, pp. 13–14.

24 Keay, *India Discovered*, pp. 64–74. Even a Buddhist shrine as well preserved as the one at Sanchi (examined by Captain E. Fell in 1819) was taken only as evidence that Buddhism had spread to an Indian periphery from a source presumed to be outside India. The claim that Buddhism had originated in India was treated as merely one more example of the Indian tendency to imagine India as the origin of everything.

25 Arthur Schopenhauer, *The World as Will and Representation*, trans. E. F. J. Payne (New York: Dover, 1969), pp. 388–89. For the presence of Indian thought in the New Testament, see Arthur Schopenhauer, *On the Fourfold Root of the Principle of Sufficient Reason*, trans. E. F. J. Payne (La

Salle, Ill.: Open Court, 1974), p. 187, and R. J. Hollingdale, ed. and trans., *Arthur Schopenhauer: Essays and Aphorisms* (London: Penguin Books, 1970), pp. 190–92. It should be noted that Schopenhauer treats Indian thought as world denying (in his vocabulary, will denying), a proposition contested in this book. Schopenhauer's relationship to Indian thought is briefly studied in R. K. Das Gupta, "Schopenhauer and Indian Thought," *East and West New Studies* 13, no. 1 (March 1962): 32–40.

26 Clark, *Shelley's Prose*, p. 238.

27 Ibid.

28 Ibid. Rammohun Roy may well be a principal member of that Brahminical Society where "Locke and Hume and Rousseau are familiarly talked of." An adequate assessment of Rammohun Roy still remains to be written. Commentary on him is not inconsiderable, and a compilation by V. C. Joshi (*Rammohun Roy and the Process of Modernization* [Delhi: Vikas, 1975]) provides more than one view of his significance. The tendency, nevertheless, is to see a strongly overdetermined figure along a single line of determination. Leask's running remarks on Roy in *British Romantic Writers and the East* are the most responsive to the complexities of his context.

Shelley's reference to "many native Indians" is not without foundation. At a meeting held on May 14, 1816, to found Hindu College, Calcutta (which was designed from the outset *not* to live up to its name), Sir Edward Hyde East found himself "struck with the enthusiasm of the prominent pundits, Sanskrit scholars, for the introduction of Western literature and science." By 1830, the Committee on Public Instruction felt justified in claiming that Hindu College students had acquired "a command of the English language" and "a familiarity with its literature and science" to "an extent rarely equalled by any schools in Europe."

Henry Derozio, the first Indian poet writing in English, was the head of the Department of History and English at Hindu College from 1829 until his controversial dismissal in 1831; he was educated at Dharamtola Academy, a school run by a follower of Hume, David Drummond. Bacon, Locke, Hume, Paine, and Bentham were important figures in the extracurricular life of Hindu College. See Manju Dalmia, "Derozio: English Teacher," in *The Lie of the Land: English Literary Studies in India*, ed. Rajeshwari Sunder Rajan (Delhi: Oxford University Press, 1992), pp. 42–62; the quotations in the preceding paragraph are from pp. 47 and 48.

29 Clark, *Shelley's Prose*, p. 238. This sentence should remain a major crux for students of Shelley and India. Leask rightly attaches considerable importance to it, referring to it as "that strange qualifying sentence" (*British Romantic Writers and the East*, p. 140) and arguing more emphatically that "the last sentence is forced, surreptitiously, to admit that the European values which are to free them [the Indians] are also those which enslave them" (pp. 119–20). Uneasiness is apparent in the awkward construction of the sentence, in the internal rhyme between "should" and

"would" that indirectly enacts, and in doing so seems to double, the frustration of a people not yet free, and in the syntactic deferral of "attain" to a horizon that is helpfully remote. "Attainment," moreover, is discouragingly restricted to "a system of arts and literature of their own." Political liberation seems significantly excluded. The final sentence may be Jonesian in its substance, but one cannot graft a Jonesian recommendation onto a Mill-Hegel view of India that has been designed to do away with Jones. Taken as a whole, the passage, with its "strange qualifying sentence," shows that Shelley, like Southey and Owenson, is a participant in two discourses and in the friction generated between them. It also displays disturbingly the strength of his commitment to the less-acceptable discourse. In exiling Prometheus and Asia to a country of the mind, bereft of any relationship to India's actuality, Shelley raises but cannot examine the question of how India was so comprehensively disconnected from itself. He also comes perilously close to the conclusion that, at least for the time being, the wisdom of India is not for India but for others better equipped to make use of that wisdom.

30   G. Wilson Knight, *The Starlit Dome: Studies in the Poetry of Vision* (London: Oxford University Press, 1941), p. 210.

9. Macaulay: The Moment and the Minute

1   G. M. Young, ed., *Macaulay: Prose and Poetry* (Cambridge: Harvard University Press, 1967), p. 718. References to Macaulay's work, wherever possible, are to this edition, cited by page number. For material not in Young, references are to *The Miscellaneous Works of Lord Macaulay*, ed. Lady Trevelyan (New York: G. P. Putnam's Sons, Knickerbocker Press, n.d.), 10 vols.; cited by volume and page number.

2   The documentary appeared in the CBC television series *The Nature of Things* (ca. 1994). The most thoughtful discussion so far of English studies in India is Rajan, *Lie of the Land*. See also John Oliver Perry, *Absent Authority: Issues in Contemporary Indian English Criticism* (New Delhi: Sterling, 1992), pp. 327–94. English literature in Indian university Departments of English remains canonically taught as well as relentlessly canonical. Teaching it within the history of imperialism or even in relation to that history, as Viswanathan recommends (*Masks of Conquest*, pp. 167–69), is not the impending imperative for which we might hope but a distant possibility reluctant to materialize. The same inertia resists Ahmad's altogether commendable proposal that English literary studies in India be situated within a cultural studies program (*In Theory*, pp. 278–84).

3   John Clive, *Macaulay: The Shaping of the Historian* (Cambridge: Belknap Press of Harvard University Press, 1987), p. 475.

4   Owen Dudley Edwards, *Macaulay* (London: Weidenfeld and Nicolson, 1988).

5   Jane Millgate, *Macaulay* (London: Routledge and Kegan Paul, 1973).

6   Quoted in Edwards, *Macaulay*, p. 123.

7   Quoted in Millgate, *Macaulay*, p. 119.

8   Clive, *Macaulay*, p. 325.

9   Müller, *India*, pp. 137–38.

10 Edwards, *Macaulay*, p. 115.

11 Brantlinger, *Rule of Darkness*, p. 81.

12 Millgate, *Macaulay*, p. 24 (italics added). The encomium and the uncritical acceptance of Mill's title endure well beyond what should have been their day. See O'Brien's reference to Mill as "the great historian of British India" (*Great Melody*, p. xxxviii).

13 Clive, *Macaulay*, p. 296. Macaulay also made use of the voyage to pick up the rudiments of Portuguese.

14 Philip Meadows Taylor, *Confessions of a Thug*, with a new preface by Nick Mirsky (Oxford: Oxford University Press, 1986), p. viii. Thuggery can be treated as a staging ground for the depiction of Hinduism's innate perversity, with the Kali cult a nightmarish version of the feminine. The fact is that many thugs were Moslem and that the principal thug in Taylor's *Confessions of a Thug* is a Hyderabad Moslem, emotionally involved in Mohurram in a way he never is in the Kali cult (pp. 106–10). His Malthusian justification of the desirability of thuggery (pp. 43–44) makes it apparent that Taylor (who is generous with epigraphs from Shakespeare to his chapters) had also read Comus's speech in Milton's Ludlow masque. Such fabrications imply that the motives of thuggery were nonreligious even to the author of *Confessions*. Nevertheless, thuggery throughout the nineteenth century was one more sign of the horrors of Hinduism, and the murderous designs of thugs under their veneer of friendliness became a metaphor for a treacherous subcontinent.

15 Millgate, *Macaulay*, p. 201n.

16 Ibid., p. 95.

17 Walter Houghton, *The Victorian Frame of Mind, 1830-70* (New Haven: Yale University Press for Wellesley College, 1957), p. 457.

18 Linda Colley, *Britons: Forging the Nation, 1707-1837* (New Haven: Yale University Press, 1992), p. 9.

19 Hay and Quereshi, *Sources of Indian Tradition*, 2:43.

20 Ibid.

21 Lata Mani, "Contentious Traditions: The Debate on *Sati* in Colonial India," in *Recasting Women: Essays in Colonial History*, ed. Kumkun Sansari and Krishna Vaid (New Delhi: Kali for Women, 1989), pp. 88–126. The original version appeared in 1987. For a critical view of it, see Sheldon Pollock, "Deep Orientalism," in Breckenridge and van der Veer, *Orientalism and the Postcolonial Predicament*, pp. 99–104. For more on the subject, see Arvind Sharma et al., eds., *Sati: Historical and Phenomenological Essays* (Delhi: Motilal Banarsidass, 1988).

22 It should be noted that Roy felt that suttee should be made considerably

more difficult rather than illegal. Abolition eventually had to come about through reformist energies in the Hindu community (Sharma et al., *Sati: Historical and Phenomenological Essays*, pp. 43–48). We could take Roy's recommendation as a commitment to cultural self-determination, but it also suited the agenda of those Orientalists who wished to expedite progressive change with the minimum of popular discontent.

23 Mani, "Contentious Traditions," p. 112; Rocher, "British Orientalism," pp. 225–31. This phase was over by the time of the debate on suttee. As the chapters on Owenson, Southey, and Shelley have shown, the Mill-Hegel discourse had come to power everywhere but in Calcutta.

24 V. J. Kiernan, *The Lords of Humankind: Black Man, Yellow Man, and White Man in an Age of Empire* (New York: Columbia University Press, 1986), p. 41.

25 David Kopf, *British Orientalism and the Bengal Renaissance: The Dynamics of Indian Modernization, 1773–1835* (Berkeley: University of California Press, 1969). Viswanathan's methodological objections to Kopf (*Masks of Conquest*, pp. 15–17) are well founded, but the same objections could be made to Schwab (*Oriental Renaissance*), and neither book is disabled by insufficient attention to the politics of knowledge. Kopf is particularly effective in bringing out the Enlightenment roots of a world humanism that might otherwise be treated as a romantic inspiration, and Schwab, more than anyone else, conveys the romance of understanding that forms the aesthetic of the romantic project.

26 Kopf, *British Orientalism and the Bengal Renaissance*, pp. 144–55, 81, 48, 96–97.

27 Clive, *Macaulay*, p. 360.

28 Stokes, *English Utilitarians and India*, p. 47; Clive, *Macaulay*, pp. 385–87.

29 Gerald Sirkin and Natalie Robinson Sirkin, "The Battle of Indian Education: Macaulay's Opening Salvo Newly Discovered," *Victorian Studies* 14, no. 4 (1971): 407–28.

30 Frederic Ives Carpenter, *Emerson and Asia* (1930; reprint, New York: Haskell House, 1968; Arthur E. Christy, *The Orient in American Transcendentalism: A Study of Emerson, Thoreau, and Alcott* (1932; reprint, New York: Octagon Books, 1963). See also R. K. Gupta, *The Great Encounter: A Study of Indo-American Literary and Cultural Relations* (Riverdale, Md.: Riverdale Company, 1987), pp. 29–41.

31 Viswanathan, *Masks of Conquest*, pp. 116–17.

32 Marshall, *Writings and Speeches of Edmund Burke*, 5:402. Burke may see a failure of imperial responsibility, but he attributes it to the narrowness of vision of the East India Company rather than to the nature of imperial management. The empire remains a mysterious gift of Providence (see afterword, n. 4) calling for respectful exploration of the meaning of the gift. Rabindranath Tagore's remembrance and adaptation of

Burke's simile in *Creative Unity* (London: Macmillan, 1922), pp. 198–99, is notable.

33 Shlomo Avineri, ed., *Karl Marx on Colonialism and Modernization* (New York: Doubleday, 1969), pp. 131–32. Ahmad in his chapter on Marx in India does not adequately examine this passage, with its troubling implication that the cost of progress is the ruin of existing structures and that the necessary agent of progress is Western dominance (*In Theory*, pp. 221–42). Nevertheless, he conveys the dimensions of a "moral dilemma" that Keats's *Hyperion*, as we have seen, addresses with tragic eloquence (p. 228).

34 Philip Mason, *The Men Who Ruled India*, vol. 2: *The Guardians*.

35 In *The British Image of India: A Study in the Literature of Imperialism* (Oxford: Oxford University Press, 1969), Allen Greenberger ably defines the parameters of these novels. They are limited to northwestern and nonurban India (p. 38); they are likely to include "a heart-rending account of the way India destroys the institution of the European family" and they portray "Hindus in general and Bengalis in particular . . . in a very harsh light" (p. 45); they regard the Moslems as an imperial people, like themselves, whom they can understand better than other Indians; and they therefore restrict their relationships with the Indian people to Moslems to "an abnormally large degree" (pp. 45–47). Rocher contrasts this preference with eighteenth-century attitudes ("British Orientalism," p. 222). As she notes, the movement from an early sympathy for "mild, meek, downtrodden Hindus" to the favoring of "virile, fearless Muslims" provides "much of the texture" (p. 245n) of Hutchins's *Illusion of Permanence* and Ashis Nandy's *Intimate Enemy: Loss and Recovery of Self under Colonialism* (Delhi: Oxford University Press, 1983). One might add that Islam's accessibility to the West lay not simply in its imperial past but, perhaps more important in its monotheism and its univocality, both of which were congenial to the aims and texture of imperial discourse.

36 Trevelyan, *Golden Oriole*, pp. 222–23, 40.

37 Emily Eden, *Up the Country: Letters Written to Her Sister from the Upper Provinces of India* (London: Virago Press, 1983), p. 294; see also pp. 35, 98.

38 Mason, *Men Who Ruled India* (London: Pan Books, 1987), p. xiii.

39 Ibid.

40 Burke's presentation of Fox's East India Bill and its connected legislation as the Magna Carta of the Indian people can be read as implying such a contract.

41 Marian Fowler, *Below the Peacock Fan: First Ladies of the Raj* (Markham, Canada: Penguin Books, 1987), p. 263.

1   Spivak, *In Other Worlds*, pp. 179–96.
2   Spear, *History of India*, 2:51.
3   Ibid., p. 53.
4   John William Kaye, *The Administration of the East India Company: A History of Progress* 1853; reprint, Allahabad, India: Kitab Mahal, 1966). Burke's reference to Britain's "glorious empire given by an incomprehensible dispensation of the Divine providence into our hands" is quoted in O'Brien, *Great Melody*, p. 581. See his introduction, p. xxxviii, for a witty but not altogether sustainable contrast between Burke's and Mill's views of history. Mill did not lecture to history. Both he and Hegel designed it to lecture to us.
5   Colley, *Britons*, pp. 169–70. The topic contrasts with the series of questions posed by the Abbé Raynal to participants in an essay competition. Indecisiveness was compounded when no prize was awarded. See Elliott, *The Old World and the New*, pp. 1–2.
6   Davies, *Splendours of the Raj*, p. 231. See also Jan Morris and Simon Winchester, *Stones of Empire: The Buildings of the Raj* (New York: Oxford University Press, 1983), p. 220. The dispute between Lutyens and Baker is narrated in detail in Robert Grant Irving's *Indian Summer: Lutyens, Baker, and Imperial Delhi* (New Haven: Yale University Press, 1981), pp. 142–63.
7   William Wordsworth, *The Prelude*, ed. Ernest de Selincourt, parallel text version (Oxford: Clarendon Press, 1926), 1805 text, 13:40–65. For the Miltonic trend in the 1850 revisions, see Rajan, *Form of the Unfinished*, pp. 137–39.
8   Spear, *History of India*, 2:59.
9   If the Renaissance is characterized as early modern, romanticism can be thought of as early postmodern. The designation might be more than argumentatively interesting. If early modernism discovered itself on the shoreline of the New World, early postmodernism can be perceived as disarticulating that discovery in the distance between imperial and revolutionary ideologies. One can even argue that the distance establishes the dimensions of a political unconsciousness whose eruptive stresses still bear on the literary realities of today.
10 Bayly, *Indian Society*, p. 3.
11 Ibid., p. 37.
12 Ibid., p. 9.
13 K. P. Jayaswal, *Hindu Polity: A Constitutional History of India in Hindu Times* (Bangalore, India: Bangalore Printing and Publishing, 1943); D. Mackenzie Brown, *The White Umbrella: Indian Political Thought from Manu to Gandhi* (Berkeley: University of California Press, 1959), pp. 18–19. See also Panikkar, *Survey of Indian History*, pp. 58–59, and Ralph Linton, *The Tree of Culture* (New York: Alfred A. Knopf, 1955), p. 497.

14 Rushdie, *Midnight's Children*, pp. 300, 356, 420.

15 P. N. Furbank, *E. M. Forster: A Life* (London: Sphere Books, 1988), 1:222.

16 Forster, *Passage to India*, p. 278. Adela returns similarly to Mediterranean "clarity" (p. 263). In describing the Mediterranean as "the human norm," Forster (via Fielding) adds that "when men leave that exquisite lake whether through the Bosphorous or the Pillars of Hercules, they approach the monstrous and extraordinary." The southern exit via the Red Sea "leads to the strangest experience of all" (p. 278). Forster's statement is notable not only in conceding that monstrosity also lies outside the Western exit but also in the map it offers us of a confined space of clarity surrounded by the abnormal. The "exquisite lake" scarcely reflects the turbulence of Mediterranean history. It reflects rather the mind's need for a central calm, a calm both defined and disturbed by the word "exquisite," with its gentle suggestions of fragility and artifice. Pound in his essay on Cavalcanti shares with Forster the use of the phrase "Mediterranean clarity," adding to it "Mediterranean sanity," which matches Forster's reference to the Mediterranean as "the human norm" (*Literary Essays of Ezra Pound*, ed. T. S. Eliot [London: Faber and Faber, 1954] p. 154). Pound's essay, first published in 1934, is vaguely dated 1910-31. The language is probably not unique to Pound and Forster.

17 W. B. Yeats, "The Statues," in Finneran, *W. B. Yeats: The Poems*, pp. 336–37.

18 Ezra Pound, letter to Ronald Duncan, November 7, 1939, in D. D. Paige, ed., *The Letters of Ezra Pound, 1907-41* (New York: Harcourt, Brace and World, 1950), p. 330.

19 Paranoia is not limited to *Midnight's Children*. Spivak suggests that the "genius of this book [*The Satanic Verses*] is more the paranoid Schreber than the visionary Blake" (*Outside in the Teaching Machine*, p. 226). Spivak is not concerned with the parodic use of paranoia. I would be inclined to give this use some weight in evoking a form of imperialism that is both nightmarish and comic. The visionary Blake is important in Rushdie's overall understanding in stressing the Urizenic ancestry of the paranoia he deflates and in contestionally asserting the proliferative energy of the fragment against the consolidating energy of the whole.

20 Wallace Stevens, "Connoisseur of Chaos," in Wallace Stevens, *Parts of a World* (New York: Alfred A. Knopf, 1942), p. 50.

21 Salman Rushdie, *Imaginary Homelands* (London: Granta Books, 1991), p. 403, and *The Satanic Verses* (New York: Viking, Penguin Books, 1988), pp. 300, 304-5, 336, 338.

22 Paul Scott, *The Raj Quartet* (New York: William Morrow, 1976), 1:28, 2:396, 3:63-64, 268, 382-83, 4:504.

23 For a translation (among many) of this poem, see Rajan, *Form of the Unfinished*, pp. 311-12.

24 Recent fictional responses to the *Mahābhārata* include Shashi Tharoor's *The Great Indian Novel* (New Delhi: Penguin Books, 1989), an entertain-

ing but too insistent parallel between the classical epic and events in our century. Githa Hariharan's *Thousand Faces of Night* (New Delhi: Viking, Penguin Books, 1992) more persuasively dreams the *Mahābhārata* into a familial text. Dreaming it into a sociopolitical text is a more formidable enterprise that, not surprisingly, has yet to be undertaken.

25 The intimate relationship between language and perception in classical Indian thought is studied by Bimal Krishna Matilal in *The Word and the World* (Delhi: Oxford University Press, 1990). Also perceptive is Hajime Nakamura's *Ways of Thinking of Eastern Peoples: India, China, Tibet, Japan*, ed. Philip P. Wiener (Honolulu: University of Hawaii Press, 1968), pp. 52–53, 60–64, 73–76, 87–88. See also Betty Heiman, *Facets of Indian Thought* (New York: Schocken Books, 1964), pp. 125, 157–77.

Index

Balachandra Rajan is Professor Emeritus of English,
University of Western Ontario.

Library of Congress Cataloging-in-Publication Data
Rajan, Balachandra.
Under western eyes : India from Milton to Macaulay /
Balachandra Rajan.
p. cm.
Includes bibliographical references and index.
ISBN 0-8223-2279-x (acid-free paper).
ISBN 0-8223-2298-6 (pbk. : acid-free paper)
1. English literature—Indic influences.   2. English
literature—History and criticism.   3. India—Foreign
public opinion, British.   4. India—Relations—Great
Britain.   5. Great Britain—Relations—India.   6. India—
Historiography.   7. India—In literature.   I. Title.
II. Series.
PR129.I5R35 1999
820.9'3254—dc21   98-30647 CIP